Knowledge Networking

Knowledge Networking

Creating the collaborative enterprise

David J. Skyrme

BUTTERWORTH
HEINEMANN

OXFORD   AUCKLAND   BOSTON   JOHANNESBURG   MELBOURNE   NEW DELHI

Butterworth-Heinemann
Linacre House, Jordan Hill, Oxford OX2 8DP
225 Wildwood Avenue, Woburn, MA 01801-2041
A division of Reed Educational and Professional Publishing Ltd

 A member of the Reed Elsevier plc group

First published 1999

British Library Cataloguing in Publication Data
Skyrme, David J.
  Knowledge networking: creating the collaborative enterprise
  1. Business information services   2. Business planning
  3. Business enterprises – Computer networks
  I. Title
  658.4'038

Library of Congress Cataloguing in Publication Data
A catalogue record for this book is available from the Library of Congress

ISBN 0 7506 3976 8

Composition by Scribe Design, Gillingham, Kent
Printed and bound in Great Britain by Biddles Ltd, Guildford and King's Lynn

Contents

Preface

This book has been a long time in gestation – nearly twenty years in fact, although when I started I did not envisage a book as the end result. The seeds were sown in 1981, when I started using electronic mail as part of a small European marketing team, whose members were working in Reading (England), Munich and Geneva, and who needed to communicate regularly with salespeople all over Europe, as well as head office in Massachusetts.

As computer networks evolved during the 1980s to connect together more people, and as they added extra facilities, such as computer conferencing, the business benefits of using them for communication and knowledge sharing became more apparent. Along with other professionals and managers within Digital Equipment Corporation (DEC) I was discovering the power of *knowledge networking*. At the time, Digital was a pioneer in large-scale peer-to-peer computer networking (DECnet), although unbeknown to most business people, a global and interorganizational network, the Internet, had already started its inexorable growth. Today, the Internet provides a very important technology infrastructure for global knowledge networking.

But knowledge networking is more than just computer networks. It is about harnessing knowledge on a global scale. Without effective means of communicating and accessing information, knowledge remains fragmented in small pieces, often in people's heads. The same is true between departments of a large organization, or of individuals who share a common interest but are geographically separated. Bring such knowledge together and the opportunities and benefits are huge. Whether you are seeking improved business performance, better public services, a better environment, the reduction of poverty in the world, or a more meaningful lifestyle for yourself, knowledge networking can help enormously.

The aim of this book is to inspire you to do so, and give you some practice guidance on your way. Because of my background it has a strong business bias, although in the nature of today's business, it is equally applicable to large multinationals, small and medium enterprises and even micro-enterprises. In fact, knowledge networking allows small enterprises to work together and compete effectively in global markets against companies many times their size. The techniques of knowledge networking are universal, so the nature of your organization, or whether you are part of one at all, does not matter. As long as you seek to gain knowledge or to use your knowledge to help others, this book has something for you.

Outline of the book

The book is divided into four parts. Part A sets the context, the changing world we live and work in. Wherever you look, organizations and institutions are under pressure, many individuals seem less certain about the future and there are doubts over the relevance of today's nation state. Individually and collectively we have still to adapt to the realities of a post-industrial knowledge economy, where the old recipes for success do not work. In the new world order, value is in knowledge and intangibles, power is distributed, careers are not for life, large organizations can disappear overnight and your business or lifestyle can be dramatically affected by developments on the other side of the world.

Part B of the book examines three main factors that are behind many of these changes. These are the role of knowledge, the impact of information and communications technologies (especially the Internet), and virtualization, where activities take place electronically over time and space rather than through physical means. While traditionalists may view these as threats, I view them as opportunities, and that is the focus taken in these chapters.

Part C of the book gets down to practicalities in a set of toolkits. Every day, I get besieged with questions (many of them coming via email from readers of my Internet website http://www.skyrme.com), such as 'how do you make a virtual organization work?', 'where is it best to start with knowledge management?', 'how do you get people to share their knowledge?'. I've been through many of these situations myself and have learnt a lot on the way, and incidentally am still learning. Over time I have codified my knowledge along several domains, such as information and knowledge management, flexible working, Internet strategies and networking skills. However, a domain view continues to reinforce narrow perspectives. Success comes from taking a more holistic approach, blending together the knowledge and skills from each domain. Therefore, Part C is organized along the dimensions of individual, team, organization and interprise (an interorganizational enterprise).

The final part of the book looks at the wider policy agenda and takes a view of how the knowledge economy may unfold.

My journey of knowledge

During my career as a professional and manager and now an independent consultant, I have read many books, articles and (more recently) web pages. It seems to me that they fall into certain genres. One is the academic genre, with lots of concepts and theory, making sure that no important reference is left out. Another genre is the practical guide, based on a single approach, with scant reference to literature. Many are domain specific and often quite narrow. Thus, you will find books on the Internet, books on intellectual capital, books on virtual organizations. Some of the better business books are written by business school academics, who have some consultancy or business experience and give practical case examples. Others are written by journalists, who blend important ideas with good storytelling. Few, alas, are written by practising managers. They are generally too busy climbing the career ladder or constrained by what they can reveal.

My own career has been somewhat hybrid. Once a researcher, then a salesperson, product manager, marketing manager and strategic planning manager, I have seen organizational life from many sides. Now my hybrid life includes writing, consulting, working in joint ventures and a little academic work, both tutoring on strategic marketing workshops and supervising MBA business research projects. It goes without saying that I am an active Internet user and through that an active knowledge networker in all my endeavours. It is this blend of theory and practice, of technology and management, of a large multinational and a micro-enterprise perspective, that I hope gives you new insights through this book.

In writing this book, I drew on many sources. In one respect it is an example of knowledge networking in practice. In part it is a coagulation of personal knowledge that was formerly fragmented. Thus it draws on many of the short pieces that I have written over the last ten to fifteen years – management reports, presentations, guidelines and check lists, frameworks for thinking, trend analyses, articles and so on. More importantly it draws on the knowledge that exists within my personal and professional network. Over the years, this network has become multigenerational, multidisciplinary, global and large. I therefore acknowledge the many knowledge exchanges, with insightful people, too numerous to name, that have influenced my thinking which is captured in this book.

Acknowledging my knowledge network

There are a few people, however, to whom I want to pay particular tribute for their encouragement and the way in which they have freely given of their time, and more importantly, their knowledge. The first of these is Debra M. Amidon, founder of ENTOVATION International, of which my company is a networked business partner. A former colleague in Digital's globally distributed Management Systems Research group, Debra, based in Massachusetts, and myself, based in Newbury, England, went our separate ways after leaving Digital. However, as is virtually inevitable when individuals work in related fields and exchange information over global networks, our paths came together again in a variety of joint projects. It was Debra's insistence that I had to write this book, asserting that it was time to share my knowledge and experience with a wider audience. When I flagged, because my consulting work was taking precedence and my very patient publisher wondered if it would ever get done, she goaded me back into action. Without her active and practical support you would not be reading this book today.

There are several other members in my inner network, whom I would particularly like to acknowledge. Jan Wyllie, founder of Trend Monitor International, has a unique talent at taking voluminous information and distilling the underlying trends, helping me sort the wheat from the chaff. Another Trend colleague, Sheila Evers, plays the role, in her own words, of being a lead balloon: 'bringing cloud cuckoo thinking down to earth'. Others whose help I have treasured include John Farago, a former board director in a large multinational and now an active networker in learning organization circles; he knows who to connect to in order to expedite knowledge networking. John Gundry, a colleague in Digital and now of Knowledge Ability, helped formulate the process and management models of Chapter 6 that helps make computer conferencing successful. Ron Smart, now based in Australia, was instrumental in getting me involved in Digital's Management Systems Research (MSR) team, and gave valuable insights into the challenges of organizational structuring within large multinationals, who wrestle simultaneously with multiple dimensions of business including products, customers, markets and geographic regions.

In my Digital days, my colleagues in our multidisciplinary 'People for the 90s team', Tony Attew, Ramsay Maclaren and Philip Scott, were a great influence. We were building and piloting the elements of self-managed teams, augmented by technology but taking on board the essential human and organizational factors. Tony Attew, in particular, as a human resources professional, taught us a lot about team process and behaviour that has stood me in good stead. That team also drew in some academic researchers who helped articulate our management and professional actions in models that are draw upon in this book. Particular mention should be made of Professor Roy Payne, then professor of organizational behaviour at Manchester Business School, Dr Barbara

Farbey, then of London Business School and Jane Cooper, then of Roffey Park College and now Director of Learning at Thomas Miller & Co.

Members of others networks since leaving Digital that have helped to inform this book include those of ASLIB's (Association for Information Management) IRM (Information Resources Management) Network and the Shipley Group whose mission is the valuation of intangible assets. In the field of telework, teletrade and telecooperation, colleagues on the European Telework Development project, most notably project director Horace Mitchell, have stimulated new thinking and identified successful practitioners. Also, there are many practitioners in the field of knowledge management, whose practical approaches to day-to-day management issues have informed me a great deal. In this group are Leif Edvinsson of Skandia, Bipin Junnarkar, formerly of Monsanto, Gordon Petrash formerly of Dow Chemical, and Elizabeth Lank of ICL.

I also acknowledge help received from those at Butterworth-Heinemann who have steered this book to completion despite my foot dragging. These include commissioning editors Jacquie Shanahan and Grace Evans, editorial assistant Sally North and production director Annie Martin, all based in Oxford. A debt is also owed to Karen Speerstra, based in Boston, who has established knowledge management as an important strand of Butterworth-Heinemann's offerings, and who has created a knowledge network of its knowledge management authors.

Last, but not least, thanks are due to another former colleague and Butterworth-Heinemann author, Charles Savage, writer of *Fifth Generation Management* (Butterworth-Heinemann, 1996). It was he who seeded my brain with the term 'knowledge networking', which struck a chord that is still resonating and guiding my actions into the future. I hope it will resonate with you as well so we can knowledge network together.

Setting the Context: An Interdependent World

Globalization, intense competition (often from unexpected quarters), demanding customers, regulatory changes, the relentless progress of technology – all are factors that recur high on the list of key challenges affecting businesses. How do they respond? Many management books, such as *Thriving on Chaos* by Tom Peters (1987), *The Future 500* by Craig Hickman and Michael Silva (1987) and *Competing for the Future* by Gary Hamel and C. K. Prahalad (1994) offer prescriptions. A common thread in these is the need for organizations to be flexible, adaptive and to continually reinvent themselves.

The harsh message is – if they don't they won't survive. The average life of most sizeable corporations is less than thirty years. My former employer, Digital, for over twenty-five years a paragon of a company that adapted, was innovative and grew rapidly and successfully, lost its way, stagnated and was finally absorbed into Compaq after thirty-eight years. Comparison of today's Fortune 500 or The Times Top 1000 with those of just ten years ago shows dramatic changes with once strong companies, like Triumph and Barings no more. When I talk to senior executives, the consistent message that comes across is that they are in the process of changing or transforming their business. And today's change is not like the change management process, described by Kurt Lewin, of 'unfreeze, change, refreeze'. It is continuous and never ending.

The single most important factor that is driving most of these changes in the business environment, and within organizations, is that of information and communications technology (ICT). It is often said that information and communications technologies are a business enabler, and should support business strategy. In my opinion, this is rather a passive attitude. Progress in ICT and other technologies is so dramatic that it is fundamentally transforming our environment, the way we live, work and the business landscape and society itself. Organizations therefore need to understand and actively embrace new technologies as a core dimension of strategy.

Perhaps the biggest change during the last decade of information technology (IT) is not continual improvement in functionality and performance – incidentally a trend that has been happening continuously since the 1960s – but interconnectedness. Today, communications and computer networks are pervasive. Organizations, governments, individuals are becoming more closely interconnected in ways not hitherto possible or economic.

Networks are not new. In earlier periods of technological development, once separate local power and gas supplies were connected into grids. Local telephone companies built interconnections with others so people could communicate outside their local area. Today many services are interconnected and interdependent, as we know only too often to our cost. A $20 switch fails in an electricity switching unit, and half of Quebec loses its electricity supply. There is a glitch in some communications software and a large proportion of eastern USA cannot communicate by phone for several hours. A snowstorm hits Chicago's O'Hare international airport and flights from all over the USA are disrupted. Hong Kong's stock prices plummet and the ripples are felt in stock markets around the world. All are examples of our daily dependency on such systems and also the interdependencies of such systems around the world, either physical systems like electricity grids or information systems, like the stock markets.

Yet when such systems work smoothly individuals, businesses and society in general gain enormous advantages, more so when such systems are global. For example, through a single point of contact, you can book travel tickets, rental cars, accommodation and more besides. Many systems, not just those of your travel agent, but those of many airlines, car rental firms, tour group operators and hotel groups are interconnected. Such networks of collaborating systems help reduce costs, distribute and share resources, and give better customer service. A feature of such a network is that value is being created through information and knowledge. To the hotelier or airline it is not having an aircraft seat or hotel bed that is valuable, but the information about it and the ability to exploit it. Thus it was widely reported that, during the 1980s, American Airlines frequently made more money from its SABRE reservation systems, than it did from flying aircraft!

Such networks, however, are relatively highly structured around a supply chain and well-defined business need. This very structured and high level of IT investment may itself limit their ability to adapt and change as the business environment changes. What is happening today is the growth of more dynamic networks, and a new layer of value on top of information – knowledge. We must also not forget the existence of many informal personal networks, often hailed as the main way that things move forward in business, scientific and other communities. We are creating not national utility grids but global knowledge networks or webs. These connect independent disparate knowledge that when combined and aggregated can lead to new knowledge and new opportunities.

A good example is that of El Niño, that recurring pattern of ocean currents that affect the climate around the world. Originally seen as purely a local unexplained phenomenon by Peruvian fishermen, the sharing of knowledge about apparently isolated unusual weather has identified it as a global phenomenon. Now scientists and economists around the world are collaborating to find out more about it, and to predict its future occurrences and impact.

Businesses likewise collaborate on an increasing scale. As well as collaborating in supply chain networks like those just described, they collaborate with business partners and even competitors in various forms of strategic alliance. To remain adaptive and innovative they need access to resources and expertise that goes beyond their own means. They need to access knowledge that they don't have and to generate new knowledge and commercialize it more quickly. Link-ups between biotechnology and pharmaceutical companies are one example of such collaboration. Mergers between content providers and Internet infrastructure providers are another. More and more collaboration is taking place globally and over computer networks, such as the Internet. Collaboration over global networks is a major theme running throughout this book.

The other major theme of this book is knowledge. Every few years there is a new strategic focus that promises hitherto unachievable improvements in business performance or a means of competitive advantage. Some initiatives are merely fads that disappear, while others become more established as mainstream business activities, perhaps after some reshaping. Total quality management (TQM) and business process re-engineering (BPR), for example, were two of the most significant management initiatives of recent years. Now another is on the scene – knowledge management. But is this something fundamental to every business or is it merely another consultant's fad? The faddists cite examples of failed BPR projects and the need for management consultancies to keep reinventing something new to sell to clients. The fundamentalists' argument is that knowledge is an important contributor to the performance, value and future prosperity of an organization. In order to maximize the benefits it must be properly managed and exploited. Too frequently, companies do not know what they know, thereby reinventing the wheel, or fail to apply best practice because that knowledge has not been shared. Already, as you will read in Chapter 2, there are many examples of companies that harness and exploit knowledge and have achieved significant business benefits. Like any innovative practice that stands the test of time, certain things must happen for it not to become a passing fad. First, the practice itself must be better understood and continuously improved through a process of ongoing learning. Second, as the business environment changes, it must be adapted and even reinvented into something better that fulfils an important need.

At this stage of its evolution, the jury is out as to whether knowledge management, like TQM, will achieve fundamental status. My own expectation is that it will, although perhaps in new configurations. For example, the current mainstream of knowledge management might bifurcate into knowledge sharing and knowledge innovation. Alternatively, knowledge management may become part of a more encompassing intellectual capital management.

What will influence the way that the themes of collaborative networking and knowledge management develop are some fundamental trends in the business and wider socioeconomic environment. This is the topic of Chapter 1.

Each chapter in Part A and Part B ends with some 'points to ponder', to set you thinking about how you could benefit from these trends and developments.

The networked knowledge economy

Many terms are used to describe the changing world in which we live and work – the post-industrial economy, information society, knowledge era, and more. My preference, and the term which reflects the orientation of this book, is the 'networked knowledge economy' – global is taken as read. Whatever term is used, this new environment has characteristics quite distinctive from the industrial era of the last two centuries.

This chapter describes the networked knowledge economy through the perspective of five major shifts or megatrends. This is followed by a review of technology, the predominant driving force behind these changes. The chapter concludes with an overview of responses that are needed to adapt and thrive in the new economy.

Old certainties no longer exist

Throughout the 1990s we have witnessed change as never before. The demise of the former Soviet Union, the fragmentation of Yugoslavia and the rise then fall of the Asian economies were typical upheavals affecting stability and predictability in our environment. Coincident with closer integration within the European Union (EU), individual regions like Catalonia and Scotland gain more control over their own affairs.

Counter-currents, not just in Europe but elsewhere, are simultaneously strengthening the need for local autonomy alongside that for closer cross-border co-operation. Where will it all end? What is the future of the nation state?

As individuals, we witness change at first hand. Life in the late twentieth century seems beset with complexity and uncertainty, resulting in a growing incidence of stress. The prospect of a secure job until pensionable age no longer exists. We live longer, but we face concerns about paying for nursing care in our old age as health services are stretched of resources.

For organizations, 'business as usual' is rarely a sustainable option. Barings, that once seemed like a bastion of stability in a flurry of change in financial markets, has collapsed in ignominy. Even apparently powerful multinationals have had to bow to the influence of outside forces, such as Shell's reversal of plans for the proposed dumping of the redundant Brent Spar oil platform in the light of concerted action by environmentalists. Everywhere you look, the corporate landscape is changing.

The changing corporate landscape

In the new economy value is shifting to service-related and knowledge-intensive industries. Health, education, finance, information systems, media and telecommunications have been growing strongly for over a decade. In the league table of companies by valuation, of the top twenty companies in the UK at the end of 1997, three were pharmaceutical companies, seven were in financial services and two count as old-style industrial companies. Table 1.1 shows a profile of British business in 1998. The story is similar in the USA where General Motors, once virtually unassailable in the top spot has seen companies like Microsoft and IBM overtake it in market capitalization. An analysis shows that during 1997 US household spending on 'old economy' items – food, cars, appliances and clothing – increased less than 1 per cent, while that for a cluster of new economy items – telephone, entertainment, cable television, financial services and home computers – rose 12.5 per cent during the same period.[1]

Further indication of this shift is evident from the new North American Industry Classification System (NAICS). It recognizes over 300 distinct new industries and has introduced a new information sector that embraces publishing, software, films, broadcasting and telecommunications.[2]

Table 1.1 New shape of UK industry

Sector	Value %
Resources – oil etc.	8.5
Industrial – chemical, engineering etc.	11.5
Consumer goods – food, telephone	9.0
Pharmaceuticals and health products	9.0
Services – retail, distribution	28.0
Utilities	5.5
Financial services	28.5

Source: FT Actuarial Share Indices, March 1998

Small business is big business

Almost all of the largest companies in the West have downsized in the early 1990s. For example, a loss of nearly 300 000 jobs. Large company downsizing is part of a broader restructuring of industry in general. As organizations focus on their core activities, they outsource more work to specialist companies. While some, like EDS in computer services, are large and so benefit from economies of scale, many are small companies in specialist niches, where such economies do not apply.

The European Commission estimate that companies with less than 500 employees account for 70 per cent of economic activity and employment within the European Union. In the USA between 1980 and 1990, at the same time that 3 million jobs were shed by the Fortune 500 companies, over 19 million new jobs were created by smaller companies. The Organization for Economic Co-operation and Development (OECD) says that small businesses represent the largest potential for economic growth.

The demise of jobs

Another trend associated with dispersion of business activity and the growth of small businesses is that of self-employment. Most employees can no longer rely on organizations to provide them with a job for life. In the USA, it is now estimated that some 25 million people are self-employed or independent contractors. Daniel Pink describes them as free agents: 'a new movement in the land – as fast-growing as it is invisible'.[3] They prefer to work for themselves rather than some large company who drives them hard, fails to give them job or personal satisfaction and has values different from their own.

Research conducted at Durham University Business School confirms a similar trend in the UK: 'The self-employed are the smallest of small business. They are solitary craftspeople, innovators and suppliers of services, often working from home, with no capital investment beyond a personal computer, a few instruments or a bag of tools.'[4]

A significant trend is the rapid growth of self-employment by professionals, particularly those who have had previous large company experience. Many draw on this experience to create innovative opportunities, often global in nature. In turn, many large organizations contract with these individuals for specialist services.

Employment in the future should be viewed not in terms of full-time jobs, but in terms of work activities that are parcelled out in the most cost-effective way to those with the necessary knowledge and skills. In the networked economy we have the opportunity to create electronic work markets, both within and beyond firms.

Continual reconfiguration

Other patterns of change are also apparent. Industry boundaries are simultaneously blurring and separating. Retailers enter banking, as banks offer property services. At the same time the financial services industry is itself segmenting into a wide variety of specialist service niches, such as credit card issuing and debt rescheduling.

Mergers and demergers are also occurring concurrently. Large companies merge to create even larger behemoths, hoping to gain economies of scale. Examples include BP and Amoco, Chrysler and Daimler-Benz. At the same time companies like Hanson Industries, ICI, Ciba-Geigy are demerging. In addition to full-scale demergers, management buyouts and selling of business units are increasingly common as large organizations reshape and focus their business portfolios. Thus Unichema, the Unilever speciality chemicals division was sold to ICI in 1997. One analysis suggests that some thirty large companies in the UK could potentially be more valuable to their shareholders by demerging distinctive businesses.[5]

Such countervailing trends demonstrate a continual reconfiguration of companies and industries. At any one time, there are kaleidoscopic changing patterns of alliances. Former partners become competitors, whilst former competitors create alliances.

Too frequently many corporate restructuring efforts do not deliver the benefits anticipated. For every merger that is successful, many more disappoint or fail. Following downsizing, the majority of companies see no sustained improvement in business performance. Simply shuffling things around rarely works in the long term. The changes in the corporate landscape are part of a broader and ever changing milieu. But few organizations have realized how fundamental these change are. They are in the middle of a fundamental change – a paradigm shift.

A paradigm shift

A paradigm shift is one that affects not just business but society as a whole. According to Peter Drucker such transformations take place over fifty- to sixty-year periods. In his book *Post-Capitalist Society*, he outlines three earlier periods of dramatic changes in the Western World:

* thirteenth-century Europe – the rise of medieval craft guilds and urban centres. Long distance trade.
* 1455–1519 – the Renaissance period of Gutenburg's printing press and Lutheran Reformation.
* 1776–1815 – The Industrial Revolution, starting with Watt's steam engine.

Drucker describes the current shift, which he reckons started around 1960 and will continue until around 2010 or 2020, as follows: 'We are entering the knowledge society in which the basic economic resource is no longer capital, or natural resources, or labour, but is and will be knowledge and where knowledge workers will play a central role.'[6]

The OECD estimates that in advanced industrial societies eight out of every ten new jobs are for knowledge workers. For many years economists have been writing about the evolution of economies from agriculture to manufacturing and services. But a more fundamental shift is not that to services but one to information and knowledge-based industries and activities. Even in manufacturing industries it is estimated that three-quarters of the value-added comes from knowledge work.

Interestingly, knowledge was a feature of the earlier revolutions and there are lessons that can still be drawn from studying them. Jean Gimpel in her study of technological change in medieval Europe showed how the Cistercians were very efficient at diffusing their technical knowledge of water power and other developments that helped improve the productivity of their monasteries.[7] Studies by some of her followers have also shown a very close similarity in the organizational arrangements and patterns of industrial evolution of today's high-tech industry in Silicon Valley and the medieval cloth industry in France.

Five megatrends

The term megatrend was used by John Naisbitt to describe a fundamental underlying trend shaping the future. In his 1982 book *Megatrends* he

identified ten key shifts that were reshaping the world.[8] Among these
were:

*   industrial society → information society
*   national economy → world economy
*   hierarchies → networking.

In a later book, he and co-author Patricia Aburdene describe ten
megatrends for the new millennium.[9] These have a more human emphasis and include global lifestyles, the decade of women in leadership, the
age of biology and religious revival. However, many of the 1982 transitions are still far from complete. I have therefore taken the three noted
above, relabelled them slightly, and have added 'virtualization' and the
evolution of the Internet to derive the five megatrends that are shaping
the networked knowledge economy.

Information and knowledge based

Information and knowledge are pervading all sectors of industry as well
as creating new industries based around them. There are several distinctive characteristics of this new economy.

1   *Every industry is becoming more knowledge intensive.* Even in agriculture,
    knowledge adds value. By combining knowledge about the effect of a
    fertilizer, soil condition, the state of plant growth (using information from
    satellite photographs), and the forecast weather conditions, farmers can
    use 40 per cent less fertilizer on their crops, yet achieve the same
    results. A new generation of combine harvesters automatically measures
    the weight and moisture content of the corn and calculates yields per
    acre. Every industry has comparable examples.
2   *Smart products.* Another manifestation of knowledge intensity comes in so-
    called 'smart products'. These use information or knowledge to provide
    better functionality or service that can command premium prices. There
    is a smart tyre that senses the load it has to carry and adjusts its
    pressure accordingly. Services can be enhanced through better customer
    knowledge. Marriott Hotels, for example, keeps track of individual
    preferences so that it can offer superior service when their customers
    check in.
3   *Higher information to weight ratios.* The value of electronics in cars now
    exceeds that of the value of the metal chassis, which itself, through better
    knowledge of structures, is significantly lighter than that of its
    predecessors. An indication of this trend at the macroeconomic level is

the trend in weight and value of US exports. At the start of the twentieth century the ratio was roughly 1:1 (1 lb avoirdupois in weight for £1 sterling in value). Today the financial value is twenty times higher, while the physical weight of goods exported is about the same.[10]

4   *Value in intangibles.* The market value of most companies is several times higher than the value of their physical assets as recorded in their balance sheets. In June 1997, the average of market to book value for companies in the Dow Jones industrial index was over five. For more knowledge intensive businesses, such as software and pharmaceutical companies, this ratio is often more than ten. This difference is largely accounted for by intangibles, such as know-how, information systems, patents and brands, whose value is not recorded by traditional accounting methods.

5   *Trade in intangibles.* The ultimate in information to weight ratios is the weightless product or service. There is a growing range of these intangibles that are traded in their own right. For example, the value of licences from patents in the US has increased from $3 billion in 1980 to over $100 billion today. Financial markets are almost wholly intangible. Futures options and complex derivatives are perhaps the ultimate intangible knowledge product, having been created through human ingenuity.

These are just some of the trends observable in the knowledge economy. A more in-depth analysis by Jan Wyllie identifies thirty-three distinctive trends, each of which has potential ramifications for individuals, organizations and governments.[11]

Table 1.2 Quaternary industries as defined by Masuda (1980)

Information industries	Printing and publishing
	News and advertising
	Information services – on-line
	Analysis
	Information processing – software services
Knowledge industries	Legal, accountancy, consultancy, design
	Research and development
	Education
Arts industries	Creators – authors, composers, artists, singers etc.
	Performers – orchestras, actors, singers
	Infrastructure – theatres, television, broadcasting, museums
Ethics industries	Philosophers
	Religion and spiritual – churches, groups
	Environment

New knowledge industries

A consequence of these trends is the creation of industries that are almost wholly information and knowledge based. Yoneji Masuda describes a whole set of quaternary industries, as distinct from primary (agricultural), secondary (manufacturing) and tertiary (services) industries (Table 1.2). While we are now starting to recognize these as distinct and valuable industries in the late 1990s, it must have taken some foresight to envisage these in 1980, when Masuda's book was first published.[12] He also described the 'information utility', in which he envisaged many of the features that we now see in the Internet and on-line communities.

New knowledge-intensive industries are being created all the time. The biotechnology industry is only fifteen years old but has more than 2000 companies and is expected to have annual revenues in excess of $100 billion by the year 2000. Other industries are emerging around the trading of information and knowledge using the Internet, as we shall see later.

Networking and interdependence

In the knowledge economy connections and collaboration add value. Connect several people together and you have multiple pathways for the creation and flow of knowledge. Combine knowledge from different perspectives and you can create new opportunities and respond to challenges in innovative ways. Networking gives organizations flexibility and responsiveness. In seeking out factors that determine organizational success, Craig Hickman and Michael Silva in their book *The Future 500* (1987) identified the 'network organization' as one of its core ingredients.

Nodes and links

The experts who have most systematically articulated the concepts and practices of networking are Jessica Lipnack and Jeremy Stamps, founders of the Networking Institute in Needham, Massachusetts. They define a networked organization as one: 'where independent people and groups act as independent nodes, link across boundaries, to work together for a common purpose; it has multiple leaders, lots of voluntary links and interacting levels'. [13]

Such organizations are informal, peer based, and horizontally structured. They have permeable boundaries, and most communications is point to point, not up and down management hierarchies. Other names used to describe organizations with these or similar characteristics include lattice organization, spider's web and holonic enterprise. For example, Samsung describes its structure as 'clustered nodes' with teams linked through networks. All these terms describe new ways of organizing in which the structure is flexible, where knowledge flows across traditional organizational boundaries and where multidisciplinary teams can be formed or disbanded quickly according to circumstances.

The notion of a network implies nodes and links. Nodes can be individuals, teams or, even, organizations. Networks operate at many levels. They act as the sources and repositories of knowledge. The links are various connecting and co-ordinating mechanisms, such as workflow procedures or meetings. As information flows across the links, new knowledge is created at the nodes, which can then be applied to meet the needs of the organization.

Networking – hard and soft

There are two defining characteristics that are fundamental in practice:

1 Networked organizations are less about organizational structures *per se*, and more about informal *human networking* processes.
2 The technology of *computer networking* both underpins and enhances human networking.

The first is illustrated by the remarks of Colin Hastings:

> No longer can we rely on the false comfort of the neat and tidy relationships between functional and hierarchical roles displayed on an organization chart, because this has shown itself to be too rigid, too slow and insufficiently innovative. When we start instead seeing an organization as a constantly hanging kaleidoscope of relationships between people, we begin to get a better flavour of what might be involved.[14]

The second characteristic was powerfully articulated by Ken Olsen, founder of Digital, a company often described in the mid-late 1980s as an exemplar of the networked organization. He writes in Digital's 1987 second quarter report:

> The companies that will survive are going to move from an environment of management control to one that allows a large number of people, all using their creative ability, their education, and their motivation to take part. Now this change won't be easy. But it has to come. And we're convinced that computer networking will be at the heart of these changes . . . and the vehicle through which these changes will be carried out.[15]

Now, in the 1990s, the ubiquitous nature of peer-to-peer computer networking, such as the Internet and intranets, means that many more companies are following Olsen's vision of the networked organization.

Innovation networks

The process of innovation illustrates the growth and contribution of networking. In the 1980s the standard model of innovation was of a linear process from research through to design, development and then manufacturing. Now, many of these processes are carried out concurrently and collaboratively through networks. For example, in an investigation of medical equipment development in Holland, Biemans found that all innovations relied on user–manufacturer collaboration. Furthermore, 76 per cent of innovations were developed within networks that also contained multiple relationships including distributors or other partners.[16]

In another investigation, Wissema and Euser determined that the secret of Compaq's success was its collaboration with dealers, component manufacturers and software developers. Their analysis of twelve innovation networks in Holland found six main reasons for collaborating: sharing costs, sharing risks, gaining additional market knowledge, complementing technical and market knowledge, serving international markets and joint development of industry standards.[17] Collaborative networks will be found at the heart of most successful innovations.

Globalization

Although brands such as Coca-Cola, Toyota and Philips are globally recognized, many industries and many companies are far from global. Even if its marketing is global, a company's manufacturing may be centralized. In retail, for every Toys 'R' Us that have expanded successfully overseas, otherwise successful retailers like Marks & Spencer have struggled hard in their overseas ambitions, or like Wal-Mart have remained largely in their home country.

Nevertheless, globalization is steadily increasing. Many large multinational companies design and manufacture at several locations around the world. They choose locations based on access to skills, markets and infrastructure. Many consumer and electronic products formerly manufactured in the USA and Europe are now manufactured in the Far East. Even there manufacturing has migrated from higher wage countries such as Taiwan and Malaysia to lower wage countries, such as China.

One company that epitomizes the globalization trend is Federal Express (FedEx). Every day it delivers around 3 million packages into 210 countries. Over two-thirds of its customers now place their orders and track their shipments through its on-line information system. FedEx regards it as equally important as its transport network. Through this network it creates global logistics networks for its customers who come to rely on FedEx for speedy delivery of components and completed goods in their supply chain. According to Jeffrey Garten of Yale School of Management: 'The marriage of information technology and transportation is a major reason that links among national economies have become so much tighter. In fact, what FedEx illustrates is not only that today's globalization is qualitatively different from its predecessors but also that it is now truly irreversible.'[18]

Global knowledge

In the industrial economy two reasons for going global were economies of scale and the need to reduce physical transportation costs by manufacturing close to key markets. Now globalization is as much a response to regional specialization and expansion of long-distance relationships and markets. Through the Internet firms can reach distant markets at a price little different from customers in their locality. Furthermore, higher value to weight ratios and networks like that of FedEx mean that global distribution is cost-effective.

You do not have to be large to be a global player. COMTECH, a small translation services company in Leamington Spa has clients all over the world, with whom it deals over the Internet. My own small consultancy company has customers in Korea, South Africa and the USA, some of whom I have never met. It is your specialized knowledge that matters in addressing global market niches.

A global enterprise takes advantage of unique skills and resources, wherever they are located. It may be the software expertise of India or the artistic weaving skills of villagers in Africa or Bangladesh. This opportunity to harness knowledge on a scale hitherto unimaginable before the Internet makes globalization attractive and exciting.

The Internet (r)evolution

From the media hype, you might believe that the Internet is relatively new and revolutionary. It is not. Its origins can be traced to ARPAnet, a 1960s USA Department of Defense (DoD) experimental network that worked on a peer-to-peer basis with no central control. It has evolved steadily from that time. What is new is that during the last few years the Internet has reached a critical mass of users in all walks of life. In turn this has fuelled significant investment in new products, services and commercial applications.

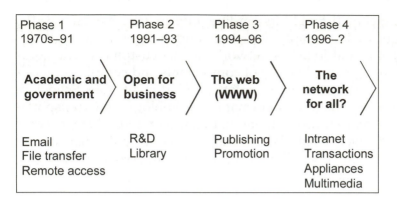

Figure 1.1   Evolution of the Internet

Evolution of the Internet

The Internet, as we know it today, has evolved through four distinct phases (Figure 1.1).

Phase 1. Initially the Internet was a tool of the research community. Academic researchers and government laboratories communicated using electronic mail (email). They could also log into a remote computer to run specialized applications.

Phase 2. Due to growth of traffic and interaction between publicly and privately funded users, it became more difficult to maintain the US Government's policy of non-commercial use. This led in 1993 to the development of a separate commercial telecommunications infrastructure.

Phase 3. The big surge in commercial use came with the arrival of the World Wide Web (WWW), followed shortly afterwards by a graphical user interface, the Mosaic browser. Developed by Tim Berners-Lee and colleagues at CERN, the Web's aim is to make it easier to share information in a distributed environment. Users can 'point and click' a computer mouse to move from page to page of information, without needing to know on which computer it is stored.

Phase 4. The Internet is now well into its fourth phase of development as a universal computer platform. The Web has evolved from a passive read-only environment, to one where users interact with a wide range of remote applications through their browsers. They can complete order forms and pay for goods electronically. Other developments are the growing use of multimedia (voice and video image) and access through low cost 'appliances', such as set-top boxes for televisions, and personal communicators (combined mobile phones and palm-top computers).

Statistics about the Internet are often mind-blowing, open to interpretation, and change rapidly. Almost every figure doubles within a year (see box). Future predictions vary widely, another indication of the dynamic nature of the evolving Internet marketplace.

The growth of the Internet

- The number of computer hosts connected was 23.5 million at the end of 1997, up from 1.7 million in 1993.
- There are 2.4 million commercial websites, expected to grow to 4.5 million by 2000.
- At the end of 1997 there were an estimated 250 million web pages, up from 70 million at the end of 1996.
- The number of users is estimated at 150 million at the end of 1998, up from fewer than 5 million in 1994. Estimates for 2003 vary from 300 to 500 million.
- 50 per cent of users are in the USA, 20 million in Europe, 14 million in Asia and the Middle East. Some 30 per cent of the US adult population have used the Internet, and of those about 20 per cent (7 per cent of the population) have made purchases over the Internet.
- Consumer transactions over the Web are expected to grow to between $300 million and $1500 billion by 2002 (depending on whose forecast you believe!).
- In the USA, more emails were sent in 1996 than mail delivered by the US Postal Service.
- After being open for general public use (1993), it took the Internet four years to reach 50 million users. In contrast, it took radio thirty-eight years and television thirteen years to reach the same number of people.

Source: Multiple surveys summarized by NUA Surveys http://www.nua.ie

---

Two specific forms of Internet have recently emerged – intranets and extranets. An intranet is a computer network, specific to an organization, that uses Internet technologies. Organizations gain the advantages of a common and easy to use interface, low cost software, and simple tools for publishing. An extranet connects selected parts of an organization's intranet to the external world. They use 'firewalls' that permit access only to authorized users, such as customers or business partners. Each user is also limited to specific areas of the intranet, according to their privileges.

The strategic importance of the Internet has taken many businesses by surprise. It opens up many new business opportunities, as is demonstrated in Chapter 4. But as with many other new developments, it is the entrepreneurial and start-up companies that are the innovators who are exploiting these. With continued high levels of supplier investment, we can expect the Internet to continue to evolve rapidly over the next few years, changing established patterns of business and communications as it does so. It will have a profound effect on knowledge work, knowledge-based products and services, and core business processes.

An interesting aspect of the Internet is the way that it has evolved with little central management. Based on a few core principles it has been largely self-organizing and has become a universal standard despite competition at one time from several proprietary networking protocols, such as IBM's SNA (Synchronous Network Access) or the formal OSI (Open Standards Interface) standard.[19] The Internet development community therefore provides a good illustration of a purposeful and successful knowledge network.

Virtualization

A key effect of information and communications technologies such as the Internet is an increase of virtualization in business activities and ways of working. Virtualization overcomes constraints of time and distance. The term 'virtual' is now appearing in many guises. Thus one view of a virtual corporation is: 'a temporary network of independent companies that co-ordinate activities to meet a common objective, such as a new product development or to meet a customer need.' This view relates to the dimension of time. However, another view relates to an organization not having a clear physical locus. Here a typical definition is: 'an organization distributed geographically and whose work is co-ordinated through electronic communications.'

Virtualness can also operate at several levels, from individual to interorganizational. These variations give rise to many types of virtuality, ranging from workers communicating with colleagues globally via phone or email, or the creation of consortia to work on a specific project. Figure 1.2 illustrates some of these types in the form of a nested hierarchy where there is a large degree of inclusivity between the levels, although not necessarily so.

Making a virtue of virtuality
Some of the common types of virtuality are the following.

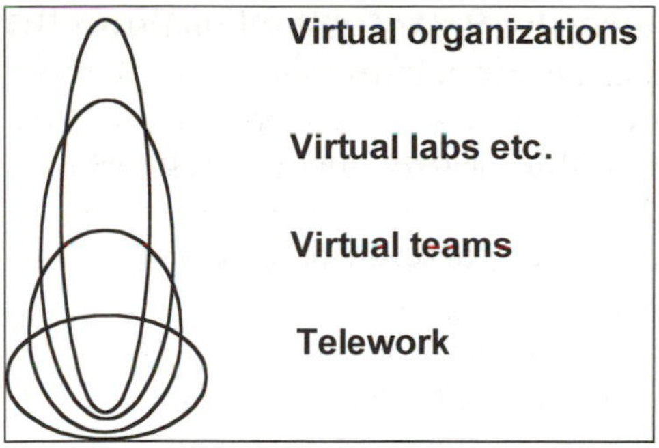

Figure 1.2 Nest of virtualness

(Figure labels: Virtual organizations / Virtual labs etc. / Virtual teams / Telework)

1 *Virtual products and services.* The cost of an electronic transaction is typically a tenth of that of the corresponding traditional transaction. Dell generates over $5 million of business a day via the Internet. Bookseller Amazon.com sells exclusively this way. Electronic markets that match buyers and sellers are now emerging in everything from Dutch flowers to second-hand cars.

2 *Virtual working or telework.* Several million people in Europe now telework for some or part of their working week. They may work from home, from telecottages, from client premises, or indeed anywhere that has telephone access, which with cellular phones is now virtually everywhere! With the ubiquitous notebook computer, it has been said that 'my office is where I hang my modem'.

3 *Virtual offices.* A related type of virtualization is the virtual office, where the physical office is replaced by office services. IBM is one of many companies that have adopted 'hot-desking'. At several of its premises, employees do not have personal workspaces, but are allocated desks whenever they are in the office. One company, Loud-n-Bow, closed its office and went completely virtual, with significant savings in office overheads.

4 *Virtual teams.* To give flexibility and to avoid relocation, many companies simply create virtual teams, where employees work at locations more convenient to them. Other examples are where several teams working in conventional office settings at different locations co-operate virtually, such as engineering teams at Ford in locations across Europe and the USA.

5 *Virtual organizations.* These can range from a stable supply network that works as a single organization, to a loose federation of independent firms that come together temporarily for specific activities. An example of the latter is OMNI, which connects 186 global relocation firms to share information and matches removal needs with truck availability.

6 *Virtual communities.* Instead of a local community a virtual community is one of shared interests, whatever the location. They are found on Internet newsgroups and discussion lists, or on an organization's intranet.

Whatever form virtualization takes, there are some common features that distinguish it from traditional forms:

* Information and communications technology allows operations to be dispersed.
* The barriers of time and space are reduced (or even disappear completely).
* Organizational structures are network-like, and more dynamic.
* The interface with customers and markets is different.
* Employees and associates (business partners, suppliers, customers etc.) adopt new patterns of work.
* The locus of knowledge is diffused. It is not necessarily in a specific place.

As a result, the geography of knowledge is quite different to physical geography. Organizations must completely rethink their geographic strategies, if they are not to be confined to a backwater of knowledge space. The topic of virtualization is addressed in more detail in Chapter 4.

Technology – a fundamental driving force

Underpinning each megatrend is the fundamental driving force of technology. Technology amplifies human capabilities. In the industrial revolution, the core technology was steam power that gave humans a 15 times improvement in price-performance over manual methods. In the knowledge era it is ICT that is boosting our ability to process information. However, the pace of improvement in the information revolution is much faster.

The rate of improvement in microchips, the fundamental component of computers, has been fairly constant over several decades. In 1965 Intel's co-founder, Gordon Moore, projected that performance doubles and costs halve roughly every eighteen months, an observation now enshrined as Moore's Law. Such improvements are almost unparalleled in the world of science and technology. The Massachusetts Institute of Technology's (MIT) landmark study, *Management in the 1990s*[20] indicated that over a ten-year period, IT showed a 25 times price-performance improvement, compared to 1.4 times for the six other most improved product groups. This rate of improvement equates to an industrial revolution every seven years!

The revolution continues

Moore's Law seems set to continue, at least through to the year 2010 (Table 1.3), although there are likely to be changes in the specific

Table 1.3 IT trends: decade on decade improvements

	1988	*1998*	*2008*
Components:			
Processor speeds	10 MHz	400 MHz	10 000 MHz
Transistors per chip	275 000	7.5 million	250 million
Memory chips	64 Kbits	64 Mbits	16 Gbit
Basic disk capacity	20 MB	1 GB	250 GB
Personal computer (typical)	PC-386 (8 MHz) 256 KB RAM 60 MB disk 14" CRT Desk-top £2500/$2500	Pentium 32 MB SDRAM 4 GB disk CD-ROM (32×) 17" CRT Desk-top and/or portable notebook £1250/$1500	10 GHz 4 GB memory 500 GB disk £1000–£2000 20" flat panel Desk-top plus palm-held integrated PC and communicators £1500/$2500
Software and applications	Basic Office Suite (word processing, spreadsheet). Profession specific	Adds database, email, Internet	Integrated voice and data messaging. Visual knowledge navigation
Users		Professionals, clerical staff have access in office	Most staff including unskilled. Professionals have several (office, home, mobile)	Everybody. Computers are consumer appliances (often for specific applications)
Typical functions	Calculations; procedures; transactions	Information retrieval; communications; decision support	Knowledge development; learning; symbiotic decision-making

Note: 8 bits = 1 byte; 1024 bytes = 1 Kilobyte (KB); 1024 KB = 1 Megabyte (MB); 1024 MB = 1 Gigabyte (GB)

technologies used. Thus X-ray lithography should replace optical lithography, leading to the development of circuits only 0.01 microns (millionths of an inch) wide by 2010, compared to around .25 microns today, and processors that are 1000 times more powerful. Thereafter, provided new applications become economic and sustain demand, investments in a variety of new technologies, such as holographic memory and molecular computers, should maintain the fundamental trend.

Sustainable trends

New products are being developed all the time. In storage today's CD-ROMs, which hold the equivalent of over 300 000 pages of typed text, will be surpassed by devices containing the equivalent of a town library. Today's bulky CRT monitors will eventually be largely replaced by slimline flat panels. There are also several underlying trends that are shaping the way that technology is used.

1   *Wider choice of formats and packaging.* Computers come in many more shapes and sizes and can even be sewed into clothing, such as training shoes and jackets. Peter Cochrane, head of BT Laboratories, frequently shows off the signet ring on his finger. It contains a microchip holding personal details, driving licence, passport and credit card. He envisages that in future, a simple handshake will transfer personal contact details. He sees the ultimate as chips embedded under a person's skin.

2   *Improved functionality.* Computer functions that today require elaborate software will become standard functions or even part of the hardware. Voice recognition technologies are maturing, making it easier to talk into word processors and other computer applications. Language translation is improving in leaps and bounds. Various biometric technologies such as retina recognition, where the computer identifies you by your eye, could well replace password protected access to computers by 2005.

3   *Multimedia and virtual reality.* Computers will touch more of people's senses through moving images, sound, etc. These can be packaged, recalled and sent to others quickly through networks. Virtual reality will move from the experimental and entertainment phase into practical business applications. Already analysts are talking virtual world maps of complex financial data. Today's cumbersome headsets will be replaced by spectacles or camera sensors that monitor eye movement.

4   *Portability and mobility.* Every year more functions are integrated into smaller sized packages. An example of this trend is the hand-held or palm-sized computer. Wireless connectivity will also replace the spaghetti of wires seen around many workplaces. Through infrared sensors, portable computers can be linked to devices such as printers or to your main desk computer.

These ongoing developments mean that computers will encroach even more into our work and home lives. Within the decade computers and the information they hold will be on tap, even more so than electricity and water. This pervasiveness presents us with many challenges on how to assimilate computing into our daily lives, without being dominated by it or overly dependent on it.

Telecommunications

Unlike computers, the average cost of telephone services has reduced only slightly year on year during the last few decades. However, there have been more dramatic reductions recently, stimulated by privatization of national monopolies, deregulation, and global competition. In February 1997 sixty-nine nations, accounting for 93 per cent of global telecommunications, signed a World Trade Organization agreement to liberalize their telecommunications regimes. From January 1998, the EU opened its domestic markets to competition. These changes are leading to improved services and reduced prices. Transatlantic telephony prices are falling 30 per cent annually, and it is now cheaper to call the USA from the UK than it is to call Italy.

Once used predominantly for voice traffic (telephone conversations), data traffic generated by computers is growing much faster, fuelled by the fast growth in the Internet. Soon the world's telephone lines will carry more data than voices. Other significant trends that affect users are:

1   *Waves complement wires.* Mobile telephony, made possible by radio waves, is the fastest growing sector in telecommunications. Price differentials with fixed lines have reduced from a factor of ten or more to only two or three. Over half of the world's phones will be wireless by 2010 and the 150 million subscribers at the end of 1997 are expected to grow to nearly 1.5 billion. New digital cordless (DECT – Digital Enhanced Cordless Telecommunications) phones will increase mobility both outside and inside buildings, as they seamlessly switch from an office base station to a cellular network.

2   *Continual enhancement of global connectivity and bandwidth.* High-speed fibre optic networks now span the globe. Recent additions are cables linking the USA to Brazil and Venezuela, and a new network in the Far East. Sophisticated terminal equipment also squeezes more capacity from a given line.

3   *New satellite systems.* In the next decade, some 1700 new communications satellite launches are planned. Billions of dollars are being invested in low orbit satellite networks. The Motorola-led Iridium initiative plans to place sixty-six satellites to give global phone coverage. Teledesic, a joint venture of Bill Gates, Craig McCaw and Boeing will circle the globe with 288 Internet satellites.

4   *Digitalization.* Telecommunications equipment is becoming increasingly
     digitalized. This allows it to take advantage of computer components to
     drive down prices, while at the same time adding more intelligence in
     both the network and the telephone. In the future networks will handle
     communications with many more devices, from photocopiers to vending
     machines.

One of the problems that has plagued more rapid uptake of new services
is the proliferation of different standards. Thus, whereas Europe has
standardized on GSM (general services mobile) for its digital cellular
networks, it is much less popular than two rival systems (TDMA - time
division multiple access; and CDMA - code division multiple access) in
the USA. This creates the need for multiple standard handsets to maintain
global mobility. However, new standards, such as UMTS (universal
mobile telephone system) means that the current barriers to global operation should diminish in future. Increasing mobility is also leading to the
acceptance of personal telephone numbers, that an individual or business
can retain for life, without the need to obtain new phone numbers when
they relocate.

The bandwidth bonanza

In line with many other industries, price reductions stimulate demand,
which in turn stimulates increased investment in networks and services.
The growing demand for networked multimedia applications over the
Internet, such as real-time video, is one stimulus for increased bandwidth.
Today's trunk telephone networks are nearly all fibre optic cables, and
while transmission speeds of 2.4 Gigabits per second are common place,
speeds of 1000 Gigabits per second have already been demonstrated. This
means that a single fibre cable can carry more than all the world's 1995
telephone traffic.

   The challenge is to deliver high bandwidth and the content it contains
to the end-user, especially when on the move or at home. High
bandwidths achievable on an office network drop rapidly as service
operators have to reach 'the last half mile' to people's homes, or go via
wireless. The first problem could be solved, for those homes without a
cable service, by DSL (digital subscriber line), that promises transmission
rates of several megabits per second through twisted-pair copper wires.
It is also expected that within five years cost-effective mobile bandwidth
will increase by a factor of fifty or more.[21] Table 1.4 shows some of the
alternative technologies and how they affect the speed of delivery of
information to the user.

   As well as higher speed connections, digital compression techniques
increase the effective bandwidth by compressing signal information into

Table 1.4 Effects of bandwidth

Connection	Speed	Time to down load 10Mbytes	Comments
Modem	56 Kbps	23 minutes	Universally available through standard telephone lines; low cost. In practice continuous speeds are lower at around 40 Kbps, so download times are higher
ISDN (Integrated Services Digital Network)	128 Kbps	10 minutes	Not universal. More popular in Europe. Line rentals cost more as does required computer expensive terminal adaptors. Good for bulk files
TI leased line	1.5 Mbps	52 seconds	Dedicated line into telephone network
Cable modem	4 Mbps	20 seconds	Needs two-way cable systems. Widely available in urban areas. Cable passes 90 per cent of US homes
ADSL (Asynchronous Digital Subscriber Line)	8 Mbps	10 seconds	Works through standard telephone copper wires. Speeds drop to 1.5 Mbps when more than 1 km from the local exchange

Note: 10 Mbytes is approximately the equivalent of a 3.5-minute video or five books. It must be realized that in practice download speeds are much slower due to network delays, or more typically overloaded computer servers on the Internet.

a fraction of its original size. We are therefore on the verge of seeing order of magnitude improvements in telecommunications functionality and price, similar to those historically associated with computers.

Convergence and connectivity

After many years when convergence of telecommunications and comput-ing did not happen as fast as many analysts expected, it now appears to be doing so. Computer Telephony Integration (CTI) allows computer systems to perform telephone functions such as automatic dialling or recording incoming voice messages. Nokia's 9000 communicator provides a mobile phone and small computer in a single device, complete with email and web browsing. There is also convergence in services, with boundaries blurring between broadcasting, publishing, on-line services and voice telephony. From a computer on the Internet you can read newspapers, see video clips and have voice conversations by Internet phone. Conversely suitable digital televisions can access the World Wide Web and on-line information services.

In the future, it will be difficult to tell the difference between what is a phone and what is a computer. The end result is that every intelligent electronic device, as well as humans, will be connected to a growing information and knowledge utility. Here, another law comes into place to complement Moore's Law. This is Metcalfe's Law (named after Bob Metcalfe, one of the inventors of Ethernet) that says that the utility of a network is proportional to the square of the number of users. Connectivity and convergence make information and knowledge available at any place, at any time. They significantly boost the capability for knowledge networking.

From computation to cognition

The role of computers has evolved continuously as improved affordability and functionality has made them more widely accessible and

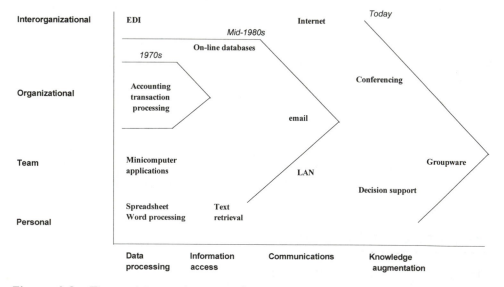

Figure 1.3 The evolving applications of computing

increased the range of viable applications. Figure 1.3 shows how the role has broadened in two dimensions – users and functions. From an early base of data processing (computation) at the organizational level, computers now handle many forms of data (text, image, sound) and are used by individuals as well as in interorganizational networks.

The next phase of this evolution of role is now unfolding. It is the development of the computer's role in support of knowledge and team working. Over the last decade we have seen the growth of its role in supporting person-to-person communications through email. Now it is increasingly supporting knowledge networking through computer conferencing and other collaborative technologies. It will also become more of a tool for augmenting human cognition. The different technologies that contribute to knowledge development and processing are the subject of Chapter 3.

New economy, new rules

The traditional economy operates on the basis of limited resources that deplete when used. In contrast, the information and knowledge continue to grow, even more so when used. For example, if I have a physical resource like a bottle of beer, and give you half, there is only half left for me. On the other hand, if I send you an electronic copy of a document, you can annotate it, add notes, return it to me, and we both have the original information – two for the price of one! Furthermore, the annotations and discussions enrich and add to our knowledge.

Knowledge is diffusable. It 'leaks' and often defies barriers and laws that try to contain it. Knowledge is intangible, yet it can have high value. How much would you be prepared to pay for the experience of Red Adair's people to stop a fire in one of your oil wells? The value of knowledge depends heavily on context. Thus the same information or knowledge can have vastly different values to different people at different times. It also has different properties and values when in different formats. When embedded in a business process it is more easily shared than knowledge in people's heads, that might be much more valuable if you can access it.

The characteristics of the networked knowledge economy, so different from those of the physical economy, demand new thinking and approaches by policy-makers, senior executives and knowledge workers alike. However, everywhere you look, you see organizations blindly following old rules and coming unstuck.

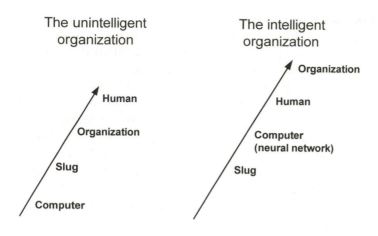

Figure 1.4 Scale of intelligence

The unintelligent organization

On a scale of intelligence, it often seems that organizations are less intelligent than the humans within them (Figure 1.4). They make costly mistakes and few survive beyond what in human terms is adolescence. Yet, according to the saying, 'more heads are better than one'. So what goes wrong?

The scales on Figure 1.4 are logarithmic. A slug (with around 1000 neurons) has hundreds of times more thinking capability than most computers. However, neural networks of computers have reasoning capability that starts to approach those of human beings in highly specific problem domains.

One problem is that of 'group think', where a herd instinct takes over from individual common sense. In the 1980s acquisition mania was in fashion. How many organizations came out with a profit on those 'strategic investments'? Another problem is that risk is shared. If a decision goes wrong then one individual is not wholly to blame. What about today's fashions? Will organizations handle these intelligently? Not if recent examples are anything to go by.

Outsourcing and downsizing

Logically, both seem a great idea. You focus on your core activities and subcontract activities to specialists who do it better and cheaper than you. However, by doing so you may lose some in-house knowledge and expertise.

Regular surveys by the American Management Association show that more than two-thirds of companies who downsize do not show any improvement in their bottom-line results. A typical example is an oil company who after bringing on stream a new oil well made many people redundant. Less than a year later, they realized that similar knowledge was needed in another part of the world. But by then this knowledge had been lost from the company. In another company a team of specialists was made redundant. Now it is spending twice what it was before to buy in similar expertise.

Outsourcing presents similar problems. Holiday Inns lost some vital information when it outsourced some software development to India. When team leaders changed, deadlines were missed. Researchers Kumar and Willcocks attributed the change to the different approaches to software development:

> The work style of Indian programmers and analysts was very different from that of their American counterparts. Compared to most US professionals who had acquired their expertise on the job, most of the Indian professionals had formal graduate level training in development methodologies. Thus, while the work style of the Americans relied upon informal learnt practices and improvisation, the Indian workstyle reflected a greater degree of methodology formalism.[22]

The original team leaders of each party had such good implicit knowledge of these differences that they could work through them together. After they moved on, the US people had to become much more explicit about what was needed. Several of the original Indian team had to go to the USA for six weeks to learn about the systems. When an organization outsources its IT, how much of its implicit knowledge is crucial but unknown to the new providers?

Millennium myopia

The problems created for computer systems when the date changes from 1999 to 2000, has turned out to be the blind spot of the century. It was known, at least to some people, that many computer programmes, those which stored dates as two numbers (e.g. 88 for 1988), could not cope with the transition of date from 31 December 1999 to 1 January 2000. Yet senior managers ignored the impact of this until it was almost too late. Estimates of the size of the problem and the costs to fix it have doubled regularly every six months, as it becomes more apparent how widespread the problem is. Even as this is written, it is predicted that a significant number of crucial computer systems will not be modified by the time of this immovable deadline, severely impacting business operations and quite likely putting many smaller companies out of business.

Fragmented knowledge

A common problem in many situations is that the knowledge needed to solve a problem actually exists, but is elsewhere. When Mercedes Benz introduced its new A-class small car in 1997, they overlooked a simple test routinely carried out in Sweden on new cars. In the so-called Elk test, a Swedish journalist swerved to avoid an imaginary elk. The car overturned and injured the journalist. Mercedes Benz had performed over 8 million kilometres of road test, but had overlooked this one. After launching the cars with great fanfare, it had to recall the car for major modifications, a costly oversight of something already known. It is even said that there were people in other parts of the organization that were aware of the Elk test.

In many organizations, knowledge is dispersed. Part of the solution to a customer problem may already be known in the engineering department and another part in the marketing department, but is not available to customer service. Important information is often held on the disk drives of individuals' personal computers (PCs). A survey in one company a few years ago found that 80 per cent of all its electronic information was held in this way, and was not readily accessible to others in the organization. Unintelligent organizations harbour fragmented knowledge. They do not know what they know.

Dangerous denials

Even where knowledge exists, as the millennium example shows, many people do not face up to the inevitable. A similar situation was true until recently in the case of the first megatrend, that of the Internet. It was only a couple of years ago that I talked to a group of MIS (management information systems) managers about the impact of the Internet. I recounted the situation in the mid-1980s when most central MIS departments had dismissed the importance of the PC, and said it would not affect them, then belatedly panicked and sought to control the inevitable. I simply substituted on an old slide the word Internet in place of PC and said the information system (IS) world was going through a comparable transition again. A senior MIS manager in the audience said: 'The Internet goes into my company over my dead body.' Interestingly, I have not seen or heard of him since! Another MIS director was widely quoted in the press as calling the Internet a 'Mickey Mouse' technology. Yet, as we now know, the Internet is rapidly becoming mainstream MIS.

Look around you. Are there dangerous denials about your environment by you or your organization? How sustainable is the environment under threat of human activities? Has your company got a blind spot like the millennium bug? Is your organization geared to the different rules of the knowledge economy? Consider your own position. Are you equipped

with the skills needed to adapt and thrive in the event of redundancy or
a life-changing event?

Dynamic environments, new responses

As well as the five megatrends described earlier, most organizations face
a number of recurring challenges:

- an ongoing need to reduce costs and increase productivity
- new competitors, often from unexpected quarters outside of their
  industry
- the changing needs and higher expectations of customers
- the need to add value and create differentiation as many traditional
  products become commodities and price sensitive
- demands for ever higher product and service quality
- the need to minimize risk – from new ventures, unexpected market
  shifts, supply chain disruption, natural disasters such as earthquakes etc.
- gaining better returns on investments, particularly in areas such as
  information technology
- the need for speed – faster responses to customer problems, shorter
  time to market for new products and services.

Most organizations are operating in a business environment that is in a
state of constant flux. Change, unpredictability and uncertainty prevail.

Organizations have developed a number of responses to these
challenges. Initiatives such as TQM and BPR have helped. But they do
not go far enough to address many of these challenges. Generally, organizations need to be more adaptive and develop new responses (Figure 1.5).

New strategies, new structures

Successful strategies will exploit the developments in technology described
earlier in this chapter. They will take advantage of the Internet and
electronic commerce to create global markets for new products and services.

Value to customers will be enhanced through information and knowledge. Information products, such as databases, and knowledge-based
services, such as consultancy, will become important ways of generating
revenues. Technology will be used to tailor services to individual
customer needs and develop closer customer relationships.

In terms of structure, responsive organizations will be those that are
more networked. Virtual teams and organizations will allow them to
create value through unique combinations of skills that are flexibly
combined as needed. The future organization is most likely to consist of

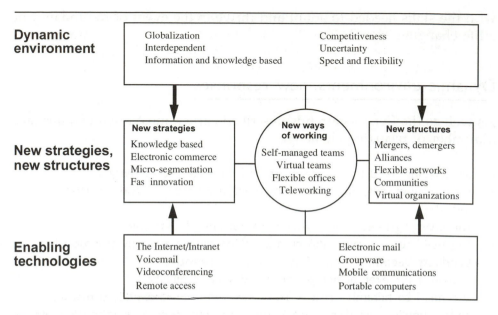

Dynamic environment

Globalization
Interdependent
Information and knowledge based

Competitiveness
Uncertainty
Speed and flexibility

New strategies, new structures

New strategies
Knowledge based
Electronic commerce
Micro-segmentation
Fas innovation

New ways of working
Self-managed teams
Virtual teams
Flexible offices
Teleworking

New structures
Mergers, demergers
Alliances
Flexible networks
Communities
Virtual organizations

Enabling technologies

The Internet/Intranet
Voicemail
Videoconferencing
Remote access

Electronic mail
Groupware
Mobile communications
Portable computers

Figure 1.5 Responses to environmental change and technology drivers

networks of self-managed teams that rapidly reconfigure to adapt to opportunity and change. Teams, not functions or departments, will become the core productive units within organizations.

In addition, success will come through wider and deeper relationships. The RSA (The Royal Society for the encouragement of Arts, Manufacture and Commerce) Tomorrow's Company Inquiry found that inclusive relationships with all stakeholders – including the wider community, employees, and customers is the key to sustained future success.[23] This is also born out by the market. In an analysis of 350 large companies, investment house Kleinwort Benson found that those companies adopting an inclusive approach outperformed the others 16 per cent in the short term and 38 per cent in the long term.[24] Furthermore these relationships will extend to those who are currently regarded as competitors. Strategies based on competitive advantage – conventional wisdom in the 1980s – may have done many organizations more harm than good. Sustainable wealth comes through creating and growing new markets, not competing in existing ones. Thus competing IT manufacturers increasingly co-operate on matters of standards, while car-makers collaborate on safety.

The innovation imperative
One of the main challenges for any organization is survival. The average life expectancy of most firms is low, around twenty years. One-third of

all businesses in 1970 had disappeared thirteen years later. Today the environment is more turbulent and dynamic, so survival becomes even harder. Yet there are companies, like Shell (founded 1907), Siemens (1847), Du Pont (1802) and 3M (1902) that survive and thrive. How do they do this? They adapt and innovate.

Every year *Fortune* does an analysis of the world's most admired companies. In 1997 it polled 13 000 business executives for this survey. *Fortune* described the top rated company, Coca-Cola, as 'ruthlessly innovative'. Other companies in the top ten include Merck, Microsoft and Intel, none of them newcomers to the list. *Fortune* notes: 'Innovation is the ingredient that all top companies embrace passionately. It abounds at ever fertile 3M; its the force behind Pfizer and galvanizes Intel.'[25]

Innovative 3M introduced 500 new products in 1996. A 1997 survey by Arthur D. Little of 700 companies in twenty-three countries showed that 84 per cent of companies believed that innovation was more crucial for their business success than it was in a similar survey carried out in 1991. They seek innovation for gaining new customers and creating new markets with innovative products, services and processes.

Of all the responses to the challenges, the most important can be summarized in two words – fast innovation. Continuous improvement initiatives give incremental benefits. What is needed in the new economy is radical innovation. It is not uncommon to find organizations succeeding in creating improvements of not just a few per cent but a factor of ten. Remember when it took days or weeks to get prescription spectacles. Now you can get them in one or two hours. It used to take BP 100 days with an expensive ship to drill a new deep-sea oil well. Now, by applying learning gained elsewhere this can be reduced to five days or less. Research at Rensselaer Polytechnic in New York State found that a key characteristic of organizations who make such breakthroughs is a free flow of ideas, in and out. In every case networking played a big role: 'the most successful researchers have wide-ranging networks of people'.[26] They have discovered knowledge networking.

Knowledge networking

Knowledge networking is not easy to define or describe. It is a rich and dynamic phenomenon in which knowledge is shared, developed and evolved. It is a process of human and computer networking where people share information, knowledge and experiences to develop new knowledge for handling new situations. Charles Savage, author of *Fifth Generation Management*, first brought the term 'knowledge networking' to my attention. It is a powerful juxtaposition of two important concepts –

that of the strategic resource of knowledge, and that of the human act of networking. Savage defines it as: 'the process of combining and recombining one another's knowledge, experiences, talents, skills, capabilities, and aspirations in ever-changing profitable patterns'.[27]

The key characteristics of knowledge networking are:

- structural components: the network's nodes and links
- links provide paths for communications, knowledge flows and developing of personal relationships
- nodes in networks can be individuals or teams
- the nodes are the focal points for activity or formal organizational processes
- the pattern of nodes and links continually changes
- density of connections exhibits many forms – some may be more circular with obvious hubs; others may be more diffuse
- individuals belong to several networks – in some they are more central than in others
- there is often no discernible boundary to a network
- networks connect to each other; links strengthen and weaken
- one-to-one and multiple conversations take place; asynchronously or synchronously
- knowledge flows in both deliberate and unanticipated ways.

In many respects knowledge networks are like biological organisms. The nodes (teams) are energized by nutrients, such as knowledge, motivation and challenge. They process knowledge, and add to their experience to develop and grow. They sense and respond to their environment through their external interactions. Connections that extend beyond their immediate neighbours gives them more sensitivity and influence. It takes only a small number of links (four to six) to connect two people anywhere in the world. Research into the so called 'small world effect' shows that just 1 per cent of long-range connections dramatically reduces the number of steps to connect two people anywhere in the world.[28] With the Internet, connectedness increases and the pipeline of knowledge is wider.

Knowledge networks take a variety of forms, and vary in how static or dynamic they are. As Lipnack and Stamps comment: 'they ebb and flow as the needs of their participants change'.[29] Because of this dynamic complexity, one might wonder how they work at all. Yet they do and bring many benefits. Networking allows rapid access to the best available knowledge, for example to solve problems or share best practice. Knowledge flows around the network and is enriched and refined by passing through many minds. New knowledge is created. This knowledge can be developed to develop better products or innovative solutions to problems. Additionally valuable working and social relationships are developed.

Knowledge networks aggregate disparate knowledge to give new insights and solve intractable problems. The El Niño phenomenon received its name since it was an apparently periodic local ocean-warming phenomenon observed by Peruvian fishermen. It was only when scientists collated their knowledge and recognized that other climatic effects occurred at the same time elsewhere in the world that El Niño was recognized as a global phenomenon. Now scientists around the world aggregate data and use modelling to predict its effects and mitigate its $6 billion impact.

Knowledge networking is a different way of working. It is about openness and collaboration across departmental, organizational and national boundaries. It's about building multiple relationships for mutual benefit. It defies traditional methods of management. There are organizational challenges in harnessing and exploiting the knowledge that is generated.

Throughout this book are many examples of knowledge networking, and especially virtual teamworking over electronic networks. Part B explores the opportunities while Part C gives practical guidelines to make it successful.

Summary

This chapter has examined some of the key trends and influences that are impacting organizations, individuals and society as a whole – knowledge, globalization, networking, virtualization and technology, especially the Internet (Figure 1.6).

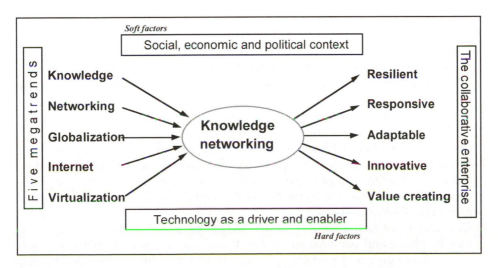

Figure 1.6   Shapers and responses in the networked knowledge economy

Many of the observations are not new. Alvin Toffler writing in the 1973 book *Future Shock* had already foreseen some of these trends and their consequences. He wrote of the pace of change and uncertainty of jobs: 'the death of permanence'. He wrote of the collapse of hierarchy and project based organizations.[30] Subsequently these things are happening, though perhaps not as fast as Toffler had envisaged. Another visionary is Douglas Engelbart. Decades ago he foresaw the possibility of inter-connecting people to hyperlinked documents of information, in a global information repository that he called a 'docuverse' (document universe). It would have hypertext links (where words in one document can be linked to other documents) so users could retrieve information and navigate around information space. Now we have such a docuverse in the form of the World Wide Web. All the trends in this chapter are inter-related, but it is the Internet that has brought global knowledge network-ing to the fore.

Points to ponder

1 What major changes has your organization gone through in the last five years? Were they predicted and planned for?
2 Which are the main companies competing in your markets today? How different are they from five years ago? Are there competitors from other industries or other countries?
3 What major changes have taken place in your life over the last five years? How well did you cope? Think about what might happen in the next five years. How certain are you of the outcomes?
4 What megatrends, other than the five covered, do you see shaping the world around you?
5 What knowledge do you need to succeed in your goals? How has it changed over the last few years? What do you need to do to keep it current?
6 Who do you network with? What benefits do you get from your network-ing?
7 If you are an Internet user, what proportion of communications takes place with people from other countries? How does this alter your perspective? If you are not an Internet user, what is preventing you from being one?
8 What products or services do you buy over the phone or via the Internet? What are the advantages and disadvantages compared to buying using conventional face-to-face methods? What would you like to be able to do or buy virtually but cannot?
9 Consider what technologies you use today compared to ten years ago, e.g. mobile phone and personal computer. What can you now do better or more easily than you could previously? How would you like technology to help you more in future?

10 Develop a blank template of Figure 1.5 (drivers and responses). Insert the key drivers and responses that you see affecting your life and work.

Notes

1 *Business Week* (1998). The new economy starts to hit home, 23 March, 36.
2 *Business Week* (1997). Vital statistics for the real-life economy, 29 December, 34.
3 Pink, D. (1997). Free agent nation'. *FastCompany*, (12), 131.
4 Durham University Business School (1997). Realising the potential of self-employment. *Small Business Foresight Bulletin No 7*, http://www.dir.ac.uk/~dbr0www/bulletin/bull_97/b7_97.html
5 Sadtler, D., Campbell, A. and Koch, R. (1997). *Breakup!: When Companies are Worth More Dead than Alive*. Capstone.
6 Drucker, P. F. (1993). *Post Capitalist Society*. Butterworth-Heinemann.
7 Gimpel, J. (1992). *The Medieval Machine: The Industrial Revolution of the Middle Ages*. Pimlico.
8 Naisbitt, J. (1982). *Megatrends: Ten New Directions Transforming our Lives*. Warner Books.
9 Naisbitt, J. and Aburdene, P. (1990). *Megatrends 2000: Ten New Directions for the 1990s*. Warner Books.
10 Stewart, T. A. (1997). *Intellectual Capital*. Nicholas Brealey Publishing.
11 Wyllie, J. (1998).The economics of intangible value. In *Collaborative Innovation and the Knowledge Economy*. The Society of Management Accountants of Canada.
12 Masuda, Y. (1990). *Managing in the Information Society*. Basil Blackwell, English; translated from the original Japanese publication, Masuda, Y. (1980). *The Information Society as a Post-Industrial Society*. Institute for the Information Society, Tokyo.
13 Lipnack, J. and Stamps, J. (1986) *The Networking Book: People Connecting with People*. Routledge & Kegan Paul; and more recently Lipnack, J. and Stamps, J. (1993) *The Team Net Factor: Bringing the Power of Boundary-Crossing into the Heart of Your Business*. John Wiley & Sons; and Lipnack, J. and Stamps, J. (1994) *The Age of the Network: Operating Principles for the 21st Century*. John Wiley & Sons.
14 Hastings, C. (1993). *The New Organization: Growing the Culture of Organizational Networking*. McGraw-Hill, p. 7.
15 (1987). *Digital Equipment Corporation Second Quarter Report*. Digital Equipment Corporation, Maynard, MA.
16 Biemans, W. G. (1992). *Managing Innovation with Networks*. Routledge.
17 Wissema, J. G. and Euser, L. (1991). Successful innovation through inter-company networks. *Long Range Planning*, **24**(6), 33–9.
18 Garten, J. E. (1998). Why the global economy is here to stay. Cited in *Business Week*, 23 March, 9.

19 Gillett, S. E. and Kapor, M. (1997). The self-governing Internet: coordination by design. In *Coordination of the Internet* (B. Kahin and J. Keller, eds) MIT Press.

20 Scott Morton, M. S. (ed.) (1991). *The Corporation of the 1990s*. Oxford University Press.

21 The European ACTS programme (see http://www.infowin.org) has several projects that have demonstrated broadmand wireless applications at 34 Mbit/sec and has demonstrated 155 Mbits/second, although only over small distances.

22 Kumar, K. and Willcocks, L. (1996). Offshore outsourcing: a country too far? RDP96/1, Templeton College, Oxford.

23 RSA (1995). *Tomorrows Company: The Role of Business in a Changing World: Inquiry Final Report*. RSA, John Adam Street, London. The Inquiry's work now continues under the aegis of the Centre for Tomorrow's Company, London.

24 Smith, G. (1997). Intangible assets in corporate valuation: an investor's view. At Business Intelligence Conference, *Turning Knowledge into a Corporate Asset*, London, October.

25 *Fortune* (1997). Most admired companies, 3 March.

26 *Business Week* (1997). Getting to eureka, 10 November.

27 Savage, C. M. (1996). *5th Generation Management: Cocreating through Virtual Enterprising, Dynamic Teaming, and Knowledge Networking*. Butterworth-Heinemann.

28 *Business Week* (1998). Do the math – it is a small world, 17 August, 77–8.

29 Lipnack, J. and Stamps, J. (1993). *The Team Net Factor: Bringing the Power of Boundary-Crossing into the Heart of Your Business*. John Wiley & Sons.

30 Toffler, A. (1973). *Future Shock*. Pan.

Identifying Unbounded Opportunities

The changes accompanying the evolution towards the networked knowledge economy are causing organizations of all types to reassess their strategies. In Part B three key areas of development that are shaping new strategic opportunities are described.

The first is the focus on knowledge as exemplified by the current interest in knowledge management and related initiatives where knowledge is a focus. The second are those opportunities created by technology, with particular emphasis on technologies that leverage knowledge. The third is really a focus on the changes brought about by the affect of technology of diminishing the importance of location. We refer to this as virtualization. It appears in various guises ranging from virtual working or teleworking to ways of selling and delivering product and services remotely via electronic networks. Together these three areas of development are contributing to the integration of 'hard' (electronic) and 'soft' (human) networking into winning knowledge-based collaborative strategies (see Figure B.1).

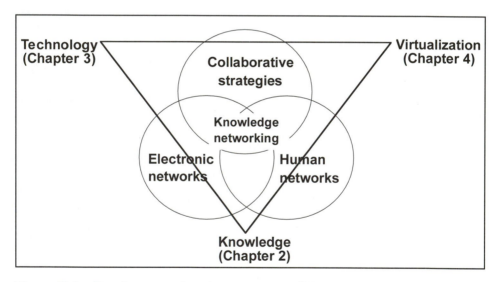

Figure B.1   Developments that shape winning collaborative strategies

This part of the book offers insights into these three significant areas. Developments are described along with examples of how organizations are exploiting them and some of the main challenges they confront.

Chapter 2

Knowledge: the strategic imperative

Every few years a new management philosophy captures the attention of strategists and business leaders. In the 1990s, such movements have included those of total quality management and, more recently, business process re-engineering. The last few years have seen knowledge take centre stage. Many consultants, organizations and suppliers have jumped on to the knowledge management bandwagon, relabelling their wares to match. Does all the hype mean that it is merely a passing fad or is it something more fundamental?

This chapter unravels the fad from the fundamentals. The origins of the current interest are traced to several well-established roots, including information management and the learning organization. The different ways in which knowledge can be applied as a core component of strategy are described in terms of seven knowledge levers. Essential knowledge processes are depicted as two knowledge cycles. One cycle consists of the processes used in innovation and the other those used in knowledge sharing. The chapter concludes with a review of opportunities and challenges.

Fad or fundamental?

It is easy to dismiss the interest in knowledge as a passing fad. Indeed, 47 per cent of British managers in a 1997 study by Cranfield School of

Management expressed this view, although studies one year later shows this figure down to 2 per cent.[1] Closer analysis shows that knowledge has been gaining importance over two decades and that many organizations have already gained significant benefits through applying knowledge-based strategies.

The momentum of knowledge

Interest in knowledge is not new. Greek philosophers, such as Plato and Socrates set out key principles that have stood the test of time. Often quoted in business circles today is Francis Bacon's observation made at the end of the sixteenth century: 'knowledge is power'.[2]

In recent times several management writers have highlighted the role and contribution of knowledge in business strategy. Peter Drucker is credited with coining the phrase 'knowledge worker' in the 1960s. Over a decade ago, he was writing about the role of knowledge in organization in some depth.[3] Other foresighted writers include Masuda (1980), Sveiby and Lloyd (1987), Nonaka (1991) and Stewart (1991).[4] Even so there was no widespread interest in the topic of knowledge among most business managers until just a few years ago.

Now the level of interest has exploded. From a mere handful of international management conferences in 1995-6, there were well over twenty-five in 1997. Each month sees the arrival of several new books. Several new periodicals devoted specifically to knowledge management were launched in 1997, including the *Journal of Knowledge Management* and *Knowledge Management Review.* My colleague Debra Amidon has traced the momentum of knowledge as a set of timelines – Hindsight, Insight and Foresight – in her *The Ken Awakening* where she writes that the momentum of knowledge management: 'has now reached a stage of critical mass of insight. Dedicated expertise across all disciplines are exploring and defining new management practices fundamental to capitalizing upon the knowledge based economy'.[5]

Established roots

The current interest stems from several well-established roots (Figure 2.1).

I   *Business transformation.* Knowledge management is seen by many
    companies as a natural adjunct to other business transformation
    initiatives, such as TQM and BPR. Property and insurance company

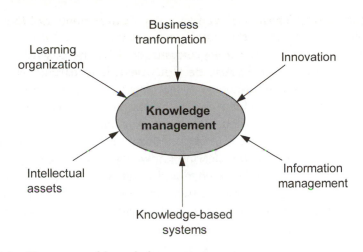

Figure 2.1 The roots of knowledge management

Source: Skyrme, D. J. and Amidon, D. M. (1997). *Creating the Knowledge-Based Business: Key Lessons from an International Study of Best Practice,* Business Intelligence

CIGNA re-engineered its underwriting processes, in which it incorporated knowledge of its best underwriters.

2 *Innovation.* The quest for better and faster innovation is leading to a focus on knowledge flows and networking in firms' innovation processes. Speciality chemicals company Unichema applies knowledge management to improve its innovative capabilities. An example is the use of conceptual modelling to map Unichema's collective knowledge of soap-making.

3 *Information management.* Professional services organizations, such as legal firms and management consultancies, have long recognized the value of well-managed information resources. Booz Allen & Hamilton's information specialists collate corporate knowledge into Knowledge Online, a networked set of databases accessible throughout the organization.

4 *Knowledge-based systems.* Those who developed and used expert systems in the 1970s and 1980s argue that they have been practising knowledge management for many years. Their systems hold the distilled knowledge of experts, captured as a set of rules for use in diagnosis and problem-solving applications. Despite their chequered history, such systems are increasingly found as part of a knowledge management programme. One example is the assessment of risk for new insurance proposals at Thomas Miller & Co.

5 *Intellectual assets.* As noted in Chapter 1, the underlying value of many companies is not in their physical assets, but in their intellectual assets such as know-how. Skandia has systematically developed measures of its

intellectual capital. These are used as a key management tool in developing its position in the insurance market.

6   *Learning organization.* The 'learning organization' has its origins in companies like Shell, where Arie de Geus described learning as the only sustainable competitive advantage. A learning organization continually develops its competence, for example by learning from its successes and failures. Learning and knowledge go hand in hand, as Harvard professor David Garvin has noted: 'A learning organization is an organization skilled at creating, acquiring and transferring knowledge, and modifying its behaviour to reflect new knowledge and insights'.[6] Companies that started with learning initiatives in the mid 1990s, such as Glaxo Wellcome and Anglian Water, have now broadened or repositioned these as knowledge initiatives.

Today's knowledge agenda draws on the skills and practices used in these different disciplines to create winning strategies based on knowledge.

Knowledge is different

One of the practical problems in developing strategies for exploiting knowledge is its complex nature. The word 'knowledge' is frequently substituted for 'information' in various methods or products. This is too simplistic and ignores some distinctive differences.

What is knowledge?

Knowledge takes many forms. There are facts, there is the knowledge to perform a certain task having learnt a particular skill, and there is knowledge that something is right, according to your personal beliefs. Many classifications have been developed to distinguish these and other types of knowledge. Most are somewhat academic and in practice matter hardly a wit.[7] Whatever classifications others use, most managers can readily identify what knowledge is important to them in their job, and what is crucial for their organization's success. Perhaps the most practice-oriented categorization is that cited by Charles Savage:[8]

*   Know-how – a skill, procedures.
*   Know-who – who can help me with this question or task.
*   Know-what – structural knowledge, patterns.
*   Know-why – a deeper kind of knowledge understanding the wider context.
*   Know-when – a sense of timing, and rhythm.
*   Know-where – a sense of place, where is it best to do something.

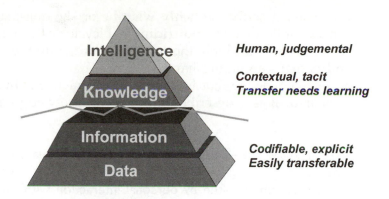

Figure 2.2 A knowledge hierarchy

Some of the more critical types of knowledge needed by managers are those that are more judgemental, such as 'know-why' and 'know-when'.

Another popular classification schema is that of a knowledge hierarchy (Figure 2.2). Amidon offers some typical definitions of its elements,[9] to which I have appended examples:

- *Data* – facts and figures. Example: 03772 41565 83385 10157
- *Information* – data with context. Example (from above data): Heathrow weather station; visibility 15 km, sky completely cloudy; wind direction north-west , speed 85 kts; temperature 15.7 °C.
- *Knowledge* – information with meaning. Example: My experience indicates that this weather will cause severe flight delays.
- *Wisdom* – knowledge with insight. Example: I will book a train through the Channel tunnel before all the other passengers find out about this more reliable alternative.

There are many such hierarchies and definitions of information and knowledge, often conflicting. For practical purposes, the precise distinctions of different authorities matter little. More important is that within whatever hierarchy is used there is a clear distinction between two types of knowledge, often referred to as explicit and tacit knowledge. According to Nonaka and Takeuchi explicit knowledge is that which 'can be expressed in words and numbers and can be easily communicated and shared in the form of hard data, scientific formulae, codified procedures or universal principles',

whereas tacit knowledge is 'highly personal and hard to formalize. Subjective insights, intuitions and hunches fall into this category of knowledge'.[10]

The concept of tacit knowledge was described in depth by Polyani who wrote that 'we know more than we can say'.[11] He used the example of a skater. Could a skater describe explicitly what he or she does, such that another person can follow suit? Like riding a bicycle, you acquire the knowledge to do so not through the written word, but the physical experience, and perhaps a guiding hand.

Another facet of knowledge that is important in practice is the degree to which it is shared. Boisot describes this axis of knowledge as diffusion:[12]

*   *Personal/individual knowledge* – known only to those who create it or conceptualize it.
*   *Shared* – diffused to others, often by personal interaction with the creator.
*   *Proprietary* – known widely within an organization, but protected from widespread external use.
*   *Public* – readily available on the open market.

Generally, tacit knowledge is the most valuable knowledge that an organization possesses. It resides in the heads of employees and stakeholders, especially customers. However, people leave organizations, and walk away with their knowledge. The crux of a knowledge strategy is therefore to seek ways of turning personal tacit knowledge into organizational knowledge. The two complementary approaches are:

1   Converting it into a more explicit form – in documents, processes, databases etc. This can be considered as the 'Western tendency' since this is the main emphasis of many European and US knowledge programmes.
2   Enhancing tacit knowledge flow through better interaction, such that the knowledge is more widely diffused around the organization and not held in the heads of a few. The Japanese and Eastern cultures excel at this type of diffusion, through various socialization activities.

Methods used in these approaches are described in Chapter 7.

Characteristics of knowledge

In Chapter 1 it was noted that knowledge defies normal economic rules. Harlan Cleveland, writing in his eminently readable book, *The Knowledge Executive*, describes six special characteristics of information or explicit knowledge.[13] It is

1   *Expandable.* Unlike other resources that are managed because of their scarcity value, the more it is used the more is generated.
2   *Compressible.* It can be summarized for easier handling and can be packaged into small physical formats.

3 *Substitutable*. In many situations it can replace physical and other forms of resource. Thus telecommunications reduces the need for physical transport.
4 *Transportable*. It can move from place to place, quickly and easily, ready for collecting when the recipient chooses.
5 *Diffusive*. It tends to leak. As technology improves, it become ever more difficult to stop reproduction and transmission.
6 *Shareable*. If it is given to another person, the first person does not lose it.

Tacit knowledge is also expandable, diffusive and shareable, but is not as easily transmitted or diffused. It is intangible and difficult to identify and describe. It is context dependent. These characteristics present some interesting management challenges. Making knowledge explicit means that it can be more readily copied, diffused and shared. On the other hand this makes it 'leaky', and it could reach undesirable parties. The increasing rate of knowledge generation means that much existing knowledge has a short 'half-life' and its value decays quite quickly. It needs constant refreshing and revalidating through use.

The knowledge agenda

Two thrusts

The strategies used in various knowledge initiatives can be distilled into two broad thrusts:

1 Knowing what you know – better awareness, sharing and application of existing knowledge, including that which originates outside the organization.
2 Faster and better innovation – more effective conversion of ideas into products and processes.

Knowing what you know

Many organizations under-utilize much of their existing knowledge, because its existence is unknown to those who need it. In one case, a department of AT&T spent $79 449 to glean information that could be found in a publicly available Bell Corporation Technical Information Document, priced $13![14] Has your customer service department spent long hours working out how to deal with a problem, when another department has the solution at its fingertips?

Lost knowledge can have tragic consequences. The crash in 1996 of a Second World War fighter aircraft and the death of its pilot could have been averted if he had known of a simple fix to a problem of losing fuel pressure when flying upside down. The fix was well known to wartime engineers, but unfortunately only came to light at the crash inquiry. A similar situation confronts the nuclear power industry. Many of the engineers who built nuclear power plants in the 1950s and 1960s are retiring, yet these plants will need to be decommissioned at some time in the future. Is there some vital knowledge, known to these engineers, that will make the decommissioning process less hazardous?

It is too easy to mislay knowledge that might be needed in the future, or to be unaware of existing knowledge that could bring business benefits today. Texas Instruments's TI-BEST programme provides a good example of the benefits of 'knowing what you know'.

TI-BEST: sharing best practice at Texas Instruments

Jerry Junkins, when CEO of Texas Instruments, issued this challenge to his leadership team: 'If only we knew what we knew. We can not tolerate having world-class performance right next to mediocre performance, simply because we don't have a method to implement best practices.'[15]

Thus was born the TI-BEST (Texas Instruments Business Excellence Standard) programme in 1994. A fifteen-member steering team was created to develop and roll out the programme. It created best practice databases containing over 500 best practices and a facilitators network. The 200 or so facilitators spend 30 to 50 per cent of their time networking, facilitating knowledge transfer from one part of the 60 000 strong organization to another. There was also a company-wide event, the ShareFair, that brought together people for seminars, knowledge sharing and the inauguration of an annual 'Not Invented Here, But I Did Anyway' award. By 1997 Texas Instruments had increased its yields at its thirteen fabrication plants to create the equivalent capacity of one new facility. Hence this benefit of sharing best practice is described by insiders as 'one free fab plant'.

Faster and better innovation

In striving for better innovation many managers I meet bemoan the lack of creativity in their organizations. In my opinion creativity is abundant. Creativity and idea creation is simply the starting point of innovation. What most organizations lack is the knowledge infrastructure and processes that converts this abundance of ideas into new products or processes. Amidon describes the percentage of ideas that are converted as the Innovation Quotient. She finds that it is 'woefully low' in most organizations.[16] Better innovation comes through increasing this ratio and in retaining ideas that might be initially discarded, but could be of benefit later.

Viable ways of doing this become apparent if innovation is reconceptualized as a set of interacting knowledge processes:

- the absorption of existing knowledge from the external environment
- the creation of new knowledge through creative thinking and interchange of ideas
- the rapid diffusion of ideas and insights through knowledge networking
- the validation, refining and managing of innovation knowledge
- the matching of creative ideas to unmet customer needs and unsolved problems
- encapsulating and codifying knowledge into an appropriate form, such as a tangible product, a description of a new internal process, training material for a new service, a marketable design, patent, etc.

Throughout the innovation process, knowledge is continually being converted from tacit to explicit and vice versa. It flows between people, gets codified into designs and databases, is disaggregated and recombined, restructured into new forms and so on. This rather complex, even chaotic, view of innovation does not easily lend itself to systematic management. Nevertheless, it is a management responsibility to coax out new ideas and steer the promising ones along an idea-to-production pipeline (Figure 2.3). In general, as knowledge progresses through the pipeline it becomes more reproducible and costs less to distribute.

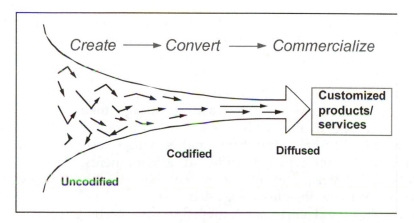

Figure 2.3   Innovation as knowledge refining

Seven levers of strategy

What can be done to secure a strategic advantage through knowledge? Analysis of many cases indicates seven commonly used levers:

1 *Customer knowledge* – developing deep knowledge through customer relationships, and using it to enhance customer success through improved products and services.
2 *Knowledge in products and services* – embedding knowledge in products and surrounding them with knowledge-intensive services.
3 *Knowledge in people* – developing human competencies and nurturing an innovative culture where learning is valued and knowledge is shared.
4 *Knowledge in processes* – embedding knowledge into business processes, and giving access to expertise at critical points.
5 *Organizational memory* – recording existing experience for future use, both in the form of explicit knowledge repositories and developing pointers to expertise.
6 *Knowledge in relationships* – improving knowledge flows across boundaries: with suppliers, customers, employees, etc.
7 *Knowledge assets* – measuring intellectual capital and managing its development and exploitation.

The core levers are knowledge in people, processes and products. In most situations winning strategies are developed by concentrating on just two or three of the seven levers.

Customer knowledge

Virtually every survey ranks customer knowledge as an organization's most important knowledge. In truth, most companies know a lot less about their customers and their markets than they claim. They place too much reliance on traditional market research. They carry out customer satisfaction surveys that tell them little of customers' real wishes and concerns. Customers can provide vital insights into the application of your products and services, but this requires forging close working relationships that surface this deep knowledge.

Companies like 3M and Steelcase encourage their researchers and engineers to spend time with the users of their products. Steelcase, a manufacturer of office furniture, makes video recordings of people working with prototypes in different environments, such as offices, airports and hotels. Through such methods, customer knowledge is deepened and new insights are gained.

Developing good customer knowledge also needs effective environment scanning and market intelligence systems to gather and collate knowledge. Such systems should cover not just customers and markets but a whole range of external factors including technology, social, political, economic and regulatory developments.

Knowledge in products and services

Almost every product is knowledge intensive, even if we don't realize it. When we buy a prescription drug, we are not buying merely a tablet but also the knowledge it encapsulates, that of the therapeutic benefits and side effects gleaned from years of extensive clinical trials. We can use genetic knowledge to create genetically modified foods, such as disease resistant potatoes or square tomatoes that are easier to pack.

Companies hold vast amounts of knowledge that can be exploited as part of their product or service offering. Such knowledge includes applications knowledge, market knowledge, and how to solve problems encountered by users. Much of this is accumulated during the product development and testing process, but is then overlooked. Only a fraction is encapsulated into the final product, leaving under-utilized a rich source of knowledge that could create additional revenues (Figure 2.4).

This knowledge can be exploited in several ways. One way is through additional paid services, such as consultancy or training services. Another way is to make the product 'smart' or 'intelligent'. There is an intelligent oil drill, which 'knows' the shape of the reservoir it is drilling, and so extracts more oil.

Products and services can be customized by combining product and customer knowledge. One example is the personalized daily news

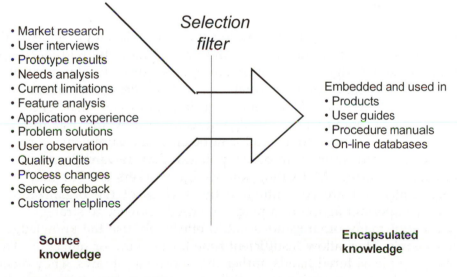

Figure 2.4 The codification filter

bulletin that combines information from many disparate sources. Another is Campbell Soups' 'Intelligent Quisine', designed for people suffering hypertension or high cholesterol. It delivers weekly packages of nutritionally designed, portion-controlled meals based on personal information.

You can also exploit knowledge that is generated as a by-product of your principal activities and turn it into a business opportunity. The Automobile Association in the UK operates motorists' rescue services, from which it builds an ever expanding database about its customers and their needs. This has helped it add many new lines of insurance business, some related to motoring needs, such as holiday travel, but others in new areas, such as household insurance. Perhaps the best known example is American Airlines' reservation system SABRE, which was run as a separate business, and in some years has made more profit for its parent company than flying their aircraft!

Knowledge in people

'People are our most valuable asset' runs the line in many company annual reports. Companies that truly believe it apply this knowledge lever through a competence or learning lens. One underlying model used in this approach is that of a repeating action-learning cycle:

- Plan: think, conceptualize, devise a set of actions.
- Act: do, gain experience of 'theory in practice'.
- Observe: record experiences, share knowledge with others.
- Reflect: consider what has been learnt and how it can be used to make improvements.

Learning programmes typically mesh competence development activities at several levels – individual, team and organization. Individual competence and knowledge is developed through personal development plans that meet the needs of individuals as well as the organization. Team knowledge is enhanced through learning processes that encourage individuals to share their knowledge in teamwork. At the organizational level the focus shifts to overall competence measurement, corporate universities and human resource policies that reward learning and knowledge sharing. Motivating knowledge workers so that they work energetically and are committed to the success of the organization is another important aspect of a people-focused knowledge strategy.

In reality, many organizations fail to effectively use the knowledge in their people. They allow insufficient time for learning or reflection. They regard people as hired hands, rather than borrowed brains. They dictate to them what to do, giving them little discretion in how they do it. It is little wonder that their employees feel undervalued, and will indeed 'walk' at the first opportunity and take their knowledge with them.

In contrast, Shell is an organization long acknowledged as an excellent example of nurturing and developing its people. It has an initiative within its exploration business to 'harness this talent' and make 'better use of this intellectual capital'. Its focus is the development of an infrastructure for learning and leverage of knowledge. There are open learning centres and databases of learning resources on the company's intranet. However, the most significant developments have been the establishment of knowledge communities and developing skills for quality person-to-person dialogue and reflection. Learning is being built into daily work activities.

One company that combines both product and people levers is that of Teltech Resources.

Teltech – people are the product

Teltech Resources of Minneapolis manages a knowledge network of some 3000 human experts whose knowledge is harnessed to tackle difficult problems. This network includes academics, industry experts and recent retirees who have specialist in-depth technical knowledge. Knowledge analysts provide a human interface between the client who has a problem, the expert network and over 1600 technical databases.

Teltech's business is based on a deep understanding of how its clients gather and use knowledge. It then develops close relationships with both suppliers and users of that knowledge. It also blends explicit and tacit knowledge. Explicit knowledge is structured according to a well-developed thesaurus of knowledge domain classifications. This also permits many synonyms, cross-referencing and multiple placements. Analysts 'act as guides in defining, clarifying and interpreting database-search results'.

In one case, a medical products developer had tried in vain to make a heart pump leak-proof in a saline solution. The answer came from an expert in submarine technology, whose equipment also operates in similar environments.[17]

Knowledge in processes

Every business process contains embedded knowledge. Ad hoc activities, previously performed by people with specialist knowledge, become codified into routine processes. It is then more readily diffused throughout an organization. Even so, much tacit knowledge is frequently needed to perform the process effectively and to deal with exceptions. Hence the explicit process knowledge is typically accompanied by training, procedure manuals and access to experts.

One way to enrich knowledge in processes is to embed backup resource material. When CIGNA re-engineered their underwriting processes, much of the contextual information that did not get coded into computer procedures was made available at the click of a mouse. Increasingly, access to human expertise is available on such systems through a 'click here for help' screen icon. This may either trigger an email or even a computer-generated phone call to a human expert. Other organizations use workflow software to blend computer held knowledge with human knowledge. The software applies rules to determine which transactions are straightforward, and are therefore handled automatically by computer, and which require human intervention.

Organizational memory

This strategic lever helps address the issue of 'knowing what you know'. It is also used to avoid repeating the mistakes of the past, and to draw lessons from similar situations or cases from elsewhere. Organizational memory exists in many places, most notably the brains of its people. But it also exists in records, filing cabinets, personal computer disk files and the physical surroundings. External sources should not be overlooked. After all, many outsiders follow an organization's actions, or have even been part of it at one time. As a consultant, I know only too well that clients use me as part of their organizational memory. They request a copy of an assignment report that they cannot now locate, since those who commissioned it have moved on!

A common approach to managing organizational memory is to capture in explicit form the most important knowledge and enter it into knowledge databases. These databases may be in document management systems, in groupware such as Lotus Notes, or as web pages on an intranet. Often such databases will not contain the knowledge *per se*, but will provide pointers to it. Examples of knowledge databases include:

*   Customer histories. These detail interactions with a given customer: products bought, sales visit reports, etc.
*   Best practices. Chevron has best practices databases and a resource map organized according to the categories of the Baldridge quality award.
*   Products and technologies. Details of the organization's various products and history.
*   Bid boilerplates. ICL's Café Vik holds information used in previous project proposals. In a typical situation 80 per cent of information for a project bid is quickly assembled from existing material, freeing up time for the bid team to concentrate on activities that could clinch the sale.

Explicit knowledge bases, however, typically contain less than 10 per cent of an organization's memory. Therefore other approaches are used to make it easier to access the minds of experts. A common example is an on-line directory of expertise, often called Yellow Pages, because they are structured by skill and discipline, not by department. Novartis have also added Blue Pages that contain details of external experts with whom they collaborate. Knowledge-sharing events provide another way of sharing tacit knowledge. Thomas Miller & Co., a mutual insurance company, runs 'knowledge in a nutshell' events. Company experts give talks on their areas of expertise and describe their experiences. These live sessions are also recorded on video for further distribution and subsequent recall.

The key to enhancing organizational memory is to make ongoing experience capture an integral part of everyday work. Techniques include decision diaries, learning histories and post-project reviews.

Knowledge in relationships

Many companies have an invaluable resource of knowledge developed through individual relationships – with customers, suppliers, business partners, professional and trade associations. When a salesperson leaves your company, it is not just their product or customer knowledge that is lost. It may be much of the customer relationship. This relationship involves shared knowledge and understanding – not just of needs and factual information, but of deeper knowledge such as behaviours, motivations, personal characteristics, ambitions and feelings. Such depth of knowledge is not easily replaced overnight.

Organizations can deepen their relationship knowledge by increasing their interaction with the outside world. This may take the form of regular meetings for knowledge exchange and sharing of databases. Toshiba collects comparative data on suppliers ranking 200 quantitative and qualitative factors. It has an active suppliers network where knowledge is shared and suppliers are integrated into future strategies. Extranets provide another way to develop wider linkages. By increasing the number of contacts with key stakeholders, at all levels and functions, you become less vulnerable to the loss of a single contact.

Relationship knowledge can also be deepened by taking a whole range of intercompany interactions to deeper levels of intimacy, and by strengthening knowledge exchange. Relationship marketing, the new vogue in consumer marketing, goes far beyond issuing customers loyalty cards. Customer relationship knowledge comes through exploring mutual interests, seeking new insights through extensive dialogue, and jointly creating new business opportunities. Activities that might previously have been considered confidential to the company are extended to involve stakeholders. These include product planning, marketing campaigns and human resource competency development. Social events also strengthen relationship knowledge. Corporate hospitality does have its benefits!

Knowledge as an asset

The final lever is that of knowledge as an asset. This builds on the notion, mentioned earlier, of measuring and managing intellectual capital. While many organizations have accountants and auditors track in detail every piece of physical plant and machinery, few devote even a fraction of this attention to intellectual capital. Yet this is much more valuable, since it includes knowledge and people.

Advocates of measuring intellectual capital have shown that its measurement provides lead indicators of future financial performance. In his book *The New Organizational Wealth* Karl Erik Sveiby demonstrates how advertising agency Saatchi and Saatchi, when apparently financially healthy, was rapidly depleting its intellectual capital. This was a precursor of the inevitable decline in its financial fortunes.[18] Information, which is arguably the most tangible intellectual asset, rarely gets proper attention. The Hawley Committee in the UK, reporting in 1996, showed a general lack of understanding of the importance of information among boards of directors, let alone having policies or practices for its effective management.[19]

The starting point of any asset-based approach is that of understanding its different components. Intellectual assets are frequently categorized into the following groups:[20]

1   Human capital – in the minds of individuals: knowledge, competencies, experience, know-how, etc.
2   Structural capital – 'that which is left after employees go home for the night': processes, information systems, databases, etc.
3   Customer capital – customer relationships, brands, trademarks, etc.

In some schemes, such as that of Annie Brooking, intellectual property is separated out as a distinct category.[21] This covers assets that are protected by law, and includes trademarks, patents, copyrights, licences and design rights.

Dow Chemical provides a good example of this knowledge lever. In 1994 it had over 29 000 patents in force around the world. However, maintaining the validity of a patent can be costly – up to $250 000 over its lifetime. Dow's Intellectual Asset Management team developed a comprehensive framework for actively measuring and managing its patent portfolio. It found many patents not being effectively exploited, and others with no obvious ownership. It took measures to exploit patents, either through internal use, licensing or sale, while allowing others to lapse by not paying renewal fees. Within three years the team had generated $125 million in additional revenues, their original target for the year 2000.[22]

Its very intangibility makes the identification and measurement of intellectual capital difficult. It also defies normal economic rules, thus creating problems for accountants who like dealing with tangibility and precision. Nevertheless, as is shown in Chapter 7, methods for its measurement are evolving. *Fortune* editor Tom Stewart says: 'You can't see it, you can't touch it, yet it makes you rich'. This lever is surely one that business strategists cannot ignore!

Knowledge processes

As the cases cited so far in this chapter indicate, a wide variety of knowledge-based strategies are found in practice. But beneath this variety, successful initiatives show a degree of consistency in their management of knowledge. This leads to the following practice-focused definition of knowledge management as 'the *explicit* and *systematic* management of *vital* knowledge and its associated *processes* of creating, gathering, organizing, diffusion, use and exploitation, in pursuit of organizational objectives'.

The emphasized words are important:

- *Explicit* – unless something is made explicit it frequently does not get properly managed.
- *Systematic* – this helps to create consistency of methods and the diffusion of good practice. Systematization also lends itself to automation, leading to additional efficiencies in handling explicit knowledge.
- *Vital* – every conversation and every new document in an organization adds to the organization's knowledge pool. Judgement must be applied as to which knowledge is critical and therefore worth managing in a more formalized way.
- *Processes* – as well as being an important dimension of management and business processes, knowledge processes are important in their own right.

The main processes are knowledge conversion, innovation and sharing.

Knowledge conversion
Nonaka and Takeuchi defined four generic processes for converting between tacit and explicit knowledge that they describe as fundamental to creating value:[23]

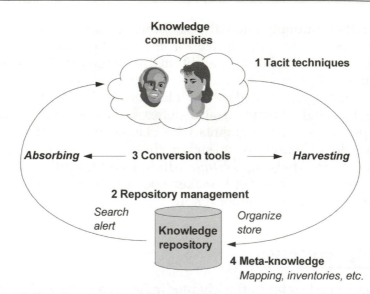

Figure 2.5   Different types of knowledge conversion process

- Tacit-to-tacit (socialization) – where individuals acquire new knowledge directly from others, through observation and dialogue.
- Tacit-to-explicit (externalization) – the articulation of knowledge into tangible form through discussion and documentation.
- Explicit-to-explicit (combination) – combining different forms of explicit knowledge, such as that in documents or databases.
- Explicit-to-tacit (internalization) – such as learning by doing, where individuals internalize knowledge from documents into their own body of experience.

Nonaka and Takeuchi describe how these processes interact in a knowledge spiral, with interaction between tacit and explicit knowledge, and where individual knowledge becomes organizational knowledge and vice versa.

Figure 2.5 shows an alternative perspective of some of the processes involved with tacit and explicit knowledge, along with more commonly used terminology. Converting tacit knowledge into explicit knowledge makes it easier to store, replicate and transmit through computer repositories and networks. When retrieved, it then needs assimilating into another person's tacit knowledge for application in their specific situation.

Knowledge cycles
Operating at a higher level than these generic processes are two knowledge cycles that relate directly to the thrusts described earlier – innovation and sharing existing knowledge (Figure 2.6). The innovation cycle

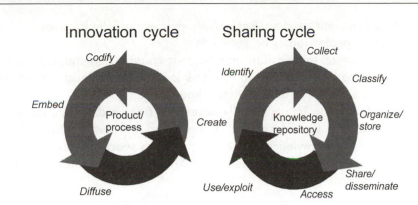

Figure 2.6 Two value-adding knowledge process cycles

on the left represents a progression from idea creation (unstructured knowledge) into more structured and reproducible knowledge, embedded within processes or products. The cycle on the right shows the processes associated with gathering and disseminating existing knowledge, having a knowledge repository as its focal point. Although the activities in each cycle roughly follow the sequences shown, continual iteration through different levels of aggregation means that the actual paths between activities are rather more complex than those depicted.

In outline the innovation processes are:

- *Create.* New ideas are created. Knowledge networking stimulates the cross-fertilization of ideas from different perspectives, and therefore often stimulates an innovation cycle.
- *Codify.* Here a prototype design or a process description is developed. This embodies the idea into a more transferable form.
- *Embed.* At this stage the prototype is further refined and its associated knowledge encapsulated in manufacturing processes and organizational procedures.
- *Diffuse.* Products are distributed in the marketplace or processes are implemented throughout the organization. Their application then generates ideas for improvements, and so the cycle repeats.

In the knowledge-sharing cycle, the knowledge management processes are:

- *Collect.* Existing knowledge is gathered either on a routine basis or as needed. Often its existence is formally recorded in a knowledge inventory or knowledge map.
- *Organize/store.* The knowledge is classified and stored, often using an organization- or industry-specific thesaurus or classification schema. This

makes subsequent retrieval easier. This process usually involves information professionals or librarians.

*   *Share/disseminate.* Information may be sent routinely to those people who are known to be interested in it – this is information 'push'. Meetings and events act as vehicles to share tacit knowledge.
*   *Access.* Information is made easily accessible from a database, for example over an intranet. Users access it as they need it – this is information 'pull'.
*   *Use/exploit.* The knowledge is used as part of a work process. It is refined and developed. Through use, additional knowledge is created and the cycle repeats itself.

A useful form of knowledge that can result from these cycles is meta-knowledge – knowledge about knowledge. Thus, some of the most useful Internet or intranet pages are those that hold directories and indexes of what other information is available. Although the processes outlined above are very much geared towards explicit knowledge or information, similar processes take place in the deployment of tacit knowledge, though in a less structured way.

The knowledge opportunity

The two thrusts of knowledge – innovation and sharing – are fundamental foundations for generating business opportunities. Sharing gets the right knowledge to the right people, in the right place, at the right time. It supports decision-making and helps to solve problems using the best available knowledge. Innovation converts knowledge into new products, services or processes. The seven knowledge levers scale up the opportunity, by widening the reach of knowledge. The processes that underpin knowledge practice are the basic building blocks of activity within a knowledge-based enterprise.

As well as following these logical and rational approaches to exploiting knowledge, let us remember that certain characteristics of knowledge mean that the greatest opportunities come from unexpected quarters. These are driven by the power of combination and by the power of community.

The power of combination

Whether knowledge is explicit or tacit, new opportunities can be created by combining different knowledge in different ways. People from diverse backgrounds regularly make connections between apparently disparate ideas. A common technique used in creativity workshops is that of word association. Participants are asked to think of associations between randomly created pairs of words. For example, the objects scissors and telephone in juxtaposition may spark ideas of a cordless phone, a telephone handset that folds open and shut, or simply cut-price telephone calls!

The arithmetic of knowledge is that of multiplication and combination, not addition. From just a few inputs, the number of different ways in which they can be combined increases factorially. With a few basic variants of colour, engine size and trim, Ford can customize over 27 million varieties of the Ford Fiesta. Now apply this arithmetic to knowledge, where there is a wider range of input choices. The number of new 'knowledge recipes' is virtually unlimited. Certain combinations will have a value out of all proportion to the value of their original inputs, due to the creative combinations used. For example, the basic ingredients used in cookery have changed little over centuries, but many new dishes are invented every day. This is partly due to the wider variety of input, such as the different varieties of a single vegetable and how it is processed and packaged, but mostly it is due to the creative skills of master chefs.

The drive to innovate through knowledge combinations is also apparent in R&D activities. For example, Du Pont deliberately seeks out collaborative research ventures, and not just for the obvious immediate project. As a result of setting up a collaborative venture with a German university to seek a replacement for CFC in aerosols, not only did it get the replacement propellant as planned, but quite unexpectedly, because different people regularly interacted during the course of this collaboration, it also gained a whole new line of catalysts. The more variety in ideas, people and products, the more likely is an innovative combination likely to arise.

The power of community

The Du Pont example illustrates how knowledge emerges and is taken forward through human knowledge networks. The human dimension adds many more possible knowledge combinations than is possible with discrete knowledge components. Furthermore, human networking brings in a new dimension – the power of community.

One knowledge-enriching practice that is gaining significant attention in knowledge initiatives is that of a 'Community of Practice' (CoP). The term emanated out of work at Xerox Parc at the turn of the decade. It refers to a group of people who are 'peers in the execution of real work. What holds them together is a common sense of purpose and a real need to know what each other knows'.[24] They are not a formal team but an informal network, each sharing in part a common agenda and shared interests. In the Xerox example, they found that a lot of knowledge sharing among copier engineers took place through informal exchanges, often around the water cooler. This happened not because management ordered it, but through individual motivation. The participants developed their own sense of community.

Developing and building knowledge-sharing communities is at the heart of effective knowledge networking. Such communities in the aerospace industry have been found to create better design through sharing and testing of ideas. In Shell participants in a K'Munity™ on deep sea drilling share expertise and contribute to reducing the time to develop new oil wells. Tetrapak Converting Technologies has created learning networks focused on its core technologies, such as packaging.

A related practice is that of knowledge ecology, a term coined by George Pór.[25] This extends the community aspect to the wider social context in which knowledge innovation and sharing can flourish. Its core notion is that knowledge is socially contextualized and its development and beneficial application depends as much on building purposeful and

Table 2.1 Contrast of knowledge management and knowledge ecology

	Knowledge management	Knowledge ecology
Orientation (Bottom-line vs Community)	Bottom-line orientation – how knowledge helps the business	Community orientation – sustaining networks and relationships from which knowledge will emerge
Metaphor (Information vs Context)	Architectural emphasis on knowledge objects and flows	Gardening – emphasis on culture, soft systems, adaptability and feedback that *inspire* knowledge flows
Elements (Architecture vs Gardening)	Actionable information	Adds context, synergy and trust to use information into actionable knowledge
Rules (Policy vs Dialogue)	Policy focus – rules for access and compliance	Dialogue focus – interpretation, understanding shared meaning and alignment
Focus (Particle vs Waves)	Intellectual matter – best promotes patents, documents, intellectual matters	Intellectual *energy* – waves, relationships, trust, meaning

committed communities as it does on rational knowledge exchanges. It thus concentrates on the context and environment as much as it does the content. It blends hard (explicit and technical) and soft (social and organizational) aspects of knowledge. It creates flows between conversational knowledge and repository knowledge. Pór makes several distinctions between knowledge management and knowledge ecology (Table 2.1).

Communities exist within and across organizations. Many existed before the knowledge agenda became fashionable. Such communities include quality circles, best practice networks, alumni clubs, professional societies and special interest groups. Although they may not have realized it, they operate as knowledge networks and link hubs of knowledge. The organizational opportunity is to nurture and support such communities, create conditions for new ones to emerge and to harness the knowledge that they generate. As they do so, each community will help grow their organization's intellectual capital – the knowledge in its people, products and processes, not forgetting relationships and the other strategy levers.

Proven benefits

Progressive companies, such as 3M, Hewlett-Packard and Glaxo Wellcome, have long appreciated the contribution of knowledge to their continued success. Many more have joined them in exploiting the knowledge opportunity.

A good knowledge initiative can achieve a range of benefits, including:

- *Avoidance of costly mistakes* – The experience of organizations losing knowledge as they have downsized or restructured, has made them more aware of the costs of 'reinventing the wheel'. General Motors uses debriefing sessions to share lessons more widely through the company.
- *Sharing of best practices* – Chevron is one of many companies that save millions of dollars a year by taking existing knowledge and applying it to similar situations elsewhere.
- *Faster problem-solving* – Using videoconferencing, workers at BP-Amoco's offshore oil platforms can tap into expertise elsewhere in the company when they have problems and minimize production downtime.
- *Faster development times* – Through learning networks and by linking customer problems to an ideas database, Schlumberger continues to improve its rate of innovation.
- *Better customer solutions* – Sales and support staff at Buckman Laboratories use K'Netix™, its computer network, to gain access to the best expertise, and so develop innovative solutions to tricky customer problems.

Examples of knowledge initiatives

- Hoffman La Roche considered the knowledge needed to prepare clinical trials documentation for the approval authorities. By developing knowledge maps, such documentation has contributed to faster time to market for new drugs.
- NEC, the Japanese electronic company, articulated its core knowledge base. This helped it redefine the company's mission as 'computers and communications', markets in which it has shown continuing success.
- Skandia, a Swedish-based insurance company, focuses its management attention on intellectual capital (the knowledge in its people and processes). This focus, with its associated tools, has helped it grow from a small regional company to number five in the world in its market segment.
- Kao, a household and chemical products company, focused on open knowledge sharing among employees. This has helped propel it into new markets.
- PriceWaterhouse created knowledge centres that act as a focal point for knowledge exchange. KnowledgeView[SM] provides a repository of best practice for different business processes. This helps its consultants access best global knowledge to provide better solutions to customer problems.
- Hewlett-Packard uses its intranet to share expertise already in the company, but not known to their development teams. This helps it bring new products to market much faster than before.

- *Gaining new business* – Consultants at ICL use its Café Vik system, to gather scattered knowledge quickly and bid on proposals that would otherwise take too long or cost too much to prepare.
- *Improved customer service* – By putting solutions to customer problems in a shareable knowledge base, Sun Microsystems has improved its level of customer service. Costs are also reduced since customers can download software corrections over the Internet.
- *Reduction of risk* – Thomas Miller & Co., a mutual insurer, combines expertise and organizational memory to better understand its underwriting risks.

The challenge ahead

Knowledge, as we have seen, has some unusual characteristics that make its management and exploitation a challenge. Different challenges face organizations, policy-makers and individuals. For organizations, achieving business benefits such as those just described requires new thinking, new organizational structures, new strategies and new practices. Surveys show that the principle barriers are organizational and management, with organizational culture often being the principal issue. Attitudes have to shift from 'knowledge is power' to 'knowledge sharing is power'. Other recurring challenges are those of information overload, lack of time and difficulties of justifying investment. To achieve success in a knowledge initiative, you need to reconcile several opposite pulls. You need to balance the widespread sharing of knowledge without it leaking such that it harms your own interests. You need an environment that stimulates serendipitous tacit knowledge sharing, yet at the same time has some formalization of knowledge processes. You need to develop organizational memory, yet be aware that sometimes it is essential to forget what worked in the past. You need to nurture knowledge networks while retaining some sense of structure and degree of formalization. All are difficult balancing acts.

For individuals, and especially those in traditional management roles, the knowledge agenda poses many personal challenges. You may regard your knowledge as your source of power, and a reason you hold your job. Why should you then share it freely? At school you were probably conditioned that sharing answers to problems was tantamount to cheating, yet that is the very behaviour you are now asked to follow. As managers you were encouraged to seek competitive advantage. Yet successful knowledge strategies require collaboration, perhaps with individuals and companies you regard as your competitors.

For policy-makers, many policies based on industrial age logic will need to be rethought. Economic measures reflect factory output more than they do knowledge creation and exploitation. Industrial policy is more often focused on attracting inward manufacturing investment rather than creating knowledge-based opportunities.

Summary

This chapter has described the role of knowledge in creating value and business benefits. It has introduced some basic concepts of knowledge, particularly the distinction between tacit and explicit knowledge. It outlined the knowledge agenda as two thrusts (innovation and knowledge sharing) and seven strategic levers, including knowledge in products, knowledge in people and knowledge in processes. The key conclusions are that:

- knowledge is pervasive and strategic
- an organization's most vital knowledge is usually customer knowledge
- most of an organization's knowledge is tacit knowledge in people's heads; therefore any knowledge initiative has to motivate and retain knowledge workers
- sharing knowledge, while a cultural challenge, helps increase overall performance
- knowledge in innovation is likely to create even larger long-term benefits
- there are proven business benefits; pioneers have already demonstrated significant bottom-line improvements
- human networking underpins the success of most knowledge initiatives; understanding knowledge networking and how to nurture communities of practice is therefore fundamental.

The knowledge agenda poses a number of challenges, for individuals, organizations and policy-makers. The toolkits in Part C give practical guidance on how to succeed in these challenges.

Points to ponder

1   Do you know off the top of your head the difference in market value and the book value of your organization – in other words the ratio of intellectual capital?
2   Do you know which knowledge is the most vital in your organization – your crown jewels?
3   Do you know who is responsible for maintaining each of these jewels – keeping them up to date, enhancing them?
4   Which of the seven knowledge levers are systematically exploited in your organization?
5   How well do you understand the needs and aspirations of your customers' customers?
6   Can you find within one minute the name of your organization's on-the-ground expert on the current political and business climate in Azerbaijan?
7   Do you write up notes of conferences you have attended and circulate them to your colleagues?
8   Do you get reward or recognition for sharing your special expertise or skill with people in other departments and organizational functions?
9   How many people are in your network? How may of these are inside your organization and how many outside?
10 When did you last do a personal inventory of your knowledge assets – your strengths, your specialist knowledge, your unique skills, your information resources, your databases, your network? How valuable is it to you? How do you exploit these assets?

Notes

1   KPMG (1998).*The Knowledge Management Annual Survey*. KPMG
2   Bacon, F. (*c*.1598). *Religous Mediations: Of Heresies*. The Latin original is 'nam et ipsa scientia potestas est', literally 'knowledge itself is power'.
3   See for example Drucker, P. (1988). The coming of the new organization. *Harvard Business Review*, **66**(1), January–February, pp. 45-53; Drucker, P. (1989). *The New Realities: In Government and Politics; In Economics and Business; In Society and World View*. Harper & Row.
4   Masuda, Y. (1980). *The Information Society as Post Industrial Society*. Institute for the Information Society, Tokyo; Sveiby, K. E. and Lloyd, T. (1987). *Managing Know-How*. Bloomsbury; Nonaka, I. (1991). The knowledge-creating company. *Harvard Business Review*, November–December, pp. 96–104; Stewart, T. A. (1991). Brainpower. *Fortune*, 3 June, pp. 44–60.
5   Amidon, D. M. (1997). *Innovation Strategy for the Knowledge Economy: The Ken Awakening*. Butterworth-Heinemann.
6   Garvin, D. (1993). Building a learning organization. *Harvard Business Review*, July–August, p. 80.
7   Since a bit is a unit of information, it has been suggested that the corresponding unit of knowledge is a wit!
8   Savage, C. M. (1996). *5th Generation Management: Cocreating through Virtual Enterprising, Dynamic Teaming, and Knowledge Networking*. Butterworth-Heinemann.
9   Amidon, D. M. (1997). *Innovation Strategy for the Knowledge Economy: The Ken Awakening*. Butterworth-Heinemann.
10   Nonaka, I. and Takeuchi, H. (1995). *The Knowledge Creating Company*. Oxford University Press, p.8
11   Polyani, M. (1966). *The Tacit Dimension*. Routledge & Kegan Paul, p.8
12   Boisot, M. H. (1995). *Information Space: A Framework for Learning in Organizations*. Routledge.
13   Cleveland, H. (1989). *The Knowledge Executive*. E. P. Dutton.
14   Oppenheim, C. (1995). Tangling with intangibles. *Information World Review*, December, p. 54.
15   Johnson, C. (1997). Leveraging knowledge for operational excellence. *Journal of Knowledge Management*, **1**(1), September, pp. 50–5.
16   Amidon, D. M. (1997). *Innovation Strategy for the Knowledge Economy: The Ken Awakening*. Butterworth-Heinemann.
17   Sources: Hildebrand, C. (1996). Experts for hire. *CIO*, 15 April, 32–40; also Teltech company literature.
18   Sveiby, K. E. (1997). *The New Organizational Wealth: Managing and Measuring Intangible Asset*. Berrett Koehler.
19   The Hawley Committee (1995). *Information as an Asset: The Board Agendas*. KPMG.
20   This model is attributed to a practitioners' working group that met during 1995–7 and included Gordon Petrash of Dow Chemical, Charles Armstrong of S.A. Armstrong, Leif Edvinsson of Skandia, Hubert Saint-Onge of CIBC, and Patrick Sullivan of The ICM Group.

21 Brooking, A. (1996). *Intellectual Captial: Core Asset for the Third Millennium Enterprise*. International Thomson Business Press.

22 McConnachie, G. (1997). The management of intellectual assets. *Journal of Knowledge Management*, **1**(1), September, 56–62.

23 Nonaka, I. and Takeuchi, H. (1995). *The Knowledge-Creating Company*. Oxford University Press.

24 Seely Brown, J and Solomon Gray, E. (1995). After reengineering: the people are the company. *FastCompany*, **1**(1), 78–82.

25 Pór, G. (1998). Knowledge ecology and communities of practice: emergent twin trends of creating true wealth. *Knowledge Summit '98*, Business Intelligence, London, November. For further information on knowledge ecology see the website of Community Intelligence Labs at http://www.co-i-l.com

Chapter 3

Technology: the knowledge enhancer

The notion that computers can enhance knowledge processes is not new. Even before modern computers were invented, scientists such as Alan Turing described how they might exhibit human thinking qualities. In the 1970s and 1980s, experts predicted that artificial intelligence (AI) systems would be prevalent throughout business, even taking over from humans most routine decision-making activities. The concept behind one type of AI system, the expert system, is deceptively simple. First, elicit knowledge from a human expert, codify it, and store it in a computer knowledge base. Then provide an interface for less knowledgeable people to dialogue with this knowledge base so that they can act like an expert. This sounds like a dream solution to a principal challenge in knowledge management, that of making individual expertise widely accessible to the organization as a whole. Unfortunately, things are not that simple. Today our views have shifted from this emphasis on 'thinking machines' to one of using machines to help humans thinking.

The different ways in which they can do so are demonstrated in this chapter which starts by positioning different knowledge technologies. There are examples of a wide variety of software tools that include text mining, conceptual mapping and intelligent agents. However, it is collaborative technologies, a category that includes groupware, intranets, videoconferencing and document management, that have delivered the most widespread benefits to knowledge practices. Opportunities of using technology to further the knowledge agenda are vast. The main challenges are not technological but are the related human and organizational factors, a theme that is further developed in the toolkits of Chapters 5 to 8.

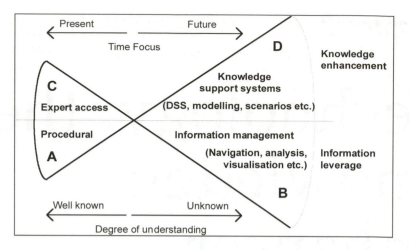

Figure 3.1   Knowledge technologies in their wider applications context

Knowledge tools

Most established applications of information and communications technologies involve automating routine procedures. They represent the codification and logical structuring of knowledge as depicted in the knowledge cycles of Figure 2.6. Their inherent knowledge is well known and expressed explicitly. However, this represents only one segment (A) of the broader field of technology applications (Figure 3.1).

Better opportunities for applying ICT in pursuit of the knowledge agenda come from the other three quadrants of the figure:

- Segment B. In these applications, technology is used to give better access to information, and to provide better ways of manipulating and interpreting it. Specific tools include text search engines and visualization software.
- Segment C. Tacit knowledge held by experts is accessed through collaborative technologies such as groupware and intranets. Communications infrastructures create rapid pathways to these known sources of expertise.
- Segment D. The individual and group processes by which knowledge is generated and developed are enhanced through tools such as group decision support systems (GDSS), modelling and computer conferencing.

Another perspective on how technology can enhance knowledge is gained from a systems viewpoint that considers the conversion of knowledge inputs into outputs (Table 3.1).

Table 3.1 Examples of ICT support from a knowledge systems perspective

	How ICT can enhance	*Examples of tools*
1 Knowledge inputs (information supply)	Scans more sources Filters according to profiles Condenses information User-oriented presentation Extracts hidden information	Intelligent agents Email filters Relevance ranked searches Concept retrieval Visual maps Data and text mining
2 Knowledge processing	Retrieves case histories Rules and induction More rapid combinations	Case-based Reasoning (CBR) Expert systems
3 Knowledge repository	Reduced cost of storage Holds most current information Single point of reference	Thesaurus management
4 Knowledge flows	Timely routing Improves workflow Alerts users of changes	Email and distribution lists Workflow software 'Push' technology Intelligent agents
5 Knowledge outputs (use/creation)	Supports thinking processes Informs decision-making	Cognitive support tools e.g. conceptual mapping, idea generation Decision support tools; meeting support; business modelling and simulation

A related perspective is that of a knowledge value chain (Figure 3.2), which also indicates a selection of supporting tools. This is a simplified schematic since there is usually not a one-to-one relationship between tools and processes. Some tools, like conceptual mapping, can be used to identify existing knowledge and gain insights, as well as creating new knowledge.

Whichever framework you use to position knowledge tools, the range of technology is large and constantly evolving as suppliers increase their investment.[1] This means that any named tools referred to in this chapter are likely to be quickly superseded by new developments. Nevertheless there are some common underlying categories and technologies that we shall focus on. Surveys of knowledge tools find the following as those most widely used: email, intranet, Internet, data warehouses, decision

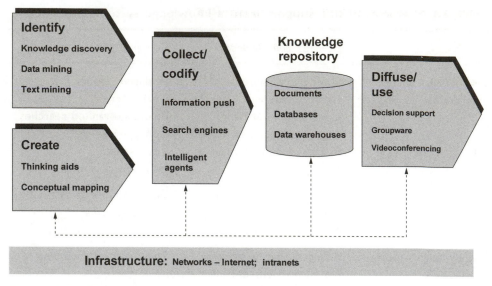

Figure 3.2   Technology in the knowledge value chain

support, groupware, videoconferencing, on-line information access and document management. Among this list data warehousing and decision support are felt to be less effective than the others.[2] The following sections reviews representative tools from the broad perspective of their ability to leverage value through knowledge. We start by considering the hubs around which knowledge activities revolve – knowledge repositories.

Knowledge repositories

The hub of an organization's explicit knowledge is one or more knowledge repositories. With the cost of electronic storage declining rapidly, it becomes practical for organizations to store larger quantities of their critical information and make it widely available through their corporate networks. Electronic knowledge repositories exist in many forms (Table 3.2). It must be remembered, however, that the best organizational knowledge repository is in the minds of its people. This helps explain why collaborative technologies are seen as the most effective knowledge enhancers.

Data warehouses

A data warehouse integrates information from multiple sources into a consistent format and makes it more amenable to analysis. For example, British Gas integrated data from twelve separate regional systems into a

Table 3.2 Examples of knowledge repositories

Repository	Typical information and use
The Internet	Comprehensive resources across many scientific and business disciplines. Uses include scientific and market research
External databases	Marketing and competitive information, general business news. Used to inform marketing and product development decisions
Document databases	Manuals, drawings, customer correspondence. Used in customer service to bring up all information related to specific customer
Data warehouse	Financial transactions, point-of-sale data. Used to discern trading patterns for target marketing, location of stores etc.

single warehouse containing information on all its 22 million customers. Data warehouses give knowledge workers access to large volumes of information that can be analysed in many different ways. This helps in decision-making, especially for marketing decisions such as store location and layout, and customer targeting.

When used with knowledge discovery tools, such as data mining, users can identify correlations, patterns and trends not previously discernible. For example, Sequent captures service engineering data, and looks for patterns and trends in performance and reliability that are then fed back into the product development process.

Document management

Document databases are another common repository for knowledge. Documents give the user more context, structure and visual impact than when the same information is reduced to standardized computer-based text. Therefore, many document management systems, such as those from Dataware and Documentum, are geared to give knowledge workers easier access to original documents, as well as adding contextual information, such as the rationale for a document, its revision status and applicability. Another feature that helps sharing of interpretative knowledge is that of 'redlining'. This allows users to add comments directly to documents, and these then become part of the document base and organizational memory.

Organization-wide document management plays an important role in helping the sharing of the most up-to-date knowledge in many applications, such as clinical trials in the pharmaceutical industry and large-scale complex projects. Construction company John Brown[3] introduced document management for the rapid sharing of information between its engineers, who are located around the world. Drawings can be retrieved and viewed on a computer screen within seconds, compared to several days in the former manual system.

On-line databases

Knowledge-intensive enterprises have a thirst for external information. Common sources are on-line databases, available through providers like Dialog and the Internet. Once these were quite distinct. On-line services used proprietary software, had heavily controlled content and bundled together access and content as an integrated service. In contrast the Internet is open to anyone and much information is free. Now the two are converging with on-line providers offering Internet access, and many reputable sources also available directly on the Internet. What is often not appreciated is the sheer volume of material held by on-line service providers. At the end of 1997 Dialog had around fifty times more content than all of the World Wide Web.

Knowledge workers traditionally accessed on-line services through an intermediary, such as a librarian. Today, more services are delivered directly to the knowledge worker's desktop computer. However, information intermediaries add value often not duly recognized. They filter, edit and refine incoming information, and know how to track down and assess sources. A survey done by the knowledge centre at American Management Systems also found that, on average, a trained information specialist could find relevant information eight times faster than the consultants they served.

Knowledge creation

There are several types of tool that assist thinking and creativity, either individually or in groups. One type is exemplified by IdeaFisher™, one of the longest established idea generation tools. It has a word repository and templates for different creative activities, such as developing a new product or choosing a brand name. New ideas are stimulated by applying well-known creativity techniques such as word association or word triggers.

Another category is that of concept or mind mapping. Users manipulate ideas by grouping them together or randomly linking them to create new ideas. Mind maps have been popularized by Tony Buzan, and a tool like The MindManager™ draws heavily on his methods. Figure 3.3 shows a mind map of this chapter. Users can drill down trees, annotate entries with notes or documents, link to other maps and create hypertext output. Another tool, Idons-for-Thinking™, uses hexagons which are colour coded

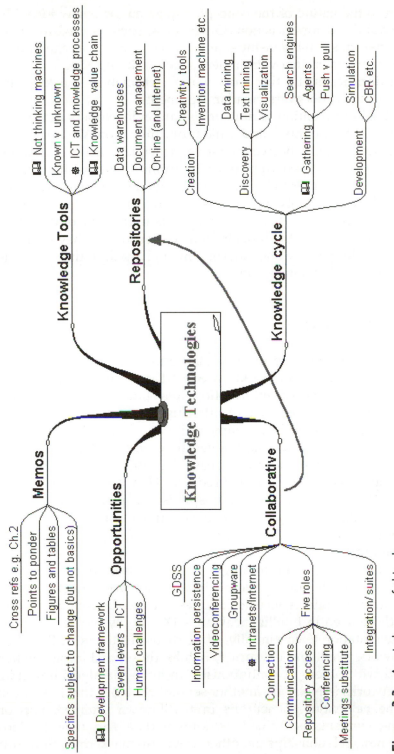

Figure 3.3 A mind map of this chapter

according to the nature of the concept, e.g. green for a new idea, blue for a strategy and red for an action. Other tools, such as Decision Explorer, focus on the causal relationships between concepts. You can specify, for example, that faster innovation needs better knowledge management, which in turn needs effective tools. Computer analysis quickly identifies core concepts and uncovers circular arguments.

In the field of invention various tools guide developers through brainstorming, selecting options and validation. Invention Machine draws on a core repertoire of ninety-five inventive principles, such as colour change or segmentation, collated from over 2.5 million patents. It steers inventors to ideas from other fields and highlights design contradictions.

Usage of creative tools within business is generally quite low. Many creative individuals feel that technology gets in the way of their thinking processes. However, as the tools become easier to use, they do provide a way of recording ideas and sharing mental models that can later be retrieved in new but similar situations.

Knowledge discovery

These tools help to identify new patterns and knowledge in large volumes of data. The simplest knowledge discovery tools are query tools that work on structured information. On Line Analytical Processing (OLAP) is one such class of tool often used with a data warehouse. It allows queries such as 'how many units of product X did we sell to customer Y in region Z during a given time period'. Marketers at Glaxo Wellcome use OLAP to query a database that contains a decade of historic information on sales of over 2500 products. They can analyse sales trends through different outlets, such as hospitals and pharmacies, and gain a better knowledge of customer and market dynamics.[4]

Data mining

Unlike query tools, data mining uncovers associations and patterns without the user having to know in advance what questions to ask. Various artificial intelligence techniques are used. Genetic algorithms, such as those used in IntelligenceWare's IXL, apply biological principles of genetic mutation to continually refine their effectiveness. Routines that do not work well are discarded, while those that work better are combined with others to continuously improve the algorithm. Artificial neural networks (ANNs) are another set of techniques that to some extent mimic the behaviour of neurons in the human brain. A network of processing elements is trained on known data and then let loose to discover new relationships in other data. In marketing, Sun Alliance started using neural networks as early as 1992 to improve the targeting of its mailshots.

Knowledge unearthed by data mining is often unexpected. One frequently cited example is that of a large US supermarket chain that discovered a strong association between purchases of a brand of babies' nappies and a brand of beer. No normal hypothesis or data query tool would have discovered such an association, but data mining revealed its existence.

Data mining is particularly good at identifying sequences, associations and clusters. Whereas humans have difficulty in dealing with more than a handful of variables, data mining tools can cope with thousands at a time and discover new knowledge that would elude most humans.

Text mining

One solution to the growing problem of information overload is that of text mining. Like data mining it identifies relationships in vast amounts of data. Concept Agent from New Age Paradigms uses the natural language techniques of syntax parsing, lexical attributes and linguistic rules are used to draw out key concepts from large documents.[5] The output is a short summary, which may include the most relevant whole sentences from the original document. Research using a similar system at BT Martlesham Laboratories has shown that summaries can be abridged to 25 per cent of their original length, while still retaining virtually all of the information in the author's abstract. Even a reduction to 5 per cent of the original retains 70 per cent of the information.[6]

A new generation of text analysis tools, such as SemioMap, provides visual concept maps from the multiple sources of text that it analyses and mines. Users can navigate their way through these maps, uncovering connections between apparently unrelated concepts and seeing how a corpus of documentation is evolving. This is one example of how visualization will play an increasingly important role in knowledge work.

Visualization

Presenting information in visual form is an increasingly common way of humans and computers working symbiotically in a wide range of knowledge work. Statistical packages, such as SPSS, use these techniques to identify market segments from large amounts of multidimensional market research data. Users can view three-dimensional images that through colour coding of individual data elements reveal groupings representing distinct clusters of customer need.

NETMAP is one of a growing class of tools that shows connections between different elements of information. A common application is identifying the communications patterns in an organization that are usually quite different from those you would expect from an organization chart. Another example is that of a citation tree in Smartpatent's patent analysis system. It shows relationships between patents, R&D activity and technological competence according to citations in various documents. Different colours can be used to show competitor activity around key technologies. Inxight's Hyperbolic Tree™ developed at Xerox offers what is termed fishbowl or hyperbolic tree views of information (Figure 3.4). A concept of interest is placed centrally on the screen, that shows links to other concepts, with the strongest and nearest links close to the centre, while more remote ones are shown in less detail. The viewer can drag on one of these to bring it into closer detail.

Three-dimensional visualization is used extensively in simulations, allowing humans to add their tacit knowledge to the explicit information presented. In the oil industry geologists and engineers visualize the geological make up of oil reservoirs and use the derived knowledge to make decisions on where and how best to drill.

Information gathering

These tools play a key role in making knowledge workers more productive by giving them rapid access to the information they need, when they need it.

Search engines

Internet users are well acquainted with search engines such as AltaVista and Yahoo! that retrieve information stored across many repositories. Users most common complaint is that too many matching hits are returned. A partial solution is to use keywords combined in Boolean expressions such as 'FIND knowledge AND management'.

More advanced search tools use artificial intelligence techniques and can accept natural language queries such as 'the role of knowledge management in customer retention'. The resultant documents are then ranked according to their relevance as calculated by various techniques, such as word frequency. Muscat, for example, complements Boolean and statistical retrieval with probabilistic retrieval, where variable weightings are assigned to every word in its database. It monitors users' interactions, and weights according to the relevance users attach to different documents. Related approaches are concept retrieval that distinguishes which concept is behind the use of a word with multiple meanings, and fuzzy logic retrieval that looks for patterns of similar though not exactly identical words. Such approaches are also being applied to the classification and retrieval of images and moving videos, as in Excalibur's RetrievalWare™ software.

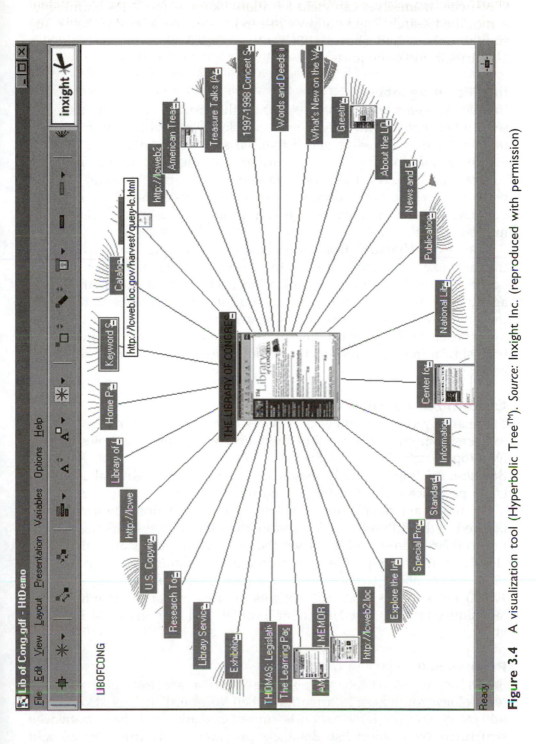

Figure 3.4 A visualization tool (Hyperbolic Tree™). *Source: Inxight Inc. (reproduced with permission)*

Searches themselves can yield additional knowledge. At Schlumberger a modified search engine allows researchers to see who else has made similar queries and shows comments recorded by previous searchers about their line of enquiry.[7]

Intelligent agents

Intelligent agents are a class of software that operate autonomously and semi-intelligently, some might even say knowledgeably. There are two main categories – passive and active. Passive agents filter and monitor incoming information streams, sorting out highly relevant material. Active agents leave their host systems and actively roam around networks, seeking out information of interest to its owner. They can then generate alerts. These are messages that prompt the user when new information is available.

Knowledge Update™ from Autonomy is an example of an active agent that acts like a personal assistant to its owner. Users create one or more agents to search the Internet and bring back relevant information. The agents are trained to perform better by rating the relevance of the items they retrieve. Unilever uses agents to keep individuals abreast of developments in their specialist fields. Associated software identifies users with similar interests, informs them and so helps them form a knowledge community.

Customized information provision

There are a growing number of services that deliver information directly to users' computers via email or the World Wide Web. Examples include Desktop Data's NewsEDGE, Dow Jones's Interactive and Reuters's Business Briefing. Typically they source material from several thousand trade periodicals, the daily press and news agencies.

An important development is that of customization. Information is tailored to the different needs of individual knowledge workers, according to their interest profiles. They then receive the top stories that most closely match their profile. For example, the customized news service First! selects about twenty stories for each user from its daily input of 17 000 news stories from 650 sources. It uses the artificial intelligence techniques just described to refine profiles and alert users of breaking news.

Push vs pull

Searching on-line databases and the Internet are examples of 'pull' technology. You access information when you need it. This also has the advantage that the information is current and may also have been well structured by a specialist database provider. In contrast, email and customized information services are examples of 'push' technology – information is pushed from source to user. With many people now receiving more than 100 emails a day, push is difficult to cope with. One approach is to throw even more technology at the problems that other technologies have inflicted! Electronic 'filters' apply rules to the headers and contents of messages and automatically route them to different files, including the waste bin.

A different form of push is that provided by companies like Pointcast or BackWeb. Information, according to a user's profile or requested sources, is downloaded on to their personal computer in background mode over the Internet or an intranet. They can then browse this information at their convenience. Despite the hype from suppliers, push strategies are what librarians have been doing for years. They call it selective dissemination! Today's technologies merely make it easier to automate.

Most knowledge workers will use an appropriate balance of push and pull. They will pull information from repositories as needed. As well as allowing retrieval through search engines, a well run repository will have information organized in a consistent structure, with suitable navigation aids such as visual knowledge trees. Knowledge workers will also allow information to be pushed at them, but by using agents, filters and personal profiles they will have the opportunity to be more selective in what they accept.

Knowledge development

Once users have access to information, there are various ways in which they can use it and process it to refine and develop knowledge. Three types of tool are now outlined as examples of the more structured processing at the right-hand side of the codification funnel of Figure 2.3.

Simulation and modelling

Computer models and simulations allow a knowledge team to share mental models and surface hidden assumptions. One class of tools is that of systems dynamics, popularized in the example of the 'beer game', an inventory management system described in *The Fifth Discipline Fieldbook*.[8] It illustrates how the best decisions are often counterintuitive to normal management thinking. Eric Wolstenholme, director of Cognitus, runs simulation workshops for managers in several industries. He describes computer based simulation as: 'virtual worlds which put a manager in control of an organization he can "fly". Just as in an aircraft simulator, he is presented with challenges and opportunities, and will probably "crash" the organization frequently to start with! The simulator provides feedback and guidance until the key principles and lessons are learned, and the organization "flies" successfully'.[9]

Simulation is particularly useful at identifying interdependencies. BP Exploration uses modelling to understand the interdependencies between key factors in North Sea oil fields – the reservoir, production platforms, operational and capital costs and commercial management. Although staff previously had access to many detailed models, such as reservoir simulation and financial spreadsheets, it was business modelling that helped the management team gain a 'big picture' overview and test 'rule of thumb' assumptions.[10]

Guidance systems

These are a specific type of decision support system, typically using expert systems, that guide users through a decision-making or problem-solving process. Despite their earlier shortcomings, expert systems are now making steady inroads into those areas of business where decisions need access to best available knowledge. Common uses are in medical diagnosis, insurance underwriting, systems fault-finding and problem-solving at customer call centres.

A typical example is that of credit scoring for loans. Previously such an application would have a simple procedural algorithm. Now it relies on inductive reasoning and rules held in a knowledge base. Michael Wolf of Swiss Bank Corporation describes how such a system has been linked to another technique described earlier – data mining. Data mining was used to identify patterns in the characteristics of loan defaulters from a large database of loan history. This was then compared with the suggested outcomes generated by the current guidance system. This approach gave insights into rules and induction processes needed to enhance the current system.

Case-based reasoning

The basis behind this technique is a knowledge base of cases, especially of problems and solutions. When a new situation arises, 'fuzzy logic' is used to match it to past cases. When cases with similar characteristics are found in the knowledge base, the solutions can be reused or adapted. In turn the current case description and its solution become part of the evolving knowledge base. The European awareness project CASTING (Case-Based Reasoning Stimulation of Industrial Usage)[11] portrays case-based reasoning as a four-stage cycle:[12]

- *Retrieve* the most similar cases from the knowledge base.
- *Reuse* the knowledge from those cases to solve the current problem.
- *Revise* and adapt the proposed solution.
- *Retain* the experience for the future.

The helpdesk at NatWest's BankLine (a desktop banking service for corporate customers), uses case-based reasoning to guide operators through a dialogue to solve customer problems (see Note 12).

Collaborative technologies

Of all technologies, it is collaborative technologies, such as the Internet, that are making the most impact on knowledge networking. Collaborative technologies enhance person to person collaboration and the sharing of organizational information and knowledge. Almost any software that allows shared access over a network can be considered a collaborative technology. However, the significant ones are more generic and universal, and are depicted on a space-time grid (Figure 3.5).[13] Examples from each quadrant will be considered starting with same-time same-place technology.

Group decision support systems

Personal computer presentations projected on to large screens are a feature of many meetings. The screen becomes a medium for sharing personal knowledge with a larger group. A limitation is that at a given time, only one person is controlling the output. In contrast, group decision support systems, such as GroupSystemsV and VisionQuest, are designed for group interaction and simultaneous input. Typical functions in such systems are:

		TIME	
		Same	*Different*
		Telephone	Email
P	**Different**	Audioconferencing	Document management
L		Videoconferencing	Groupware (conferencing/forums etc.)
A			Internet/intranet
C	**Same**	Meeting support software	Notice boards
E		Group decision support systems	Team rooms

Figure 3.5 Positioning of various collaborative technologies

- Brainstorming – users enter their thoughts which are added to a shared list.
- Categorization and grouping – a facilitator groups and reorders the ideas.
- Voting and preferences – participants weight or prioritize ideas, from which average rankings are generated, or they can vote on a proposal, anonymously if preferred.
- Issue exploration – commentary is added and topic relationships determined; in some systems relations are depicted visually as concept maps.

Such systems can make meetings more productive than conventional ones. Decisions are reached faster, often in less than half the time. The involvement of every participant helps to achieve greater consensus and ownership of the outcome. The assumptions behind decisions are recorded and become part of the organization's knowledge base.

Although these systems continue to grow in popularity, they are still far from being widely accepted in many organizations. Their success depends critically on user acceptance and expert facilitation.

Information persistence

Technology supporting the bottom right quadrant of Figure 3.5 is usually 'low tech'. The note left on somebody's desk, the department notice board, and the shift log book are examples. The information they contain remains in one place over a period of time. In knowledge management there is growing recognition of the importance of such information persistence. By keeping key information permanently visible, recall and idea stimulation is higher. Many organizations are developing this notion by devoting team rooms for projects. Charts and whiteboards act as a vehicle for knowledge development, such that team members dropping in get a sense of a project's current status and issues, and can add their own updates.

Steelcase is one company that has taken information visibility and persistence a step further. In its new executive suite, the walls are lined with large-screen flat displays which allow senior managers to see important information whenever they are there. Some information is relatively static, but since the panels are updated in real time, managers can view the latest sales and business statistics.

Videoconferencing

The same-time different-place quadrant contains technologies that aid simultaneous communications over a distance. Telephones are universally used but videoconferencing is rapidly becoming an essential tool for knowledge networking.

It is commonly reckoned that effective communications relies roughly 10 per cent on words, 20 per cent on voice and tone, and 70 per cent on 'body language'. Videoconferencing adds in this important visual element to conversations. It creates as near a face-to-face experience as is possible over a distance. Videoconferencing systems come in many forms. Some are camera and monitor systems used in rooms to link together two or more groups. A recent development is low-cost desktop conferencing that uses a standard personal computer with a small camera mounted on the monitor. Callers can see each other in image windows, and at the same time share application windows. Hence they can converse at the same time as jointly manipulating a document or spreadsheet.

For example, design teams at Ford based in the UK, US and Germany work together as part of a 'virtual global design centre'. They talk through designs while using shared electronic whiteboards. Video-conferencing played a significant role in reducing car design cycles from three years to two. A good example of the use of videoconferencing for knowledge networking is BP's virtual teamworking project (see page 113).

Groupware

Groupware is a technology that transcends space and time. The term was invented by Doug Engelbart at the Stanford Research Institute in the 1960s as the use of computers for 'the augmentation of human intellect'. Its focus was to help knowledge workers share their expertise, particularly in a distributed environment. Engelbart's prototype hypertext system that later became Augment had email, computer conferencing and shared-screen editing. Computer conferencing allows users to go to on-line topic files or a bulletin board and add their own notes to a thread of conversation.

Today there are over 300 groupware products, of which Lotus Notes and First Class are among the best known. There are also a growing range of World Wide Web conferencing tools such as Caucus and O'Reilly's WebBoard. Compuserve's forums and AOL's communities provide similar facilities in on-line services. Groupware has several features that enhance knowledge networking:

- Multiple data types are handled – free form text, graphs, images, voice and video.
- They combine both email and 'bulletin board' functions.

- Messages are displayed as threads of conversation, so it is easy to distinguish original postings and replies.
- Users can switch between different views, for example to see records relating to authors, customers or topics.
- Conferences or discussion lists can be public or private, allow entries to be posted directly or via a moderator (who checks for suitability).
- Most have a web interface; Domino, the latest version of Lotus Notes allows files to be published in WWW format and can take web pages as part of a Notes database.

Groupware features widely in many organizations' knowledge programmes. For example, Thomas Miller and Co., a manager of mutual insurance companies, found that Lotus Notes significantly improved knowledge sharing among its employees and agents around the world. Its databases aggregated formal information, about geographic regions, the types of risk managed and customers, alongside emails and informal discussion. This helped its member companies make better risk decisions, develop proposals faster and get closer to their clients.

Intranets and the Internet

In the last few years the proportion of large companies that have installed an intranet has risen from less than 10 per cent to over 70 per cent. They are an important part of the infrastructure of many knowledge initiatives, offering several benefits for knowledge networking:

- *Easy-to-access and use.* The use of WWW browsers gives a familiar and easy-to-use interface to information and applications.
- *Universal access to information.* Information can be kept on any 'server' on the network, and can be accessed from anywhere within the intranet.
- *Rapid publishing of information.* Individuals can easily publish information pages from their word processors.
- *Person-to-person interaction.* Intranets simplify interaction between people in different locations through email and computer conferencing.
- *Scaleable networks.* As organizations restructure, it is easy to add or remove servers to the overall network.
- *Access to external information and knowledge.* Intranets usually have gateways to the external Internet, which give access to a rapidly growing global information resource.

In addition, implementation is relatively low cost compared with other groupware solutions, because of the wide availability and low cost of most Internet software. Intranets link people to information and people to people. For information, an intranet can simultaneously be a formal electronic library and an informal publishing medium. For person-to-person interaction, an intranet provides a place for making personal connections, communicating and community building. By themselves, intranets do not create or share knowledge. The key to a successful intranet implementation is good content, a well designed information architecture and good information management.

Many companies use an intranet to stimulate organizational knowledge flows. Perhaps the world's largest is AT&T's, whose 80 000 users can access thousands of different areas of information. It also has conferencing facilities that allow knowledge communities to evolve and work effectively. At Hewlett-Packard, an intranet is core to its corporate strategy.

Intranet boosts knowledge sharing at Hewlett-Packard

The Hewlett-Packard (HP) intranet has more than 2500 computers that act as web servers. It transmits more than 1.5 million electronic mail messages daily. Lew Platt, HP's Chief Executive describes its contribution: 'HP's corporate culture has always encouraged open communications among employees. With the advent of the corporate Intranet, information sharing has taken off like never before'.

Platt comments that HP was using an intranet in 1989, long before the name was invented. He views it as offering tremendous opportunities for HP to increase its intellectual capital by sharing and leveraging knowledge.

One use of the intranet is in product management, where design teams, manufacturing and product management teams all share the same information. This has resulted in better forecasting, improved scheduling of products and faster time to market. Hewlett-Packard's intranet has over 100 internal newsgroups. Topics discussed in these 'virtual conversations' cover everything from computer architecture to problem tracking. Another application is Electronic Sales Partner, which gives sales representatives access to over 10 000 up-to-date documents. It is also used as an extranet, in which customers can access selected information directly and communicate with HP personnel.

Perhaps the most important benefit of HP's intranet is that it encourages increased collaboration. It enables people to work more co-operatively across organizational boundaries.

Sources: Hewlett-Packard's website (http://www.hp.com); Platt, L. (1995). The corporate intranet: a new model for conducting business, real people doing real business, *Business Week's* Futures Executive Conference, San Francisco, (December 1995).

The Internet extends the reach of an organization's intranet to the outside world. Even though more facilities might be available, response times are generally slower, and the information may not be as well managed or reviewed as that internally. Nevertheless it is widely used to expand an organization's access to information and knowledge.

With the wide range of collaborative technologies available, it is easy to dismiss email as an old-fashioned and unsophisticated technology. But this is not so. It is still the most heavily used application on the Internet. In many companies it has already taken over from the telephone as the primary means of business communications. Its functionality has increased significantly in recent years. You can attach documents, images and voice messages. You can send a message to a distribution list that delivers to every participant in a knowledge network. You can manage files and folders, and have them indexed by a search engine for efficient retrieval. Let us not forget that more information sharing and knowledge development probably takes place through email than any of the other technologies or tools mentioned in this chapter.

Five roles of collaborative technology

Collaborative technologies fulfil five overlapping roles in knowledge development:

1   A knowledge connector – they connect people to information and people to people. The Internet provides many starting points to find appropriate information or expertise.
2   A tool for improved communications – constraints of geography and time are overcome. Conversations are recorded as organizational memory.
3   Access to information repositories – from a single computer users can access terabytes of dispersed information. Furthermore much of that information is more comprehensive and up to date than if individuals manages it themselves.
4   A vehicle for active knowledge exchange – conferencing facilities, both synchronous and asynchronous, allow workers to share knowledge and collaborate in its ongoing development.
5   An alternative to conventional meetings – meeting support systems capture additional knowledge in face-to-face settings. Groupware lets participants contribute to virtual meeting at times and places of their choosing.

Collaborative technologies must be appropriately chosen and used. Asynchronous electronic communications cannot replace sensitive face-to-face negotiations. Neither groupware nor videoconferencing can wholly replace a highly interactive meeting that engages people emotionally. As a general rule, collaborative technologies come into their own where a wide variety of perspectives and knowledge is needed and participants are geographically dispersed. Many implementations of groupware and videoconferencing have not met expectations. This is due to insufficient attention to human and social factors during implementation. In BP's virtual teamworking project, the largest proportion of spending was not on technology but on addressing these factors.

Integration and suites

Since collaborative technologies form a central plank of knowledge management initiatives, many suppliers of these technologies are combining several functions into one software package. One example is the extension of groupware into the same time dimension. Ubique's CoWorker, for example, is an add-on to Lotus Notes that lets like-minded people connect in a real-time conversation. Just as today we see office suites such as Microsoft Office or Lotus SmartSuite that integrate what were previously separate tools, we can expect similar moves with knowledge tools. Thus, Dataware has extended its document management system into a full knowledge management suite that associates documents with experts, whose details are held in a directory of expertise. Open Text's Livelink integrates document management with intranets, and adds user commentary and conferencing facilities.

The technology opportunity

The wide range of tools described in this chapter show that there is hardly any aspect of knowledge work where technology cannot lend support. Individuals and organizations should continually think about how they work with knowledge and where technology can have the most impact.

Collaborative knowledge work

Knowledge work involves a wide range of activities, including accessing information, classifying and organizing it, thinking, and communicating with others. An organization that is thinking strategically about using

	Person–computer	Person–person	Computer–computer
Active **knowledge**	Expert systems Intelligent agents	Videoconferencing Meeting support (GDSS)	Neural networks Intelligent agents
Information **push**	Web publishing	Email	Automated transactions
Information **pull**	Document management Information retrieval Internet/Intranet Knowledge bases	Computer conferencing Expert networks	Data mining

Figure 3.6   A knowledge development framework

technology to enhance its knowledge capabilities should therefore have a broad spread of technologies that help knowledge development (Figure 3.6).

The following are some examples of how knowledge technologies have been exploited in a range of collaborative applications:

- *Scientific research.* Scientists can more easily keep abreast of their colleagues' work and offer informal critiques. Glaxo Wellcome's intranet with desktop videoconferencing helps its research groups share research results and discuss DNA sequence diagrams. This makes knowledge networking more effective and helps lead to drug breakthroughs.[14]
- *Sharing best practice.* Rover Group's GLEN (Global Learning Electronic Network) gives each shopfloor operator access to best practice in manufacturing and production, with specific case examples from other parts of the group.
- *Collaborative design.* Teams from different organizations and locations bring different perspectives to create innovative products. It is easier to solicit inputs from users about proposed features.
- *Faster and better problem-solving.* Price Waterhouse's KnowledgeView[SM] gives their business consultants access to best practice. Its unique thesaurus allows comparison of business processes across a range of industries. This helps them deliver better customer solutions much quicker than when the knowledge was dispersed and fragmented.

- *Faster project proposals.* ICL's Café Vik knowledge repository holds proposal templates and project knowledge that can quickly be assembled to create customer proposals. It allows salespeople to assemble more finely tuned proposals quickly and economically.
- *Improved customer services.* All a company's expertise can be accessible from the front line. Buckman Laboratories gives every employee a portable computer that lets them tap into the company's knowledge network K'Netix™ wherever they are. This gives them access to information resources, discussion forums and email. This helps them comes up quickly with the best solutions to customer problems.

These applications illustrate the value of making information readily accessible. Knowledge, previously dispersed, can be quickly aggregated and applied. Additionally, communications pathways provide access to experts, who supplement information with context-specific advice.

Information technology knowledge levers

Another way to think about opportunities is to consider each of the strategy levers described in Chapter 2 and consider how technology can enhance them (Table 3.3).

The human challenge

Several challenges need to be addressed if the application of knowledge technologies is to be successful. The first is the perceived problem of information overload, itself a consequence of technology proliferation. While information customization and intelligent agents offer some relief, a clearly thought out personal information strategy, as discussed in Chapter 5, is probably the best antidote.

A second challenge is to recognize that many of the tools described deal only with explicit knowledge or information. Yet the best knowledge in an organization is tacit knowledge in people's heads. Therefore, most technology needs complementing with non-technical processes and methods that help tacit knowledge transfer.

The largest challenge is that which has for years afflicted implementation of ICT systems in general. It is inadequate attention to human and organizational factors. This challenge is accentuated with knowledge management systems since knowledge networking is a very people focused activity. The introduction of technology needs to be sensitive to the needs and working patterns of those whom it is intended to help.

Table 3.3 ICT and knowledge levers

Knowledge lever	Typical ICT levers	Example
Customer knowledge	Data mining to extract buying patterns Customer dialogue on focus discussion lists Registration and feedback forms on websites	Microsoft software developers monitor discussions on relevant Internet newsgroups, even though they are public forums and not managed by Microsoft
Products and services	Internet websites for latest product information and updates On-line enquiry points for customer service	Federal Express allows customers to track the progress of their package through the Internet
Knowledge in people	Knowledge elicitation in expert systems On-line discussion lists or forums that give access to expertise Expert directories on intranets	Medinet gives users access to medical expertise through the Internet. They ask questions of a doctor
Organizational memory	Intranets and groupware holding project histories Document management systems giving access to product information	Hoechst Celanese's idea bank holds ideas and results of research, available for use at any time in the future
Knowledge in processes	Workflow software that codifies best process practice Current procedures and forms on an intranet	Sales representatives at Cadence Design Systems use an intranet-based systems that guides them through a sales process supported by a one-stop sales support encyclopaedia
Knowledge in relationships	Extranets that give customers access to internal experts Special forums for specific account teams and customers	Relationship managers at Chase Manhattan can access customer knowledge held on multiple legacy systems
Knowledge assets	Asset management systems Executive Information Systems	Engineering company S.A. Armstrong use a pbViews executive information system to monitor key measures of intellectual capital

Even greater dangers lurk ahead if we unwittingly put too much reliance on technology without understanding the consequences. The millennium bug has been a timely 'wake up' call. In the near future we are likely to see more information and knowledge exchange over computer networks taking place between intelligent agents. If we abdicate too much responsibility to them, we could be in for another rude awakening. A sobering thought is that artificial intelligence will surpass human intelligence by about 2015. How will we cope then?

Summary

This chapter has demonstrated how a wide range of technologies can enhance knowledge activities. Of all those discussed it is collaborative technologies, such as groupware and intranets, that have the greatest knowledge leverage and organizational impact. They connect people and allow them to collaborate in ways hitherto not possible. They provide conduits for knowledge flows and give universal access to information, wherever it happens to be.

Knowledge technologies directly affect the way that people work, either individually or with others. Since styles of knowledge work are very personal, organization-wide implementation of knowledge technologies is likely to pose even greater difficulties than implementation of other ICT systems. Achieving success requires attention to organizational and human factors, aspects that feature prominently in the toolkits described in Part C of this book.

The opportunities afforded by knowledge technologies are limited only by human ingenuity. In particular, some of the best opportunities come from exploiting the dimensions of time and space in creating effective virtual environments, the topic of the next chapter.

Points to ponder

1 Has your organization successfully deployed artificial intelligence applications? If so, what did you learn about the kinds of problem they were most suited to?
2 What techniques (e.g. data mining, on-line conferences) do you use to discover new knowledge about your customers?
3 Where do you most frequently need quick access to tacit knowledge where videoconferencing might be a help?

4   Do you have knowledge bases where you can quickly find a) solutions to customer problems? b) product ideas that were shelved, but may be useful in future? c) your best expert on doing business in China?

5   Do you know where to find key corporate policy documents? Are authorship, validity and ownership clear? Are there contact details to ask more detailed questions?

6   Can everybody in your organization easily communicate and send documents to each other via email?

7   Can you do the same with your key suppliers and customers in a confidential way?

8   How reliable and accessible is your organization's IT infrastructure (access to critical applications, email, intranet) – as reliable and consistent as the telephone? What about when you are on a business trip abroad?

9   On your intranet or groupware system, can users find the information they require within three mouse clicks of the home page?

10 What is your track record of success with new IT systems? Are applications using the technologies described in this chapter being initiated by the IT department or business users?

Notes

1   An analysis done by Trend Monitor International in 1997 identified thirty-three main categories (http://www.skyrme.com/updates/u16.htm). Its knowledge tools monitoring service continues to refine and develop knowledge tool schemas (http://www.trendmon.demon.co.uk).

2   Sources include '20 questions on Knowledge', a survey by Ernst & Young/Business Intelligence, summarized in Chapter 2 of Skyrme, D. J. and Amidon, D. M. (1997) *Creating the Knowledge-based Business: Key Lessons from an International Study of Best Practice,* Business Intelligences; Chase, R. (1997). The knowledge-based organization: an international survey. *Journal of Knowledge Management,* **1**(1), September, 38–49; Murray, P. and Myers, A. (1997). *The Facts about Knowledge.* Cranfield School of Management, The Cranfield/Information Strategy Knowledge Survey, cited in *Information Strategy,* September 1997.

3   (1996). Engineers create a global office. *DEC Computing,* 10 April, 13; also application note at http://www.documentum.com/jbrown.htm

4   Chang, P. and Ferguson, N. (1996). The data warehousing boom. *Conspectus,* February, 2–3.

5   New Age Paradigms at http://www.nipltd.com

6   Natural Language Group, BT Laboratories, Martelsham. See information at http://www.labs.bt.com/

7   Merline, K. (1998). Schlumberger creates cutting-edge KM network. *Knowledge Inc.,* **3**(3), March, 1–5.

8   Senge, P. M., Roberts, C., Ross, R. B., Smith, B. J. and Kleiner, A. (1994). *The*

Fifth Discipline Fieldbook: Strategies and Tools for Building a Learning Organization. Nicholas Brealey.

9   Eric Wolstenhome, Cognitus Limited, Harrogate, England, 1997.

10 Application note, Cognitus Limited, Harrogate, England, 1997.

11 CASTING: Case-based reasoning. Project web pages at http://www.ace.co.uk/casting/overview.htm

12 Dempsey, M. (1996). Phone service transformed. *Financial Times*, FT-IT, 6 November.

13 Johanson, R. (ed.) (1991). *Leading Business Teams*. Addison-Wesley.

14 Additional source material – Silicon Graphics application note at http://www.sgi.com

Chapter 4

Virtualization: networking knowledge globally

Virtualization exists in many guises. It happens where workers communicate through a computer network to distant co-workers as part of a virtual team. It happens in a virtual organization whose participants come together temporarily to meet a specific market need. Or it may be any one of a number of similar practices that replace conventional arrangements with new virtual forms. The megatrends identified in Chapter 1 are also factors in creating an increasingly virtual world. Globalization and networking lead to greater collaboration between widely separated business units and organizations, while advances in ICT make this easier to do cost-effectively. The restraints of time and geography that have traditionally influenced how we work and trade are rapidly diminishing.

Opportunities through virtualization come through reconfiguring activities in space, time and structure. After considering these three dimensions this chapter describes specific types of virtualization, including virtual products and services, virtual working, virtual organizations, teams and communities. It concludes with some perspectives of knowledge-based opportunities that exploit virtualization.

Three dimensions of virtualization

It may seem paradoxical that knowledge networking requires people to work closely together to share and combine their knowledge, yet virtualization usually means that they are physically apart. A partial answer to this conundrum is that improved global communication allows knowledge networking on a much wider geographic scale than was previously possible. The cost of communicating electronically is usually only a small fraction of that for face-to-face contact, even for people who live in the same locality. Location is one of the three key dimensions of virtuality (Table 4.1). Any organizational strategy developed today that does not fully consider how to exploit these dimensions is unlikely to be sufficiently stretched or secure.

Table 4.1 Dimensions of virtualization

Location (space and distance)	Local → Global
	Global → Local
	Distributed → Centralized
	Concentrated → Dispersed
	Physical → Virtual
	Fixed → Flexible
Time	Synchronous → Asynchronous
	Specified → Flexible
	Limited hours → All hours
Structure and processes	Sequential → Parallel
	Procedural → Object oriented
	Aggregated → Dispersed
	Stable → Dynamic
	Hierarchical → Networked

Rethinking location

In the networked economy global becomes local and local becomes global. Individuals can more easily seek jobs or work opportunities outside their immediate locality. A freelance graphic designer in Finland, for example, supplies his services to me in Newbury, England, with a quality and level of service as good as any I could get locally. You can buy products over the Internet, where your shop is a mouse click away, yet may be located the other side of the world. At the same time that the

Internet opens up global opportunities, it also means that remote suppliers can compete with you in your local markets.

Surprisingly the Internet can also help strengthen *local* communities. When a local community in Lapland went on-line it had the twofold effect of building a greater sense of community in isolated villages, while at the same time allowing them to participate in the global economy.

Location can also be exploited by dispersing previously centralized activities into different locations, taking advantage of where the best expertise is available. In 1990, Digital created an award winning disk drive by distributing the development across seven specialist design teams, working in Israel and the USA. Conversely, many organizations have replaced distributed customer response points with centralized telephone call handling centres. When you call a local Dell support number in Europe, your call will most likely finish up being answered from Ireland by a knowledgeable person speaking your language.

The location of an activity does not have to be discrete as in a call centre. Activities can be chunked and dispersed in a myriad of ways. Intelligent networks that automatically reroute calls, even to teleworkers at home, offer organizations much more resilience and flexibility in the way they operate.

Many activities can now substitute physical presence with so-called 'telepresence', where tasks are carried out over a communications or computer network (Table 4.2).

Although lack of personal contact limits tacit knowledge exchange, telepresence offers significant advantages over its physical counterparts. Travel can be reduced or avoided altogether by using electronic communications. You can attend meetings virtually through video links. You can use computer conferencing for meetings that might not otherwise take place because of scheduling difficulties. An added advantage of such virtual meetings is that they encourage contributions from those who are more reserved in face-to-face settings. Participants can also make consid-

Table 4.2 Replacement of physical presence with telepresence

Conventional	Telepresence
Face-to-face conversations	Email
Meetings	Videoconferences (live)
	Computer conferences
Document exchange, post	Electronic file exchange
Retail shopping	On-line shopping
Accessing information in libraries	Database access

ered responses, rather than making off-the-cuff remarks. As audio and videoconferencing continue to improve, limitations compared to face-to-face interaction will continue to diminish.

In practice, most work activity is best conducted through a mixture of both physical and telepresence. The optimum balance will vary according to circumstances, business needs and personal preferences. For example, most workers in virtual teams cite the positive benefits of having a face-to-face meeting early in its development, so that team members can get to know and trust each other in person before working virtually.

Time shift and reduction

Many information-based activities can take place virtually without incurring the time delays inherent in their physical alternatives. A message sent to the other side of the world by email arrives at its destination in minutes rather than the days taken by post. Electronic wallets can transfer funds without the delays built into the conventional banking system.

Many knowledge-based activities that have traditionally needed simultaneous action by two people can be replaced by asynchronous activities over networks. Each individual carries out their part of the interaction at a time (and place) convenient to them. Despite how it might at first seem, email or voicemail is often quicker than the telephone to complete simple communications. The reason is the avoidance of telephone tag, in which two people wanting to converse keep calling each other without making contact. Email also has the added advantage that messages can be more easily forwarded and duplicated.

The ability to communicate and store information synchronously creates opportunities to use time flexibly. Many teleworkers, for example, adjust their working days around their domestic needs and personal preferences. They may intersperse work and domestic activities, such as doing a few hours work, then taking children to school and the dog for a walk, going shopping, then resuming work later on.

Along with rising customer expectations, businesses are increasingly open twenty-four hours a day. When some supermarkets in the UK started all night opening, they found stores as busy at 2 or 3 a.m. on a Saturday morning as on a typical weekday. An on-line store never closes. It may not be staffed continuously, but this matters little if customers can browse, select goods and place orders. More time critical responses can be handled virtually by service representatives in those parts of the world where it is normal working hours. Businesses need to think of creating twenty-four hours a day channels to knowledge – to people as well as databases.

Different time zones can be exploited in the growing practice of 'sunshine operations', such as moving design work around the world according to time zone. When European engineers go home at the end of their working day, the designs are transmitted electronically to the Far East, where in turn they are transferred to the West Coast of the USA. The work on a project never stops, and the time-to-market for a new product or a project is shortened.

Flexible structures and processes

The third dimension of virtualization involves the reconfiguration of organizational structures. Because of physical limitations, many work processes are serial, with work being passed from one person to another in sequence. The use of shared knowledge repositories makes it possible to perform activities in parallel. Thus, marketing, engineering and commercial department personnel can simultaneously work on the same bid proposal document. As various sections are completed, the collaborative document evolves. Boeing and its various subcontractors designed the 777 aircraft frame on a shared computer-assisted design (CAD) system, and so reduced the time normally needed to move paperwork and drawings from stage to stage.

These examples also illustrate the trend of thinking from a process perspective to an object one. The objects in these cases are documents or design specifications. Hoffmann La Roche specifically selected documents as the focus for improving its performance in the clinical trials approval process for new drugs. It uses document prototypes, very skeletal at first, as focal points for the ongoing assembly and evaluation of the required information and knowledge.

Other restructuring opportunities result in virtual organizations or virtual teams. In markets that are dynamic and knowledge intensive, advantages can be gained by more frequent reconfiguration of supply chains than is usual in relatively static markets. Different suppliers can be selected according to their specialist knowledge to create product customization, or for their local knowledge and service capabilities. Management consultancies face different problems with each new customer assignment and rapidly assemble new teams from the pool of available talent.

Many specialist publications work in a way that combines two of these concepts – flexibility of structure and object orientation. The German magazine *Teleworx* reconfigures its virtual team for each issue, using specialist freelancers knowledgeable in the themes to be covered in a particular edition. The object, in this case the publication, is where the different streams of knowledge are converted into words and images that

coalesce into the final document. Few of the journalists, working virtually, have ever visited the magazine's office.[1]

Virtualization recipes

The move to virtualization has been developing rapidly over the last few
years and has attracted a corresponding vocabulary. Indicative of this are
book titles like *The Virtual Corporation*[2] and *Virtual Communities*.[3] Both are
incidentally highly thought-provoking visions of the future, but draw on
practices that are already visible today. Like any knowledge recipe (see
page 63) there is an endless number of ways in which the variables of
Table 4.1 can be combined. Organizations who think creatively about
them can significantly change the dynamics of their markets, as several
of the examples described shortly demonstrate. Activities that are mostly
likely to yield strategic opportunities through virtualization have the
following characteristics:

- High information handling content (e.g. market analysts).
- Intensive telephone work (e.g. telesales).
- Extensive travel (e.g. salespeople, field engineers).
- Large numbers of client site meetings (e.g. consultants).
- Creative and analytical work (e.g. writing).

Some of the different ways in which organizations can create opportunities from virtualization are now considered.

Virtual products and services

There is rapid growth in the volume of products and service being both
virtually over electronic networks. On-line sales are more than doubling
every year and are expected to surge to over $300 billion a year business-
to-business and $20 billion or more to consumers by the year 2002. Even
so, this will still represent less than 10 per cent of all consumer sales and
be less than sales made by telephone. Electronic commerce is bringing
about these changes:

- *On-line marketing of traditional goods and services* – travel, computer
  products, books and gifts are the most highly traded products. Computer
  maker Dell now generates sales of more than $5 million a day from its
  website. Small specialist suppliers particularly benefit. Climb Limited, a

supplier of outdoor equipment, did as much business in its first year on-line as one of its shops, at a fraction of the overhead.

- *The marketing and delivery of information based goods* – business information services and publications are often now sold only in an on-line format, not hard copy. The encyclopaedia *Microsoft Encarta* on CD-ROM with on-line updates has totally transformed a business once dominated by suppliers of voluminous tomes, such as *Encyclopaedia Britannica*, costing up to a hundred times more. Potential purchasers can also sample goods before purchase. Many CDs sold from CDNow's website have segments for sampling. Much software is already delivered by downloading over the net.
- *Emergence of new information and knowledge products* – virtual flowers and greetings cards makes it easier and cheaper to show that you are thinking of relatives and friends in distant parts of the world. Dispensing on-line advice is a growth industry. Customers who may be reticent or overwhelmed by a face-to-face visit to a professional quite happily share their problems with on-line lawyers and doctors. New knowledge providers like Bright act as packagers and outlets for specialized knowledge, either in the form of information or on-line master classes or consultancy sessions.
- *The creation of electronic markets* – the Internet has seen the rise of on-line shopping malls and on-line directories, providing single points of entry to supplier's websites or actually handling transactions on their behalf. Some, of which Barclaysquare was an early example, that merely emulated the physical retail mall in an on-line format but with fewer goods, have had limited success. In contrast, those that have specialized in niches or have exploited the characteristics of the medium such as Auto-by-Tel have prospered. There are now also on-line auctions, which widen the access to potential sellers and buyers, in everything from cattle embryos to secondhand yachts. eBay has over a thousand categories of goods in its classified sections, in which potential buyers bid against each other.

Many of these developments are driven by lower costs of doing business and increased geographic access. Many on-line transactions, such as issuing tickets or processing an order, cost a tenth or less of conventional ones. Cisco, a supplier of computer networking products, reckons that it saves it over $250 million a year by Internet trading.[4] Even these benefits are insignificant compared with what can be gained by developing and exploiting knowledge from such transactions.

Knowledge enrichment

As organizations embrace Internet commerce, their strategies evolve through several stages, each one deepening the customer relationship and increasing their capability to exchange and absorb knowledge. Many start by putting existing literature on-line. This 'brochureware' often creates delays in downloading large images and provides little useful content for prospective purchasers. Many organizations compound the problem by making it difficult to communicate with them through their website. They omit email addresses, and many that are given route enquiries to 'webmasters' and not to knowledgeable sales staff.

Intelligent catalogues provide more knowledge exchange. Saqquara, as used on Xerox Computer Products web pages, guides users through product choices that meet their application needs. Tracking users' needs and interests also provides useful knowledge to suppliers. Either through individual profiles, typically gained through a registration form, or by monitoring what information users access, suppliers can generate customized offers or links to further information on-the-fly. Suppliers can get closer to customers by cutting out the intermediary. Unilever provides consumers with advice on perfumes. This helps engender brand loyalty and also gains useful consumer feedback. Marshall Industries, a supplier of electronic components, appeals to its main influencers, electronic design engineers, by providing over 300 000 data sheets on its website.

The ultimate dream of many marketers is the segment of one, where the supplier knows each customer intimately. One of the most cited successes of on-line trading, bookseller Amazon.com, exemplifies relationship knowledge in several ways. Not only does it offer more titles (over 2 million compared to 100 000 in a typical large bookshop) but it also holds much more information and knowledge on-line than is found in a typical book store. It shows readers what other titles purchasers of a given book have also bought. It provides on-line reviews, both from established reviewers but also other customers. It can also inform customers by email when new books are published by their favourite author. Combined with discounts and good customer service, it has built a loyal set of customers in just a few years of existence.

Effective on-line marketing focuses on information needs and knowledge exchange. It provides buyers with the knowledge they need, knowledge that is often sadly lacking when buying conventionally through a shop, where much depends on the knowledge of the particular salesperson you encounter. On-line, the best available corporate knowledge can be aggregated. Consumers can visit more stores in a given time, and shop for the best information and prices. They can compare notes with each other in specialist forums. The successful on-line marketer will link into these and other independent knowledge hubs. They will also make their own on-line presence informative and engaging, so that the customer maintains a dialogue that continues to enrich their market, customer and relationship knowledge.

Telework

The second example of virtualization is that of virtual working or teleworking. Telework has attracted interest since the early 1980s, when Jack Nilles coined the term telecommuter, a person who commutes to work via telecommunications and not travelling. Despite popularization by writers like Francis Kinsman,[5] the practice really started to take off only with the widespread adoption of notebook computers and mobile telephones. Today, a number of different arrangements are considered as telework (Figure 4.1), with the teleworker whose base is their home and who only occasionally goes into the office being the minority.

The most common situation is where a person works some of the time from home and the rest in other locations, not just their base office but also customer sites. Another common arrangement is that of the telecentre, known in more rural areas as a telecottage. It is a managed office facility where you can rent workspace, computing equipment and Internet access. A recent phenomenon is the growth of resort telecentres that promote themselves as places to combine work and leisure. For example, Crete Resort Offices provides both business centre accommodation and telework facilities from a local luxury hotel. Office services include bilingual secretaries, email and messaging services: 'You do not need to bring a thing. Not even a paper-clip.'

Teleworking offers many advantages. For individuals, the top three advantages are personal productivity, reduced commuting time and better quality of personal life.[6] It also allows them to carry on working, even after a family house move or the arrival of a baby that needs looking after.

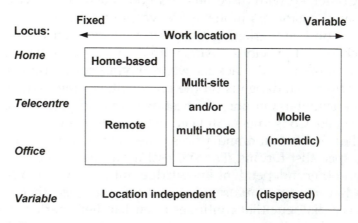

Figure 4.1   Different types of telework

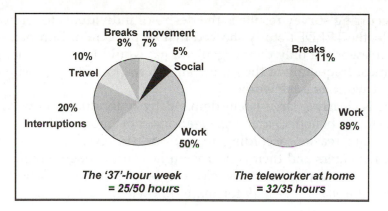

Figure 4.2   Relative productivity of office and home workers

Their employer also gains by retaining their knowledge that would otherwise have been lost. Other benefits for employers are:

- *Savings in office space and costs.* Most teleworking schemes reduce the space required for a given number of workers by 30 per cent or more.
- *Increased productivity.* Various companies have reported savings of 40 per cent or more.[7] Audits conducted by the author at Digital[8] indicate how a thirty-five hour week at home can be much more productive than a thity-seven-and-a-half hour week in the office, since teleworkers avoid travel time and the interruptions of an office environment (Figure 4.2).
- *Avoidance of relocation costs.* People can change jobs and work together without having to move home, a typical saving of $50 000 or more.
- *Less absenteeism.* Teleworkers usually take off less time for illness, partly since they may carry on working at home whereas they would spreading germs in an office.
- *Access to new sources of skill.* For example, the KiNET project in the Grampian region of Scotland, has illustrated the cost-effectiveness of using local skills to outsource CAD work from the home counties.[9]
- *Organization flexibility.* As companies restructure or projects change, individuals can continue to work virtually without relocating to another office.
- *Resilience.* An organization that works flexibly is more resilient to unexpected events (e.g. travel strikes) or disasters (fires, terrorist bombs). Digital's business continued with minimal interruption after fire destroyed its main Basingstoke office in 1991.[10]

Despite the advantages, uptake of telework is relatively low. It is estimated that fewer than 2 per cent of Europe's population telework, although the actual figure may be higher due to the prevalence of informal teleworking by individuals outside formal programmes. One of the most recurring survey results is the desire of individuals to telework. For example, the TELDET study showed that 40 per cent of Europeans would like to telework, if only their organizations would let them. The question asked most frequently at the European Telework *On line* website is: 'how can I get work as a teleworker'?

There is clearly a large latent demand by individuals. So why, despite the business benefits, are organizations not more enthusiastic? The number one reason, according to various surveys, is the attitudes of middle managers and their concerns on how to manage remote workers. Properly introduced, these obstacles can be overcome, making teleworking a natural *modus operandi* for many knowledge activities.

The virtual office

Conventional office buildings are often inefficiently used and badly designed for knowledge work. At any one time you may find only 25–30 per cent of individual workspaces actually occupied during normal office hours. The effective utilization rate of this space drops to only 3 per cent if you also take into account non-working hours, holidays etc.[11] What other organizational asset is so inefficiently used? More organizations are therefore converting personal space into shared space and using 'hot-desking', where individuals do not have their own desk, but use whichever is available when they come into the office. At Proctor & Gamble's new facility near Cincinnati there are no private offices for senior executives. Work areas are open spaces with rollable filing cabinets, so that team space can be quickly reconfigured.

Furthermore, most offices offer little in the way of diversity needed for different types of knowledge work need. In an analysis done as part of Digital's flexible work programme, the need for over thirty different work environments was identified, ranging from individual workspace, small rooms for informal meetings, casual meeting space, formal project rooms etc. Yet most office buildings have only a few of these environments, typically individual cubicles and managers' offices. No wonder that knowledge worker productivity in such offices is low!

Architects and office designers are at last responding to the need for better knowledge working environments. At Proctor & Gamble there are 'huddle rooms' where teams can quickly group in a brainstorm and wide corridors with easy chairs that allow people to stop for discussion. Although design helps, the success of the flexible office depends on the motivation and attitudes of those who populate them.

The ultimate flexible office is a totally virtual one. That is what software company Loud-n-Bow achieved in 1995. With many of its professionals working at client sites, the rationale for occupying an office became less

---

ROMPing – the creative way to work

The HHCL and Partners advertising agency has a totally flexible office with no enclosed areas. Believing that fixed desks kept employees apart, it initiated ROMP (Radical Office Mobility Programme). There are no personal desks. Employees, including the boss, must find a new office every day. The rompers toolkit is a mobile phone, a portable PC and a personal locker.

HHCL's meeting rooms have no chairs, so meetings are short and straight to the point. As well as 20–30 per cent more space efficiency, interaction among creative staff is now much higher. The whole area has a buzz about it. People walk about and connect.

With HHCL's help the BBC who featured ROMPing in its *Money Programme* encouraged a small experiment in a more traditional firm, the Pearl insurance company. As well as no personal desk, three different rooms were provided. The first is a customer room, based around a kitchen design, to put employees in the mode of thinking customer. The second is a fish-tank room, to inspire creative thinking, and the third the Pit Stop, for fast quick discussion. It is not to be used for more than five minutes at a time. Its design and lack of seating encourage this. Although the employees in the experiment adapted to this, it was felt inappropriate for the whole firm. The main benefit achieved was improved customer service through reduction in end-to-end service time. But this improvement was also attributed to the fact that the pilot group was created from different functions serving the customers. By bringing them together and empowering them as a team, they worked through customer issues until they were resolved, rather than passing them from department to department.

Source: BBC, *Money Programme*, 8 March 1998, 28 June 1998.

---

clear cut. It took a deliberate decision to close its office and operate entirely using the Internet. As a result facilities costs were slashed by over 80 per cent, and general administration costs significantly reduced.

Virtual offices represent a change in perspective from the office as a physical facility to that of the provision of a range of office services. Several suppliers now provide such services, which are particularly attractive for knowledge nomads. The Virtual Office in London will answer the phone in your company's name and, depending on prearranged instructions, divert the call to mobile or fixed phones, route to voicemail or transfer the message to email.

In conjunction with teleworking the virtual office provides an opportunity to rethink organizational space arrangements. A common misperception is that people need to be close to each other in a physical space to share knowledge effectively. While this is true, studies have shown that in conventional settings personal interaction diminishes significantly when people are further than 10 metres apart. Therefore, other than for casual encounters or for very close teamworking, a teleworker making effective use of technology can be as effective as a person based in an office. In fact, since visits are consciously planned, the quality of knowledge networking is often better.

The virtual corporation

Another type of virtualization is that of the virtual corporation or virtual organization. Many interorganizational arrangements where there is collaboration over time or space can be termed virtual, including joint ventures, or 'hollow corporations' that outsource most of their activities. In the knowledge-networking context the most relevant type, especially for smaller firms, is where several organizations pool their complementary resources and knowledge. One such example is Agile Web. This is a network of twenty-one engineering companies in eastern Pennsylvania. It combines skills and resources from the network to meet a wide variety of customer needs, and so bid on business that would be beyond the reach of any individual member. A new virtual organization is created from network members for each customer contract (see also page 232).

In many cases, virtual corporations evolve naturally out of working relationships that have developed between different individuals and companies over many years. While these virtual corporations are in relatively stable networks, others may be created uniquely for a given project. The latter is particularly true for collaborative research in the European Union's Framework research programmes, whose virtual organizations are also geographically dispersed. Companies and universities from several countries combine expertise by seconding staff, either part-time or full-time, to the collaboration. The project team becomes a virtual organization. European Telework Development (ETD) is such a virtual organization.

Virtual operations

Other forms of virtual organization replace physical activities with virtual ones. Examples are found throughout the whole gamut of business activities, for example in:

ETD – A pan-European virtual teleworking enterprise

ETD is a good example of several principles of virtualization in practice. It is one of over 150 projects supported under the European Commission's (EC) ACTS (Advanced Communications and Telecommunications Services) programme.[12] Like all EC-supported research projects partners must be drawn from different countries of the European Union. Even before its formation participants in the ETD consortium worked virtually over electronic networks.

1 The idea for ETD was first discussed using email between people in the UK, Denmark and Belgium; the two main proposers of the initiative first met through the Internet.
2 The main team was enlisted using similar methods. A core team of people from six countries jointly developed a proposal on-line over several months, before ever meeting face-to-face.
3 Management and co-ordination takes place through a combination of closed email distribution lists, and what is effectively a team intranet operated over the Internet. Team documents are initially developed in WWW format for ease of access, compatibility and sharing.
4 The project uses a media service provided by NEWSDesk,[13] itself a company that provides virtual services by delivering press releases electronically.
5 The project embraces a mix of formal documentation, structured databases, bibliographic data and on-line discussion groups. It uses a wide gamut of Internet facilities, including email, the Web,[14] list servers and a back-end database engine that generates WWW resource pages on-the-fly.

The project runs as a virtual corporation, with its own ethos, procedures and computer systems (managed remotely from a location in the west of England). Participants come from both large and small organizations, including one-person companies. All are teleworkers, some working exclusively from home, some working only occasionally from home. Much of its work is commissioned directly on-line, often to subcontractors who have not met project partners face to face. Their ability to communicate electronically and perform the work satisfactorily is what defines their suitability, not their geographic location.

- *Virtual research.* In pharmaceutical research, virtual chemistry has replaced test-tube chemistry as the primary tool in the hunt for new drugs.
- *Virtual production.* Manufacturing processes are simulated and validated before production lines are built. In Ford's C3P project, production engineers across several sites manipulate three-dimensional images in a virtual factory to test feasibility of assembly rather than doing physical prototyping.

- *Virtual recruitment.* Companies are hiring candidates interviewed virtually. Often this is done through videoconferencing. Over half the respondents in an Ernst & Young survey claim to have employed 'virtual' candidates.[15]
- *Virtual education and training.* There is growing use of distance learning, where course material and tutor advice is given over the Internet. In the Global Executive MBA programme at Duke University, students from different companies and locations also form collaborative virtual teams for project assignments.

The growth of virtualization in all spheres of organizational activity is blurring distinctions between virtual organizations, virtual working and virtual teams.

Virtual teams

Virtual teams are a microcosm of virtual organizations. Like them, they can be virtual in time, space or configuration, or combinations of all three. For example, when Buckman Laboratories wants to solve a technical problem, any of its 1200 employees around the world can contribute. The team may exist only until the problem is solved, perhaps a matter of hours.

Another type is where team members are distributed, such as a team created at NCR to develop their next generation computer system. Over a period of nearly a year, people from San Diego, South Carolina and Illinois worked as a team. When they met virtually they sat around a virtual table, created by a high bandwidth video link which gave the appearance of other people sitting opposite at the same table. This setup was dubbed 'the worm-hole'. Whirlpool is another company whose on-line systems connect designers around the world. Once highly US focused – in 1987, 96 per cent of its sales were in the USA – it is now a global supplier with 40 per cent of its $8 billion revenues coming from outside the USA. Its vision is to create global designs, getting the best expertise of their employees around the world, while keeping design teams locally based. Previously designers relocated to Michigan headquarters for a period of six months from Whirlpool locations in Brazil, India and Mexico.[16]

Teams are the nodes in knowledge networks. Like all networks that adapt to changing needs, teams may come and go, change in size, enlist new members, and alter their collaborative links according to the knowledge needed. Virtual teams are dispersed in space, with information and communications technology the glue that allows them to work together. Virtual teamworking at BP provides a good example of how such teaming contributes to improved knowledge flow around the organization.

Knowledge networking at BP

BP is an organization that has gone through much restructuring in recent years. From over 130 000 employees in the late 1980s, its workforce before its merger with Amoco was 53 000 employees operating as a 'federation' of eighty-seven business units across the globe. Information technology has made it possible to replace centralized teams with a more decentralized organizational structure.

One initiative that spawned from BP's restructuring was virtual teamworking. BP has many virtual teams that are empowered to make decisions, which they do by networking intensively and sharing its knowledge. The technology that makes this possible is multimedia email, document management, Lotus Notes and an intranet. All are seen as essential infrastructure for stimulating knowledge exchange through a global knowledge network.

A key technology that changed the nature of their virtual teamworking is videoconferencing. In 1994, following a proposal by external consultants, BP committed to an eighteenth-month $12 million pilot project. One hundred and fifty desktop virtual team kits that included PCs with videoconferencing and scanners were installed around the world. It allows individuals to communicate with each other more naturally, seeing visual expressions and body language. What was also quickly discovered was that a face-to-face video interaction also generated a higher level of trust between two remote workers.

Virtual teams can be created in an instant. A team at the Andrew oil field in the North Sea oil field can share knowledge with colleagues in the Gulf of Mexico. Furthermore, if there is a problem on a remote site, such as an oil rig, the camera can be trained on a piece of equipment. Thus, though it was once common practice to fly an expert out to the site, many problems can be solved quickly and effectively through a video link.

Knowledge team leader Keith Pearse highlights several ways in which knowledge sharing has improved:

- Speed of completing a knowledge transaction − instead of sending emails to and fro, the shared document facilities allow a dispersed team to complete a joint document in minutes rather than days.
- Making connections that might otherwise be difficult because of travel cost or time considerations. Virtual multiway 'meetings' with suppliers have taken place that would otherwise have incurred extensive travel.
- More regular and sustained communications − without the necessity to travel, such interactions can take place more frequently. There is more 'intimacy' and understanding in the relationship than would be achieved with email alone.
- Higher levels of commitment. Commitments made 'face-to-face' by videoconferencing were more likely to be kept than those made by ordinary email.

A critical success factor in the success of virtual teaming was the use of coaches working with users. In fact, over half the budget for the project was spent, not on technology, but on behavioural and organizational aspects.

Virtual communities

Local communities give people a sense of identity and belonging. Their inhabitants supply each other with local services and support each other socially. A virtual community does the same, except that instead of being rooted in a physical place, it is a locality in cyberspace. It is a community of shared interest. Such communities emerged in the 1980s based around bulletin board systems. Today they exist on the Internet in newgroups, email discussion lists and conferences and on company intranets or groupware systems.

Communities come in many shapes and sizes. Some are open to anyone who cares to join, attracted by the topic of interest. Others are closed, in that they are by invitation or subscription. Some are simply focal points for chat or questions, while others have more specific ambitions. Some allow uninhibited access (which often brings in its wake undesired advertising), while others work through a moderator who vets inputs before posting them for public viewing.

The WELL and beyond

One of the first electronic communities, and still going strong, is the WELL (Whole Earth 'Lectronic Link). Rooted in the culture of the San Francisco Bay area, it is an open-ended and self-governing community that started in 1985. Attracting people from a wide diversity of backgrounds, many of them professionals, it hosted computer conferences on a wide range of topics – education, arts, recreations, computers and entertainment. It went on to the Internet in 1992 where over 260 separate conferences are hosted. Its introductory web pages emphasize that it is not just another website or collection of web pages: 'More than just another "site" or "home page" the WELL has a sense of place that is palpable. Civility balanced by a high degree of expressive freedom has resulted in sometimes startling contrasts in atmosphere from conference to conference. Each conference has a distinctly different sense of place and style, and a loyal group of participants'.[17]

One spin-off of the WELL was the Global Business Network (GBN), created in 1986, that drew together planners and strategists from companies like ABB, AT&T, Volvo, BP and Bell South. This group used a mix of face-to-face meetings and on-line conferences to develop scenarios of the future. Through GBN, company executives and leading thinkers in a variety of fields would openly share their knowledge and insights. This interplay of knowledge generated new thinking about the future. It also led to increased collaboration between GBN members. For example, Shell and PG&E worked on a joint project to provide compressed natural gas as a fuel.

Whatever your interest, there are places on the Internet where you can meet like-minded people and different ways in which you can do it. Popular with professionals or business people are highly focused discussion lists. There are over 50 000 of these, ranging from 'Law and Business in Israel' to 'The Learning Organization'.[18]

As well as communities of common interest, there are now business communities focused on a specific set of activities, such as a car or house purchase, or planning a business trip. They are organized by suppliers, trade associations or intermediaries who draw around them complementary suppliers. Such communities are changing the nature of both traditional and on-line markets. For example the conventional recruitment market is dominated by suppliers who advertise for jobs. In contrast the website of Career Mosaic lets job hunters seek suitable opportunities among over 200 participating employers. They can file their CVs on-line and Career Mosaic helps them find matching opportunities. It also provides links to career advice and offers a one-stop shop for job seekers' needs, including advice on courses and writing CVs. The evolving nature of Internet-based communities, such as Geocities, provides valuable insights for those developing knowledge communities within organizations, a topic covered in Chapter 6.

Community networks

Community networks are another fast developing form of electronic community. They often start from a need for regional and economic development. Typically, they provide on-line facilities in a local community for commercial, educational, social and cultural purposes. Thus, the Manchester HOST started in a disused warehouse to provide on-line services for local community groups (see page 265).

Other community networks are initiated to exploit knowledge. The Tuscany Hi-Tech Network links small and large companies with the local universities of Pisa, Siena and Florence. With a decline of its traditional industries, this region of Italy needed to rethink how its indigenous talent could be better used. The result has been a community that connects research centres, businesses and public institutions. They co-operate as virtual departments in four application areas and seven core competencies, including cultural assets, the environment, biomedicine, robotics and space research. One outcome is a virtual science park that promotes co-operation across the different institutions and diffuses its knowledge around the locality, especially to smaller enterprises.[19]

Another community that has developed from local origins and now participates in the global networked economy is Taitverkko, a co-operative in Finland.

The Järvenpää Co-operative

Some 35 kilometres north of Helsinki, around 100 inhabitants of Järvenpää have pooled their skills in Ok Taitverkko Järvenpää (the Järvenpää Skillnet Co-operative). It is co-owned by small businesses, freelancers, unemployed professionals and craftspeople, and non-profit community organizations. The skills they offer include environmental consulting, urban planning, legal services, sales and marketing, translation and graphic design. By working virtually on the Internet they attract business from well beyond the confines of their local community.

Lars Tollet, an architect by training, was a founding shareholder of the co-operative in 1993. Local people expressed interest in working close or near to home as teleworkers but also having a neighbourhood office with advanced telecommunications and computer equipment. Tollet has put the experience gained in helping to set up this community to help other similar groups in Finland. As the National Co-ordinator for Finland in the European Telework Development project, he works with other co-ordinators based in eighteen countries across Europe.

Another member of the co-operative is Sonny Nakai, a native of Tokyo. He came to Finland in 1970 and after studying graphic arts at the Helsinki University of Industrial Art, set up his own design studio named IN-Design in 1986. It joined Taitverkko in 1995. He works with international commercial clients producing brochures, annual reports, advertisements, corporate magazines and designing trademarks. Designs are prepared on his Apple Mac computer and sent over the Internet to his clients across five continents.

The co-operative operates as a series of 'know-how' teams, which develop and co-ordinate the specialist skills of its members. It maintains a skills register of members and actively networks with other co-operatives in Finland. While not all its members telework, Tollet feels that by operating as a community network and working virtually with clients, they have helped bring work into the locality and have also drawn the community closer together.

Creating the virtual opportunity

The forms of virtualization described in this chapter are evidence of the growing dispersion and mobility of business activity. As ICT infrastructures improve, location independence increases. This creates a double-

Table 4.3 Opportunities and threats of virtualization

Dimension	Knowledge-based opportunities	Implementation issues and threats
Location	Creation of knowledge hubs as market attractors in cyberspace Resourcing talent globally Packaging knowledge for remote delivery, e.g. via on-line conferences	Being attractive to quality knowledge providers Competition from regions with better and lower cost skills Sharing tacit knowledge over a distance
Time	Capturing knowledge for instant access and reuse later Asynchronous knowledge development around objects Instant access to tacit knowledge through twenty-four hour knowledge networks	Loss of access to knowledge originators over time Changing value of knowledge over time Synchronization interdependencies Balancing supply and demand through time zones and business cycles.
Structure	Creating virtual teams or organizations with complementary skills Reconfiguring knowledge flows dynamically according to needs Aggregating knowledge from disparate sources	Developing trust in virtual teams Identifying and rewarding individual contributions Encouraging knowledge sharing across organizational boundaries

edged sword for individuals, businesses and policy-makers. On the one hand, it lets them access distant resources and markets. On the other hand, this same flexibility means that outsiders can more easily come and compete in their territory.

Beyond the obvious strategies of saving costs through tele-substitution and accessing global markets and resources, the best ways of exploiting virtualization come through innovative ways of manipulating its three dimensions. Table 4.3 indicates just some of the possibilities as well as some of the challenges.

Virtualization means that most conventional organizational activities can be restructured in many different ways to take advantage of global knowledge. This calls for a radical rethink of the existing *modus operandi* by every organization. For many forms of virtualization, it is not the large established organizations that are exploiting these opportunities, but innovative smaller companies, such as Amazon.com, AOL and Geocities.

Points to ponder

1   What current operations or new developments are constrained by access to skills? Could some of these be sourced remotely?

2   Which activities or customer services are suffering from time delays or slowness compared to competitors? Could more advantage be made of 'sunshine' operations?

3   Look at your core business processes. How centralized or decentralized are they? Should they be reconfigured?

4   Consider your Internet web presence. How easy is it for potential customers to reach experts? Are you gaining customer knowledge through this channel?

5   Do you have an on-line interactive forum where customers can have a dialogue with your product developers and applications experts?

6   In which electronic business communities do you and other senior professionals in your organization participate? Are you maximizing the use of these as knowledge hubs to create business opportunities?

7   Do you have a formal teleworking programme in your organization?

8   How much does your office space and facilities cost? What is its utilization level? What's stopping you creating more flexible offices?

9   How effective are the virtual teams in your organization? What stops them from being more effective?

10 Are there customer opportunities that you failed to close, because of lack of necessary resources or skills? Would collaboration with other individuals or organizations have helped?

Notes

1   Pesch, U. (1998). On-line collaboration in the production of Teleworx magazine. *Proceedings of On-line Collaboration '98, Berlin*, June, pp. 57-9. ICEF.

2   Davidow, W. H. and Malone, M. S. (1992). *The Virtual Corporation*. HarperBusiness.

3   Rheingold, H. (1994). *The Virtual Community: Finding Connection in a Computerized World*, Minerva Press.

4   A good description of the general impacts of electronic commerce, together with examples, will be found in US Department of Commerce (1998). *The Emerging Digital Economy*, April. US Department of Commerce. Also at http://www.ecommerce.gov

5   Kinsman, F. (1987).*The Telecommuters*. John Wiley & Sons.

6   Telecommute America Survey for Smart Valley Inc., Decisive Technology, http://www.svi.org (October 1997).

7   Taylor, J. (1995). The alternative office. *Flexible Working Conference*, IBC (November) citing Hughes, Sun, AT&T, 3Com and others. See also *Financial Times*, 8 September 1993.

8   *Computing* (1995). Adapted from Fears slow down teleworking, 27 April, 46.

9   Michael Wolff, KiNET Associates, Lethen, Scotland (1995).

10   Flexible Working Practices Team (1993). *Case Study: The Crescent*. Digital Equipment.

11   Lloyd, B. (1990). Office productivity – time for a revolution. *Long Range Planning*, **23**,(1), February, 66–79.

12   European Commission (1996). *ACTS Programme Guide*, DGXIII-B. European Commission. See also http://www.infowin.org (ACTS Information Window) which has project descriptions of each project.

13   http://www.newsdesk.com

14   The main website is http://www.eto.org.uk

15   Ernst & Young/HRFocus Survey at http://www.ey.com (April 1998).

16   Hildebrand, C. (1995). Forging a global appliance. *CIO Magazine*, 1 May 1995.

17   The WELL is at http://www.well.com

18   Several lists and directories of lists exist, e.g. Liszt at http://www.liszt.com lists over 17 000 newsgroups, 50 000 mailing lists and 30 000 IRC channels; or MIT's 'List of Lists' at http://www.tile.com/listserv/index.html

19   Bianchi, G. (1996). Galileo used to live here. Tuscany hi tech: the networks and its poles. *R&D Management*, **26**(3), pp. 199–211.

Toolkits for Tomorrow

Part B described challenges and opportunities that are affecting organizations of all types and size. Some developments, such as the Internet, are already having a dramatic impact on many aspects of business life. Others, such as telework, are being adopted in a more evolutionary manner. Whatever your position, and wherever you are, you cannot afford to ignore these changes. You may have a choice as to whether you work in a virtual team or not. You may decide that using the Internet is for someone else or you may decide that some of the opportunities discussed earlier offer significant advantages for you, your colleagues and your organization. Either way, you need to make informed choices, and if you embark on a new way of working or doing business, do whatever you can to be successful.

This part of the book provides some practical tools to help you make informed choices and be successful in the networked knowledge economy. In general, it is about optimizing and aligning resources that are crucial for success. The most important of these resources are information and knowledge, technology and people. The chapters in this part consider in sequence the individual, then the team, the organization, and the collaborative interprise, such as a virtual corporation. To be successful at each level needs a holistic approach that integrates work with effective management of the resources just mentioned. This can be represented as a matrix (see Table C.1) that shows some of the topics addressed in each chapter.

Table C.1 Some of the topics addressed in each chapter

	Work	*Knowledge*	*Technology*	*Organization*
Individual (Chapter 5)	Knowledge work; networking	Competencies development learning	Workstations; productivity tools	Knowledge; skills; flexibility
Team (Chapter 6)	Tasks; processes	Communities	Groupware; applications	Team-building; virtual teams
Enterprise (Chapter 7)	Globalization; core processes; knowledge-based strategies	Knowledge management; IRM; IC measurement	Intranet; email	Cultures; structures
Interprise (Chapter 8)	Collaborative alliances	Sharing; protecting	Internet/ intranet	Virtual organizations

There is naturally overlap and significant interaction between the different boxes of the matrix. It is the management of these interfaces that presents the greatest challenge and reward.

If this were a hypertext medium, such as a web page, and not a book, these elements and relationships could be dealt with in any order to suit the reader. Confined here as we are to a linear sequence, this part of the book follows this structure row by row. Each chapter concentrates on decisions and methods for working in an environment that is global, networked and knowledge intensive. A key feature of each toolkit is that it invites you to become actively involved. There are questions to stimulate your thinking and activities to work through. Use the toolkits as a practical way of planning your work.

Chapter 5

The knowledge networker's toolkit

Your knowledge and skills are your greatest assets. Are you making the most of them? Are you using them to fulfil your ambitions, while leading a balanced lifestyle and avoiding overwork and undue stress? In today's dynamic environment, where the future is uncertain and job security minimal, those who survive and thrive will be those who take charge of their career. They will understand their capabilities, chart a course for their future, work smarter not harder, and network extensively to achieve their aims. In short, they will be knowledge networkers.

This chapter considers what you as an individual need to do to succeed in a networked knowledge world. Your starting point is knowing more about yourself – your values and what is important to you. You then need to consider how to manage your key activities and resources – work, time, communications, information, your network, technology and your workspace. Last, but not least, you need to focus on managing and developing your intellectual capital.

It is not the intent of this chapter to be a primer on personal development, self-improvement or career planning. There are many books that do that much better.[1] The main focus is on those aspects that are inherently different in the networked knowledge economy – virtual working and working with information and knowledge as core resources.

Characteristics of successful knowledge networkers

In an analysis of high-performing knowledge workers, Keeley and Caplan identified nine recurring characteristics:[2]

1   *Initiative taking* – they will act beyond the defined scope of their job.
2   *Good networkers* – they will directly tap into the knowledge and expertise of their co-workers.
3   *Self-management* – they have good control over their use of time, making and meeting commitments and career development.
4   *Effective teamworkers* – they coordinate their activities with coworkers and assume joint responsibility for the outcomes
5   *Demonstrate leadership* – they formulate and state common goals and work to achieve consensus and commitment to them.
6   *Supportive followers* – they support their leaders in achieving their goals through taking the initiative, rather than waiting for specific instructions.
7   *Broad perspective* – they see their work in its wider context and take on board the perspectives of other stakeholders.
8   *Show-and-tell* – they present ideas persuasively.
9   *Organization savvy* – they are aware of organizational 'politics' and negotiate their way around to promote co-operation and get things done.

This shows the importance of broadening your horizons beyond your specific job role, working across organizational boundaries and engaging in teamwork and networking. Job advertisements tell a similar story. Self-motivated people with interpersonal skills, who are achievement oriented, flexible and adaptable are highly sought after. Behaviours and transferable skills are as important as any specialist knowledge. This is understandable. Changing markets, technologies, methods and customer needs means that much of today's specialist knowledge rapidly becomes obsolete. Adaptability and a capacity to learn and assimilate new knowledge are therefore crucial.

To be a successful knowledge networker therefore requires a range of capabilities as represented in Figure 5.1. The top layer of the inverted triangle represents surface knowledge that is explicit and visible. The deeper you go, the more tacit the capabilities, and the longer it takes to acquire or change them. At the bottom are values and beliefs. These determine our overall approach to life and work, and shape our everyday actions and decisions. They are deep seated and difficult to change. Hence culture change in an organization is usually reckoned to take at least three to five years. Along the right-hand edge of the triangle are

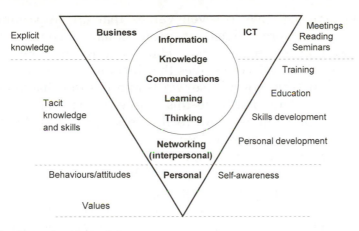

Figure 5.1   Triangle of capabilities

shown ways in which these layered capabilities are developed. Notice that training, so widely practised in many organizations, is usually most effective only at the upper layers.

Activity 5.1: Develop your own capabilities triangle

Use your own words to describe your capabilities and specialities. Be sure to distinguish explicit (surface) knowledge and your deeper (tacit) knowledge.

Know yourself

Uncovering your personal values is usually a good place to start. It also gives practice in an important generic knowledge process – that of converting tacit knowledge into explicit. A common approach used by career counsellors is to ask you to think deeply about your past (Activity 5.2).

Activity 5.2: Articulate or reaffirm your core values

1   Think of what you have accomplished and done well throughout your life. Write them down. A timeline is a useful tool for this.
2   Which of these did you also enjoy doing? What particular aspects of the activities did you like?
3   What were the circumstances – working environment, boss, co-workers, personal situation etc.?

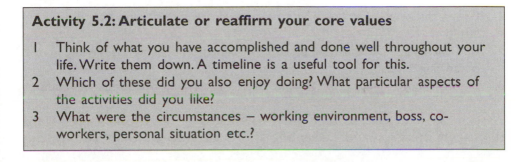

You should arrive at five to seven values that are important to you. Commonly found core values for professionals include recognition, autonomy and achievement. Brian Hall, a long-time investigator of values, has identified 117 core values that include duty, respect, account-ability, esteem and self-worth.[3] Use words and phrases that are meaning-ful to you. If you have not done this before, it may take considerable effort to really pull out the few really important ones. Discuss your findings with your spouse or a close confidant.

Having ascertained your values, look more widely at different aspects of your personality. Most professionals will have encountered one or more of the many personality profiling techniques that exist. Most involve you responding to a battery of questions about your preferences in different situations. Some involve in-depth personal interviews with trained counsellors. Popular tools are the Myers-Briggs Type Indicator (MBTI™)[4] and neurolinguistic programming (NLP).[5] Among other things, they will help you understand how you absorb information and make decisions. For example you may prefer a logical argument or you may rely on your intuition. You may like visual representations or you may prefer to listen attentively. The point about any kind of profiling is that it reveals individ-ual preferences. Many problems in work situations arise because these preferences are ignored. If you are sensitive to your own and your colleagues' preferences, you can improve the quality of your communica-tions and develop more harmonious working relationships.

Your thinking style

As a knowledge networker, you spend a lot of time thinking. So it is important to understand something about your own thinking style. One useful tool for this is the Thinking Intentions Profile (TIP) developed by Jerry Rhodes and Sue Thame.[6] It is based on research into 'skilful think-ing', carried out at Philips from 1977 to 1981. By responding to a set of forty-eight questions, individuals can ascertain their preferred thinking styles, which are grouped into three categories coded by colour:

1   Green thinking – *Creating what's new*: imaginative, divergent, lateral, intuitive.
2   Red thinking – *Describing what's true*: information seeking, classifying, organizing.
3   Blue thinking – *Judging what's right*: deciding, forming opinions, evaluating.

Associated with each colour are two modes – 'hard' and 'soft'. Hard represents precision and a scientific approach; soft relates to feelings and an artistic approach. Thus soft green is imaginative, while hard red is analytical. This approach has been further developed by SmartSkills into a set of diagnostic aids and also toolkits for various kinds of professional and management activity, such as task analysis decision-making or strategy development.[7]

Activity 5.3: Understand your knowledge processing styles

Think about how you absorb information and make decisions. Write down your preferred ways of gaining knowledge. Write down what thinking processes and preferences guide your decision-making. If possible, use a profiling tool, such as one of those mentioned.

As you go through the rest of the activities in this chapter, you will probably find that you need to adapt them to match your style. For example, if you are a green thinker, you may prefer to visualize activities rather than complete written details. Whatever your style, the main consideration is to be conscious and explicit about what guides your actions.

Work smarter, not harder

The smart workers focus on outputs and results. They recognize the distinction between outcomes and efficiency and effectiveness (Figure 5.2).[8]

As an example, your inputs on a piece of work might be information, knowledge and time spent. Your output might be a report. Your efficiency is how quickly you complete it, e.g. measured by number of words per day. Your effectiveness, though, depends on the outcome – what benefits are achieved by acting on your recommendations.

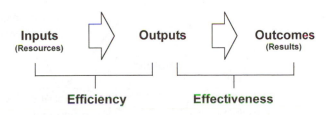

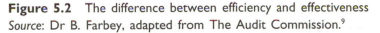

Figure 5.2 The difference between efficiency and effectiveness
Source: Dr B. Farbey, adapted from The Audit Commission.[9]

Activity 5.4: Goals and effectiveness measures

Take a typical project you are working on. What are its inputs and outputs? What are the outcomes you are trying to achieve? What measures do you have against each of them? Now try to describe them in terms of knowledge, who uses it and how it is transferred and used.

Research conducted by Barbara Farbey when at the London Business School indicates that effective managers and professionals take a holistic view of their situation and simultaneously manage several key resources (Figure 5.3).

In thinking about your work tasks, consider the relative intensity of thinking, information processing and communications. List your tasks and rate them against these characteristics. Also identify what kind of tasks you prefer doing and are better at. Think about which tasks are best done individually and which are best done in teams. Make sure you include personal development activities in your task list, such as learning and developing your network.

Time is a precious resource. Unlike knowledge, which can be reused, time once past is irretrievable. Review periodically your use of time: plan vs actual. Think of what needs doing in different time planning periods – for example a three to five year career period, a six months to one year project period, a month, a week, a day. Develop time planning approaches consistent with your thinking style. Stephen Covey is quite critical of time management systems that concentrate on activities, and suggests a focus on *relationships* and *results*. His simple but effective planner distinguishes the urgent from the important and links activities

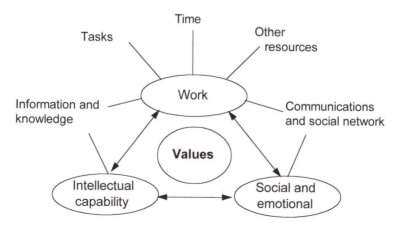

Figure 5.3   Factors that need managing well (after Farbey)

to key objectives.[10] Common time traps that knowledge workers fall into are underestimating how long developmental activities take, not realizing how disruptive interruptions are to thinking, and switching context too frequently between different types of task.

Manage the information glut

One of the problems facing many knowledge workers is that of information overload, coping with the growing volume of information that comes your way. A study commissioned by Pitney Bowes revealed that many employees now process over 150 emails a day and that 60 per cent of managers and professionals feel overwhelmed by this volume: 'today's corporate staffs are inundated with so many communications tools – fax, electronic mail, teleconferencing, postal mail, interoffice mail, voice mail – that sometimes they don't know where to turn for the simplest tasks'.[11]

The problem can even lead to a physical illness known as Information Fatigue Syndrome.[12] Current trends point to no improvement in this situation. For every intelligent agent that filters out unwanted information, another is likely to gather you even more! You will therefore need to devise a good personal information management strategy that gives you 'the right information, in the right place, in the right format, at the right time' (Figure 5.4).

Your personal preferences and styles will help determine what approach works best for you. Try the following approach:

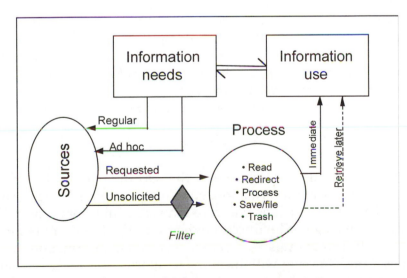

Figure 5.4   Elements of a personal information management strategy

1   Clarify your information needs. What are your goals, priorities and critical decisions? What information and knowledge do you need to support them?

2   Develop a sourcing strategy. Consider what periodicals or databases you need to scan regularly, and what you can seek out just when you need it. Identify the best content sources, including people, for each of your information needs.

3   Clarify what you want 'pushed' at you (e.g. via email) and what you want to 'pull' when needed. For which information is it essential to be alerted about changes? Err on the side of 'just in time' pull rather than wanting to see everything.

4   Work out how and when you will process information. There are only a limited number of things you can do with incoming information, e.g. use it immediately, file it or throw it away. You may want to use software filters to automatically preprocess incoming electronic information. This turns push into pull. If you don't need to work on a given folder right now, then that's an email you don't yet need to read.

5   Set criteria for what you want to file and save. Why do you want to keep it? For me it is seminal articles, essential reference material and work in progress. For most of the rest, I rely on the Internet and other sources so that I can access what I need when I need it.

6   Create a personal filing system, with a well-designed structure, that is appropriate with your work activities and areas of knowledge. File things away as soon as you can. Don't leave them in a 'to read' pile. For computer held information, use search tools such as Discovery AltaVista or Verity Personal that index all the information held on your personal computer – whether word processed documents, emails or presentations. They are a boon for careless filers like myself.

7   Refine your information. You might, for example, codify information into different categories, e.g. fact, opinions, examples. As you collate it and use it, synthesize key concepts and messages.

8   Review your information on a periodic basis. Prune ruthlessly based on use. Some people tab their files with a colour code the last time they accessed a file. If they don't access it, they don't keep it!

As a general rule, the less you keep, the less the overhead of management, or of misplacing information. New information is being created all the time that others, such as database managers and librarians, are paid to index and manage. Why duplicate their effort? Also, don't fall into the trap of analysis paralysis – seeking ever more information to make decisions. Good thinking with incomplete information is better than poor thinking with too much.

> **Activity 5.5: What sort of information manager are you?**
>
> Review a recent significant project or decision. List what information you felt you needed to do your best, how you went about finding it, how you processed it, and how it affected the outcome of your task. What have you now done with this information and how might you use it again? After reviewing the check list, would you do something different next time you are in a similar situation?

Communicate effectively

Each of us spends a lot of time communicating, but how often do we step back and ask how effective we are at it? Poor communications is often cited as a primary reason for failed projects and ineffective teams. Are you using the best medium for the message? In one study it was found that ineffective media were used in one-third of all business communications.

A good starting point is to understand your preferred style for receiving different classes of communications. You may be a listener rather than a reader. You may prefer to receive graphs rather than tables of data. Make those who communicate with you aware of your preferences. For example, when in a meeting, Bob Wiele and his colleagues at SmartSkills place cards on the table in front of them that show their thinking colours. This immediately gives a visible cue about how they process information. Activity 5.6 can help you gauge your communications patterns and effectiveness.

> **Activity 5.6: Analyse your communication preferences**
>
> Take a short period, say a few days, and for each communication, list who initiated it, the medium used, its purpose, duration/length, degree of interactivity, outcome and comments on effectiveness. Is there a pattern in those communications that were effective and those that were not? Could similar or better outcomes be achieved in less time with different media? Are there people with whom you should be communicating with more frequently but are not?

Review your communications log and determine what communications media and technologies are most appropriate for different types of communications. Consider:

- *Content* – purpose of communication, type (e.g. request, advocacy), length, precision, degree of formality, security.
- *Time* – frequency, duration, pattern (e.g. lengthy information vs interactive vs bursts).
- *Space* – location of recipient, accessibility.
- *People* – number of recipients, their preferences, role, styles, feedback.

As a result you may elect to use email for most routine communications to minimize the problems of 'telephone tag', but initiate regular face-to-face or videoconferencing meetings for project progress reports.

Good communications is fundamental to effective knowledge sharing. It occurs when the recipient clearly understands what the sender intended and acts accordingly. This requires dialogue, not monologue. Here are seven tips for effective dialogue:

1 Plan your messages or conversations beforehand – clarify your purpose, jot down an expected outcome, and note the topics to cover.
2 Make sure the environment is conducive to good communications – reduce background noise, divert incoming telephone calls.
3 Begin by introducing yourself (if not known to the recipient), establish rapport. Make sure that it is an appropriate time to converse.
4 When conveying information, first set the context; start from common ground and what is known. Make one point at a time and wait for feedback.
5 When receiving information listen carefully; don't jump to conclusions. Practise active listening, play back your understanding and ask clarifying questions (which also gives you time to think and process what you have heard).
6 Summarize, especially action points – this gives time to reflect and confirms mutual understanding.
7 Follow through. Did you commit to an action? Note it in your diary. Failure to keep even minor promises will influence the way that people judge and trust you.

Email and other on-line technologies require even more attention to ensure that communications is effective. Since email is not simultaneous, there is no immediate opportunity to check how well your recipient has understood your message. Here are a further seven tips for improving electronic communications effectiveness:

1 In general, restrict each email to just one topic. This allows the recipient to process each one differently, such as forwarding one to a team, filing in different folders or replying directly.

2 Use meaningful titles. Avoid the standard reply, e.g. 'Re: Our Meeting', when the topic has moved on.

3 Avoid copying all recipients by default. For many emails, replying to the sender alone is sufficient.

4 Reply to emails by making your comments adjacent to copies of just the parts of the received email that are relevant.

5 Keep them short and informal, perhaps add some humour, to reflect a conversational style. Emails are not for essays. If appropriate, send documents as attachments with a covering email.

6 Follow a logical structure – state your purpose, develop your message logically and be clear about what you expect the sender to do.

7 Make use of efficiency aids on your mail software – distribution lists, filters, filing in multiple folders and the use of standard replies.

Spending a little effort in improving the structure and readability of emails that you send, will bring significant benefits to the recipient, and make an overall contribution to the effectiveness of your communications.

Activity 5.7: Your email effectiveness

Take a selection of emails (say five to ten) you have just received. Was the intent of the sender clear? Did you understand what they were communicating? Was it clear what action you should take? Now review a corresponding number of emails you have recently sent.

Beyond email, there are useful techniques of netiquette (network etiquette) for participating in on-line and discussion lists. For example, Rinaldi's *Guide to Netiquette* has special sections for email, websites and discussion lists.[13]

Working on-line in a global context also requires a greater sensitivity to other geographies and cultures. Don't assume that your home town is the centre of the world, or that other people's values are the same as yours. Enter an open dialogue to help you discover those with whom you are communicating. This knowledge alone helps richer dialogue later.

Develop your network

Your personal network, which may run to hundreds of people, is the key to leveraging knowledge. Their knowledge can help you, and yours them.

Every person in it is a potential link to many more. Your network is dynamic. At different times different people are closer to you, both intellectually and emotionally, than others. Your network needs active managing. Review the following points to consider how you might manage it more effectively:

1   Understand the extent and shape of your network. With whom do you have the closest relationships and most regular contact? Draw a network diagram, with a circle representing you at the centre, surrounded by two to three concentric circles representing closeness to you. Draw links that show the nature and frequency of communication. What needs to change?
2   Determine how its composition might be strengthened. Is there other knowledge that you need access to? Are there others who can help link you to influential people or new business opportunities? Ensure that your network has a good mix of different thinking styles, generations, organizations and people with different cultural perspectives. It may seem difficult and uncomfortable but diversity strengthens your overall capabilities.
3   For your closest network associates, do you really know what motivates them? Find out about their plans and aspirations. Then you can help and support them. Too many business meetings get bogged down in task detail, ignoring these simple questions whose answers might well help the task proceed.
4   Keep activating your network. If you have not been in contact with an important member for some time, make a point of communicating with them. Some people work through their contact base, say twenty names a week, throughout the year. A short call asking: 'How are you? What are you doing? Can I be of any help to you?' is all that it takes. Don't just call when *you* need help.
5   Engage your network in your activities, even if you could do them by yourself. For example, on nearly all my consultancy contracts, other than the very smallest, I actively team up with a colleague. This helps strengthen the relationship, as well as giving backup should I fall ill.
6   Reciprocity and trust are the watchwords of effective networking. You get out what you put in. Use the game theory principle of tit-for-tat that has been shown to be effective in many business situations. You respond as they behave. Start off positively. Be proactive and helpful, and a good networker will respond in kind. If they do not, nudge and encourage them, but if that fails, then abandon them. If they take advantage of you in some way, send a strong signal to them to make amends. Be fair but clear. You only want people in your network who give as much as they get.

It is also useful to cultivate as part of your network people not directly involved in your work, in order to provide other kinds of practical or emotional support. Finally, a social network should be warm, friendly and informal. Therefore, you should create opportunities to meet in a relaxed setting, say on a boat trip or at a barbecue.

Activity 5.8: Deepening your network relationships

For each person in your inner network, check your diary to see when you last had an informal 'getting to know you better' session with them, that lasted two hours or more. If it was more than three months ago, schedule such a session.

Be techno-wise

Information and communications technologies are your vital tools. To maximize your effectiveness, you need to choose them with care and mould them to your individual situation. The technology check list draws together some key selection principles, first through some key consider-ations (1–5), then through a decision and implementation process (6–10).

A typical basic product set for a knowledge networker consists of a high-specification multimedia personal computer plus telecommunica-tions equipment and services. The computer will have generic office software (word processing, spreadsheet, presentation software etc.) and may have personal or shared peripherals such as a printer, scanner, video-conferencing camera.

As you tailor technology to meet your needs, you will be faced with multiple, often conflicting, choices. Do you need a desktop PC, a notebook, a palmtop PC or some combination of all three? Think about where you work and the complications of synchronizing files if you use more than one computer. Should you go for multifunction devices that combine fax, scanner and printer in a single package, or have separate devices? A general rule of thumb is to choose combined functions where saving money and desk space is important, but to go for separate devices where you need higher performance. In all the choices you have to make, the essential first thing to do is be clear about how you work and what functions are most critical in leveraging your effectiveness.

Whatever the choice of technology the most important practical consid-erations concern how you use it. With communications technology you need to have an explicit call handling strategy. When and where will you divert incoming telephone calls? Do you want to give callers a single number rather than separate office, home and mobile numbers? Be

> **Technology check list**
>
> 1 *Organizational context.* Are you located with co-workers or part of a virtual team? Are there company standards and constraints? How soon might your work or co-workers change?
> 2 *Task analysis.* What is your pattern of ICT for communications, document work, specialist applications, Internet etc.? What is personal and what is shared?
> 3 *Location/workplace considerations.* Where do you work? How fixed or variable are your work locations? Is the locus of your work your office, home, somewhere else or location independent?
> 4 *Personal needs and working style.* Are you a technology enthusiast or pragmatist? What is your tolerance level of new technology?
> 5 *Critical success factors.* What are the key aspects of communications, information and knowledge, and other uses of ICT that are important for your success?
> 6 *Your basic product set.* Select a basic combination of products and services that makes a sensible base for tailoring and adapting to your needs.
> 7 *Specific product selection.* From catalogues of products and services, apply selection criteria to guide you in selecting the most appropriate options.
> 8 *Holistic review.* Check that the solution selected meets your needs 'in the round' and is sufficiently well integrated i.e. that each component works well with the others.
> 9 *Clarify supporting mechanisms.* How will technical support, backup and security be provided?
> 10 *Continuous improvement.* Gain proficiency in the use of the products and services. Devote time for learning and practice.

conscious about security and loss of data. Although portable computers are vulnerable to theft, more data is probably lost by inadequate backup procedures that are only discovered when your hard disk crashes or you accidentally delete important files.

As your work becomes more virtual and location independent, there are a number of products and services that you need to seriously consider:

- Cordless (DECT) phones for mobility around the office.
- Telephone charge cards, that for the world traveller often give cheaper and more reliable access than mobiles.
- Adaptor kits containing essential power plugs and telephone socket converters for round-the-world connectivity.
- Audioconferencing. Often regarded as the poor step-cousin of

videoconferencing. However, it is more universally available, quicker to set up when away from the office and lower in cost.

Activity 5.9: Does technology work for you?

Consider how extensively you use technology in your job. Does it make your work easier? If not, why not? What functions do you find you use the most frequently? Can you upgrade the technology to do these better? What technology causes you the most problems? Are there improved solutions?

Manage your workspace

Most professionals devote insufficient attention to their office environment. Yet it can have a profound effect on productivity. If you have control over basic conditions such as temperature, air flow, ventilation, lighting and outlook, you are more likely to work efficiently. Ergonomic studies show the importance of good posture and seating when using computers workstations. Indeed there are now EU regulations and guidelines governing visual display unit (VDU) usage. Screens should not reflect glare from windows or lights, eyes should be level or look downwards to the screen, and wrists should have a surface to rest on in front of a keyboard. All this is fairly basic, but often ignored. Likewise, layout should allow you to move easily from one work area to another.

For knowledge work, space in which to think and space in which to meet are two important work areas. The former should be purposeful, and the latter inviting and informal. If your office does not let you do this, invest in an easy chair and low table, and do it whatever the corporate facilities policies! Choose colours that stimulate the right mood. Make sure that your office has a range of environments to meet your various needs and moods. Many conventional offices are lamentable for purposeful knowledge work.

If you work at home, there are other factors to consider as well. Ideally, you should have a separate room devoted to office work. Make sure you have sturdy furniture and sufficient work surface and storage space. It's amazing how space for those office essentials, like stationery, mounts up when you just cannot walk round to the office stationery cupboard! Unlike an office where you are likely to get up and walk around a lot to meet colleagues and have meetings, at home you may be sitting in your chair for longer periods. Therefore an ergonomic office chair, with lumbar support and plenty of adjustment, is a wise investment. Finally, do not overlook important safety equipment, including two fire extinguishers, one dry powder and one for electrical fires. Insurance, planning regulations, employment contracts and taxation matters are other practicalities that home workers, whether self-employed or corporate employees must also address.[14]

Personal development

Knowledge and intellectual capital need constant updating and refreshing to maintain their value. As with thinking styles you will have your own learning style and preference. A well-known model is that of Honey and Mumford.[15] Individuals use several modes of learning but tend to have a dominant mode based on one of the following four learning styles:

*   Pragmatist – acts quickly, learns by doing.
*   Activist – learns through concrete examples and experience.
*   Reflector – observes, takes in multiple perspectives.
*   Theorist – conceptualizes, integrates observations into their mental models.

Each represents one part of a typical learning cycle – planning, doing, reviewing, understanding. Once you understand your preferred learning style, take practical steps to introduce learning activities into your timetable. The more these can be made part of your daily work, the easier it is to get into the habit of continuous learning. For example, if you are a theorist, make sure you have time to read and put your activities into conceptual frameworks. If you are more of a pragmatist, pick activities that will give you practice at a skill you need to develop.

There are five keys to continuous learning:

1   Identifying a learning need.
2   Developing a learning event.
3   Identifying learning resources.
4   Scheduling time to do it.
5   Making time to review and to practice.

And this process repeats itself for every part of your knowledge and skills base. Learning events need not be long – ten minutes is often ideal. Your learning resources could be other people as well as printed or visual material. A week or so after a learning event, review it and record how well you learnt.

There are various tools and techniques that can help you learn as you work. One is active note-taking. Ignore presenters when they tell you not

---

Activity 5.10: Developing a learning plan

Select one or two areas of knowledge that you need to develop. What is the best way for you to develop this knowledge – through a course, through hands-on experience, through knowledge exchange with a member of your network? Now schedule a specific time slot within the next month to accomplish it.

---

to take notes because there are handouts. Research shows that retention levels jump from 10 to 30 per cent if you write something down rather than just listen, and increase even more if you subsequently present or practise what you have heard. In a similar vein, don't be afraid to make copious notes in publications that you read, even books. Such notes, representing your own interpretation and reference frame are often more useful than the original document.

Another underrated but very practical tool is a learning log. Just as organizations capture and share lessons as part of their knowledge management, as an individual you can likewise benefit from learning from your daily experiences. A log book helps you learn in a systematic way.

Creating a learning log

In a hard-backed notebook, draw a line across each page about three-quarters of the way down. Divide the part of each page above this line into three columns headed 'Margin', 'Main text' and 'Ideas/actions' respectively.

The central column is for your regular note-taking. In it make sure that you highlight outcomes. Use the margin column for topic subheadings and navigation pointers. These may only emerge later in a conversation or meeting. Use the right-hand column for three Is – Ideas, Implications and 'I will' (actions). Again, some may not be added until later when you review your notes. Actions may be requests by others or self-initiated. A reason for separating them into this column is to give quick visual record of how much time you might be committing.

The bottom part of the page is your review and reflection section. Record here what you have learnt. Did outcomes happen as planned? If not why not. Note what would you do different next time. Also add feelings, thoughts, and ideas for doing better next time.

Revisit these pages regularly, looking for patterns and adding further reflections. A log book used in this way becomes more than a record of your activities and meetings. It becomes an active tool where each page is a contribution to your growing intellectual capital.

As you may have already discerned, despite my very intensive use of computers, my own diary, time planner and learning log books are in fact kept on paper. They are with me almost constantly and available for instant reference.

> ### Activity 5.11: Recording your intellectual capital
>
> Itemize the main items of intellectual capital you have, Using Table 5.1 as a guide. For each write down (e.g. in six columns) who might it be valuable to, its current value, how this is likely to change if not updated, how it could be made more marketable and valuable, and how you could leverage this value.

Your intellectual capital

As part of your career planning, you have probably already documented your skills and experience in a CV. A review of your intellectual capital takes this a stage further. You explicitly record your intellectual capital (IC) in different categories. The customer, structural, human capital model outlined in Chapter 2 can form a good basis. This is expanded in Table 5.1 from an individual perspective.

Table 5.1 Categories of personal intellectual capital

Human (competencies)	Experience (applied knowledge)	Accomplishments, successful situations
	Knowledge	Professional fields, industries, markets
	Skills	Technical, professional, IT, on-line, transferable skills
Structural	Processes	Methods you have developed, refined
	Network	Know-who, your contacts, the IC you can mutually leverage Information resources Your personal databases, files, codified knowledge, articles
Customer	Relationships	Number and depth of your personal customer relationships
	Reputation	Successful assignments, projects; credentials based on experience
Other		Any other IC that has value if exploited, e.g. copyrights, designs.

By developing an inventory along the above lines, you start to gain a perspective of your important personal assets and how you might develop and exploit them. Typically you will find that your structural capital is low. Concentrate on converting more of your other forms of capital into this more explicit form. As the knowledge economy develops, there will be more ways for you to make such explicit knowledge tradable, for example through knowledge exchange networks or knowledge markets, such as those described in Chapter 10.

Leveraging your intellectual capital

As a knowledge networker you must both grow and exploit your intellectual capital. This requires a certain amount of self-marketing and influencing others. Selling yourself and your knowledge is an intangible sale. You cannot package and market it like a soap powder, nor would most professionals want to. The key is to let your reputation attract people to you. This can be done as follows:

- Presentations at internal seminars and external conferences.
- Writing 'white papers' or 'thought pieces' that provoke discussion among your peers and managers about critical business issues.
- Publishing in journals, periodicals and your professional and trade press. Paradoxically external publication is often a good route to better internal recognition. It shows that the outside world values what your write.
- Making your experience known in directories and databases. If your company's knowledge base has an expertise directory, make sure you are properly represented in it.
- Active contribution to subject matter discussion lists or databases.
- Creating your own web page, even if it a personal page within a company's intranet. Focus on what you know and how it helps your reader, rather than satisfying your ego.
- Public relations. Be willing to be interviewed for press, radio, television or video, including your organization's newspapers or videos.
- Create short 'how to . . . ' guides. Do it in such a way that the reader knows that what they are reading is just the tip of your intellectual iceberg. Beneath it you have a lot of tacit knowledge waiting to surface!

This is how you package and present yourself to the wider world. Your selling proposition must be clear on how others can take advantage of your knowledge. This means articulating how you will transfer it in a given situation. Are you a facilitator, whose skill elicits the sharing of knowledge by others? Will you package your knowledge in the form of training or workshops? Will you act as a mentor and learning resource to others? Whichever mode is best for you, the linchpin of your proposition is to specify how your skills and knowledge can improve organizational performance. Your intellectual inventory should provide illustrative examples. And as you complete a successful project, remember to add it to your inventory!

The millennium manager

Some of you will be taking the management career path. In the knowledge economy the role and skills of managers is different. Most will manage knowledge workers who know more about a subject than they do. Their role is one of managing the context and environment so that knowledge workers are motivated and work well in a team. Research by Martin Tampoe identified three primary motivators, other than money, as common amongst knowledge workers – personal growth, operational autonomy and task achievement.[16] Managers must therefore create business challenges and personal development opportunities to satisfy these motivators. They must provide positive feedback and create a sense of community. They must also create events and situations that facilitate socializing and joint learning activities. Some of the shifts contrasted with conventional management styles are:

*   Telling how → telling what: prescribing the outcomes, not the methods.
*   Controller → coach: helping workers learn as they carry out their tasks.
*   Directing → enabling: giving workers autonomy but supporting them as needed.
*   Input measures → output and outcome measures: managing by results.
*   Detailed measurement → motivation: enthusing with vision and encouragement.

This is a more hands-off and strategic style of management. Individuals are empowered to manage their day-to-day activities. More than ever, managers will succeed through 'soft' interpersonal skills and especially communications skills. Networking is also a key success factor. In a study by Fred Luthans of 400 managers over a four-year period, successful managers spent 48 per cent of their time networking, compared to other managers where the figure was only 8 per cent.[17]

As companies globalize and virtualize other key capabilities are being able to work across international borders and having cultural sensitivity. In many multinationals today it is unlikely that individuals will reach higher levels of management without having gained experience in several countries.

The knowledge leader

In the new millennium, successful organizations will need leadership, and in particular knowledge leadership, throughout the organization. Leadership is more than management. It is about vision, creating the future and motivating others to succeed. Knowledge leaders help their companies to succeed through exploitation of knowledge. Successful knowledge leaders, according to research,[18] are:

- Challenging – they challenge the status quo.
- Visionary and inspiring – they have a vision of how knowledge could transform their enterprise.
- Clear communicators – they have simple messages, reiterated in many different ways; they use anecdotal examples to inspire.
- Involved – they participate in teams, network extensively, build relationships and attract support.
- Leaders by example – they get involved personally and start experiments.
- Learners – they have a thirst for new knowledge; they learn from both successes and failures.

Many of these attributes are the same as for successful knowledge networkers, though with greater emphasis on nurturing and developing human resources rather than information or knowledge resources. Therefore, knowledge networkers who build up their capabilities and effectiveness through applying the lessons of this chapter are ideally placed to be the knowledge leaders in the successful organizations of the future.

Whichever path you choose, if you have followed the activities in this chapter and devoted time to your personal and emotional development you should be well placed to face the future with confidence.

Check list for action

Analysis and envisioning

1 Understand yourself. Take various profiling tests and clarify your values, goals, and needs.
2 Consider what aspects of your domestic, social and business environment, help or hinder your progress towards your goals.
3 Review your effectiveness. For each of the factors of the effectiveness model (Figure 5.3) rate your effectiveness on a scale of 1 (poor) to 5 (excellent).

4 Rate your achievements and progress on your on-line capabilities, your intellectual capital inventory, your learning goals/diary and your self-marketing.

5 Taking account of your values and personal preferences, describe your ideal working environment and type of work.

Optimizing your working environment

6 Compare this ideal environment with your current situation. What needs to change and what do you plan to do about it?

7 Prepare a timetable for filling in the critical blanks in your analysis of items 1–4.

8 Review your information management, communications and technology. List five specific areas for improvement e.g. a new practice, new software or training, and schedule into your timetable for the next month.

9 Select a mentor from your network. Arrange a meeting specifically for the purpose of gaining feedback on your approach to the topics addressed in this chapter – understanding yourself, improving your effectiveness, developing your skills and knowledge.

10 Plan your next career move. How different a job or environment is it to what you are doing now? What knowledge and expertise will you exploit? What will stimulate the move? When?

Notes

1 Examples of books covering this area include Pedler, M., Burgoyne, J. and Boydell, T (1994). *A Manager's Guide to Self-Development*. McGraw-Hill; Bolles, R. N. (1998). *What Color Is your Parachute: A Practical Manual for Job-Hunters and Career Changers*. Ten Speed Press; Covey, S. R. (1992). *The Seven Habits of Highly Effective People*. Simon & Schuster.

2 Kelley, R. and Caplan, J. (1993). How Bell Labs creates star performers. *Harvard Business Review*, July–August, pp. 128–39.

3 Hall, B. P. (1994). *Values Shift*. Twin Lights.

4 Myers, I. B. (1993). *Introduction to Type*. Consulting Psychologists Press

5 NLP was developed by Richard Bandler and John Grinder in the 1970s. Bandler, R. and Grinder, J. (1981). *Frogs into Princes: Neuro Linguistic Programming*. Real People Press provides a popularized introduction. Further resources can be found at http://www.nlpresources.com

6 Rhodes, J. and Thame, S. (1998). *The Colours of Your Mind*. Collins.

7 The full TIP and other material is available from SmartSkills, Collingwood, Ontario. See http://www.smartskills.com

8 The concepts in this section are based on an unpublished study on 'Professional effectiveness' conducted by Dr Barbara Farbey when at the London Business School.

9   Audit Commission (1986). *Performance Review in Local Government: A Handbook for Auditors and Local Authorities.* HMSO.

10 Covey, S. R. (1992). Habit 3: put first things first. In *The Seven Habits of Highly Effective People*, Simon & Schuster.

11 The Institute for the Future and the Gallup Organization (1998). *Workplace Communications in the 21st Century.* Pitney Bowes. See http://www.pitney-bows.com/pbi/whatsnew/releases/messaging_1998.htm

12 Reuters Business Information (1997). *Dying for Information?* A UK and world-wide investigation conducted for Reuters, in which 41 per cent of respondents felt that they suffering from information overload. A survey a year later (1998), *Glued to the Screen*, showed that 61 per cent were feeling information overload, with 80 per cent believing it will get worse before it gets better.

13 Rinaldi, A. H. (1996). *The Net: User Guidelines and Netiquette.* http://www.fau.edu/rinaldi/net/index.html

14 Various telework associations provide useful guidelines on these matters. See for example *The Teleworking Handbook* (1998). TCA. This is also published in several national editions in different langauges.

15 Honey, P. and Mumford A. (1992). *The Manual of Learning Styles.* Peter Honey Pubications.

16 Tampoe, M. (1993). Motivating knowledge workers. *Long Range Planning*, 26(3), pp. 49–55.

17 Luthans, F. (1998). Successful vs effective real managers. *Academy of Management Executive*, **2**(2), pp. 127-132.

18 Skyrme, D. J. and Amidon, D. M. (1997). Knowledge leadership. *Creating the Knowledge-Based Business*, ch. 3. Business Intelligence.

Chapter 6

The knowledge team's toolkit

The fundamental organizational units in the networked knowledge economy are knowledge teams. They are the hubs that gather, develop and apply knowledge to create value. Because of globalization and better communications, an increasing number of teams are virtual teams.

The core of this chapter emanates from a set of principles that were first developed in 1998 when I was part of a self-managed team. They were subsequently adapted for virtual teams[1] and have been further refined in this chapter to take account of knowledge. Altogether there are twenty-five core principles. They cover team composition, commitment, processes, technology and knowledge. Before examining the principles, the chapter starts with a review of the thinking behind them: what makes teams successful. To round off the chapter there is practical guidance on the related topic of creating and nurturing knowledge communities.

The activities in this toolkit are designed for the team as a whole, rather than as individual exercises. They are something to do and discuss at team meetings.

Knowledge teams

A group is not a team

Just because people work in the same group does not mean they are a team. Conversely, people from different groups can work together as a team. A team is a cohesive entity whose members share a common purpose and are committed to each other's success. Katzenbach and Smith, authors of a highly regarded book, succinctly state the case for teams:

> Savvy managers have always known that real teams – not just
> groups of people with a label attached – will invariably
> outperform the same set of individuals operating in a non-team
> mode, particularly where multiple skills, experiences and
> judgements determine performance. Being more flexible than
> larger organizational groupings, they can be more quickly and
> effectively assembled, deployed, refocused, disbanded.[2]

There are many different types of team, including management teams, specialist teams, cross-functional teams and project teams. Some teams, such as an airline crew or a medical team apply and reapply a well-established body of knowledge. Other teams, particularly in development work, are more varied in composition and structure, evolving as their work progresses. Some are permanent. Others are temporary. Some have members who work with each other daily. Others are virtual teams whose members come face to face only occasionally. As organizations become more flexible and work more on a project basis, their teams will work more virtually and change more frequently. Whatever the type of team, there are recurring characteristics in those that perform well.

High-performance teams

Teams that achieve very high levels of performance not only achieve work goals but also team cohesiveness. At the same time every team member is successful at meeting his or her personal goals and ambitions. The visible manifestation of success is an aura of enthusiasm, energy and commitment laced with fun and enjoyment. Such teams:

- are empowered and self-managed
- put teamwork and the team ahead of individual stardom
- assume collective responsibility – members represent the team as a whole
- have members who are committed to each other – they share knowledge, support and coach each other, exhibit trust, discretion and responsibility
- dynamically change roles and tasks to achieve desired results
- value diversity; ideas are challenged; debate is intense
- continually test the boundaries of freedom
- are never satisfied with the *status quo*; they seek innovation, continuous learning and improvement
- receive support and encouragement from management.[3]

Table 6.1 Characteristics distinguishing high performance from other effective teams

	Reactive	Proactive	High performing
Perspectives			
Time horizons	Past and present	Present and future	Timelines and trajectories
Focus	Action	Anticipation	Innovation
Motivation	Reward	Achievement	Excellence
Knowledge	Given, unchallenged	Sought, experienced	Created, challenged
Strategy	Predefined	Evolving	Emergent
	Operational	Customer oriented	Value focused
Organization and processes			
Structure	Hierarchy	Heterarchy	Network
Roles	Defined/stable	Assumed	Negotiated/dynamic
Relationships	Competitive	Collaborative	Mutual commitments
Communications	Inward and vertical	Outward and lateral	Open and extensive
Development	Targeted improvements	Systematic continuous learning	Team challenge
	Task focus	Process focus	Innovation focus
Work management	Command and control	Workflow and co-ordination	Pattern filling
Leadership style	Directive	Coaching, facilitation	Self-managed
Use of technology	Procedural	Informational	Team knowledge
	As needed	Regular sensing	Exploratory

Table 6.1 contrasts some of the factors found in high-performing innovative teams with those who are otherwise effective, but merely reactive or proactive.

Activity 6.1: What sort of team are you?

Review Table 6.1. Each individual should independently plot where they think the team is against each characteristic (row by row). Then come together and discuss differences. For each characteristic you deem important, and where you are only reactive or proactive, discuss what is stopping you becoming a high-performing team. Is it something within or beyond the team's control?

High-performing teams focus as much on people and processes as they do on tasks. This is a particular challenge for those working in many innovative environments, such as research or engineering, which are frequently too task focused. By ignoring the social context, team dynamics and processes, many teams fail to achieve their full potential, while their members suffer stress and burnout.

Creating the context

Team performance is heavily influenced by the individuals within them and the organizational context within which they operate (Figure 6.1).

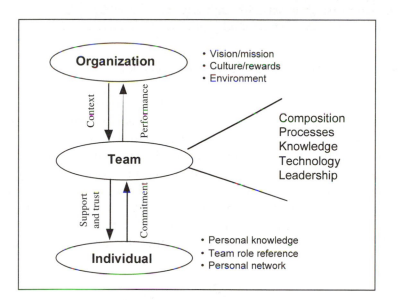

Figure 6.1   Key elements that determine team performance

The organizational context is covered in the next chapter. Regarding individuals, a good team player is one who:

- contributes knowledge and is effective, along the lines described in Chapter 5
- has team roles that match their expertise and personal preferences
- values every other team member for their contribution and has positive expectations
- learns from other team members, from the results of their own actions, and from collective experience
- demonstrates a high level of trust

- builds mutually supportive relationships, with a corresponding degree of give and take
- keeps commitments they have made; where circumstances prevent this, other team members must be informed as soon as possible
- represents the whole team and does not criticize colleagues in public
- expresses their feelings and recognizes the feelings of their team colleagues.

Activity 6.2: The team context

At one of your team meetings, consider how well the organizational environment supports your team goals and needs. Discuss what makes an ideal team member. Contrast your list with that above.

Teams are nodes in knowledge networks

A knowledge team is as a node in a knowledge network (Figure 6.2). The node is the focus of a knowledge intensive task or group of tasks. It is where knowledge is gathered, developed and converted into useful outputs. In a virtual team, the node is not in any single physical location but is dispersed. The links between teams can be formal work processes, overlapping responsibilities and activities, or personal connections, both formal and informal, such as in a community of practice. The strength and breadth of these links determines the capacity to share and develop knowledge through the network. Our principles are therefore designed

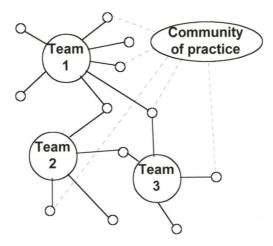

Figure 6.2 Teams as nodes in networks with multiple linkages

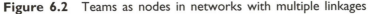

to create effective knowledge processing nodes that tap into the flows in the knowledge network.

Twenty-five principles for effective teams

The team toolkit is based around twenty-five key principles, divided into five groups:

1   Teams and teaming – creating the composition and structure of a team.
2   Team commitment – vision, mission and other factors that build team commitment.
3   Team processes – especially communications and building trust.
4   Team technology – that bolsters communications and knowledge processes.
5   Team knowledge – the vital resource and output of a knowledge team.

Each group of the toolkit is now considered, with the key principles first, followed by discussion and further guidelines.

Teams and teaming

1   Teams are the organizational units that create focus and harness individual talents. Create a network of knowledge teams to develop your organizational knowledge and achieve success.
2   The most productive knowledge teams are small multidisciplinary teams of five to seven people with a variety of backgrounds and personality traits.
3   Larger teams are usually loosely federated groups or committees which may be used to pass information (often ineffectively), motivate, or provide a sense of identity. They are rarely effective work teams. Use larger groupings to create cohesion, reinforce values and to provide networking and knowledge sharing opportunities, but not as the primary unit for organizing work.
4   Every knowledge worker should belong to at least two separate teams. This helps the organization achieve cross-functional co-operation; it provides knowledge-sharing links between different teams and it helps the individuals gain a broader perspective.
5   An individual can have one or several roles in the team. These roles can change and be exchanged (for example during holiday periods, to balance workloads, or to broaden individual experience). Distinguish the role from the person.

Teams are organized around a set of tasks. Ideally a team is chosen according to the mix of talent needed to perform these tasks. Diversity in perspectives, culture, age and gender also helps in tackling challenging assignments and making innovative breakthroughs. In the networked organization, many teams will be self-forming, by attracting people with the right motivation and expertise. It also helps if several members of a new team have previously worked together.

Teams are dynamic. As new needs emerge, workload grows or tasks change, team composition must adjust accordingly. If a team gets too large split it into two comparable or complementary teams. Regularly review the team's network connections. If communication patterns are denser between teams than within a team, consider redrawing boundaries. Regular restructuring will also help the diffusion of knowledge around an organization as individuals move between teams. This dynamic, though, has to be balanced against the time taken to build team commitment. Some 'slack' should be built into the network. A certain amount of duplication or overlap should not be viewed as bad. This slackness permits a higher quality of output, plus a resilience to cope with the unexpected.

Roles and relationships

As well as specific task roles, there are a number of team roles that need filling. These roles include co-ordinating work, scheduling, liaising, planning, budgeting, etc. In particular there are knowledge roles to fill, such as the knowledge gatherer who scouts for external knowledge, the knowledge analyst who interprets client needs and the knowledge manager who organizes the team's knowledge resources. Some of these roles can be shared responsibilities, while others are performed by one person. Teams run into problems when these roles are not initially assigned or where there is role ambiguity. On the other hand, some overlap in roles is useful, so that people can learn from each other and provide cover during a colleague's absence.

Meredith Belbin's research into teams identified eight roles other than specialist:[4]

1   Plant – who stimulates the team with new ideas, often unorthodox views on solving problems.
2   Resource investigator – who networks and brings external information into the team.
3   Monitor-evaluator – the analyst who logically evaluates situations.
4   Team worker – people oriented, who supports other members and helps foster team spirit.
5   Completer-finisher – painstaking, attention to detail and seeks closure on loose ends.

6   Implementor – organizing ability, turns plans into practical procedures.
7   Chairperson – helps the team move forward by drawing on the strengths of each individual.
8   Shaper – a dynamic person who prioritizes and shapes direction of team effort.

There are obvious similarities with individual personality and thinking styles. Thus the red thinker (the logical person) is more likely be a monitor-evaluator or completer-finisher. Belbin's formula for a successful team is a good chairman, one strong plant, and a general spread in both team roles and mental attributes. He also found that the cleverest teams (with many plants) were often the least successful. They vie with each other intellectually, but fail to address crucial team processes and communications, both internally and with their clients. Add a team leader and team effectiveness considerably increases. If your team is not performing well, check if it has just resource investigators and plants, leading to a talking shop, or just team workers and implementors who plod on in an orderly way but fail to grasp new ideas.

Activity 6.3: Your team characteristics

Review the principles and the set of roles. How closely does your team follow them? How many other teams does your team actively link to through personal membership? What are the interdependencies? Do you need skills or role behaviours (Belbin) in your team that are absent? How can you change your team and its composition to fill these gaps?

Team commitment

---

6   Every team must have a defining purpose if it is to act as a team and not as a group. It must have its own vision, mission and goals which reinforce those of the organization.
7   Every team should develop a strong set of cultural norms and values. Hence regular team meetings should take place. A set of working principles should be developed (print them on a laminated card).
8   Each team should identify other teams carrying out related or dependent activities. It should draw a network diagram with:
    (a) itself (and its mission) at the centre
    (b) an inner ring of teams (nodes) where interdependencies are high (formal relationships)
    (c) an outer ring of collaborative teams (mostly information sharing).

9   Each team should make its core processes explicit. Identify the
    sequencing of main activities and their interdependencies (who
    provides what to whom)
10 Individual members of teams should maintain their personal and
    professional networks, even beyond the immediate requirements of
    current activities.

Achieving team commitment is the most challenging, yet the most rewarding, of team-building activities. Teams that have high commitment have in place a keystone of high performance. They have a compelling vision, a distinctive mission, clear goals and a realistic plan of action, all set within the context of the organization's mission and strategy.

From vision to reality

In developing commitment, work from the abstract to the specific, along the following lines:

- *Team vision.* This should be inspirational, and a pointer to the future. Capture the essence in a memorable phrase, such as 'knowledge in motion' (for a logistics team).
- *Mission.* Avoid commonly found bland statements such as 'best in customer service'. A good mission statement reflects the team's *raison* d'être and ethos. Thus, it might describe your core competencies and activities, the customers you serve and what benefits you deliver to them.
- *Norms and values.* Describe the ethics and standards of behaviour that can be expected from the team and from each other, e.g. respect for the individual, honesty, valuing diversity, a commitment to quality, etc. Express them in the form 'Our (or my) commitment to you is ... '. Many will follow directly from reaffirming some key principles from this chapter.
- *Goals.* These are tangible measurable objectives, both short and long term, for each project or area of responsibility. Good goals are stretching. They are not merely extrapolations of the present. Make sure you have goals for developing and exploiting the team's knowledge assets.
- *Tasks.* Allocate and sequence tasks to achieve team goals. Remember to allocate roles for team support tasks and for virtual teams, take account of which locations are best suited to what types of task.
- *Decision-making.* Agree what decisions need team consensus and what is delegated to individuals.
- *Identity.* This is how a team portrays itself, internally and externally. Identity manifests itself in slogans, logos, communications, job and role titles and generally how the team describes itself.

These aspects of team organization should be developed by the team as a team. Visions and missions are not dictated. They should evolve from within the heart of the team.

Team-building – where face to face matters

Teams commonly go through a sequence of development steps before they become fully effective. One model that provides a useful framework for team development that is consistent with the twenty-five principles is the Drexler/Sibbet Team Performance Model. It blends both the social and task requirements of team-building through seven stages:[5]

1   Orientation – *why* are we here?
2   Trust-building – *who* are you?
3   Goal/role clarification – *what* are we doing?
4   Commitment – *how* will we do it?
5   Implementation – *who* does what when where?
6   High performance – *what* are we capable of achieving?
7   Renewal – *why* continue?

It is important to iterate between each stage. In the early stages build relationships and get to know each other's strengths. In global teams, explore your cultural differences. Hold meetings at different locations around the world, and not just at corporate headquarters.

Commitment grows through high levels of communication and interchange of ideas. Even in those organizations where computer communications is the norm, it is found that teams which come together regularly in person typically outperform those who don't. Face-to-face meetings provide an effective way of deepening relationships.

Team development takes time. Do not assume it will occur naturally. Schedule time for 'away days' and allocate time for team development at every team meeting. Using skilled independent facilitators also helps considerably. Make your meetings invigorating and motivating:

• Celebrate team and individual successes.
• Continually re-examine team processes – review their effectiveness and scope for improvement.
• Reflect and review – at the end of each agenda item, allow time for each team member to offer some words of reflection on what they have learnt.
• Explore differences of opinion. Delve beneath the surface, explore assumptions, and validate that commitments are realistic by analysing progress and task dependencies.

Through such team-building processes, a common language develops, helping to create team identity and shared understanding.

Team processes

> 11 Communicate, communicate, communicate – frequently, both within the team and to your wider network. Think about the best media for each type of communications and apply the techniques of effective communications (Chapter 5). If you are in a virtual team, make sure you also communicate socially in between face-to-face meetings.
>
> 12 Develop clear mutual understanding through active listening and 'playing back'. Monitor feedback and be sensitive to lack of response. After face-to-face meetings reaffirm decisions or understandings in a follow up email.
>
> 13 Recognize the unpredictability and fuzziness of decision-making processes. An action taken might imply a decision taken. Be guided by your mission, values and principles. Understand which types of decision are fundamental and should be agreed up front, and develop simple formal processes for these. Otherwise keep formality to a minimum.
>
> 14 Learn together – all the time. Coach each other. Critique each other's actions and output. Share your respective knowledge and skills. Reflect and learn from your successes and failures.
>
> 15 Build trust in depth. Although formal relationships within and between teams are best cemented by having agreed written processes ('rules of engagement') on key interdependencies, aim for higher trust and openness rather than higher formality. Adjust your frequency of communications according to criticality of the linkages.

Communications is the most fundamental team process. It underpins all the others. Whole team communications builds on those for individuals described in Chapter 5. Each team should develop its own set of communications principles taking into consideration:

- Accessibility – who can be contacted when and where, taking account of different time zones and individual movements.
- Preferred media – for routine, confidential and urgent messages. Many teams find email or groupware the most convenient medium for most communications since it is any time, any place.
- Regular communications – such as diaries, project and activity reporting. Use a standard structure and format to make it easier for users to find what they want.

- Team storage – where to find current team documents, e.g. processes, contacts, schedule, assignments, outstanding items – so that the latest team knowledge is readily accessible.
- Patterns and styles – deciding what types of communication are private, what is for the team, what's public?
- Role of meetings, especially whole team meetings – many virtual teams have regular (say weekly or biweekly) whole team meetings using audioconferencing or videoconferencing.

Communications in Ford's virtual teams

Ford has many designers in virtual teams. Richard Riff manages one programme that has five project managers and twenty other people who report directly to him. They are located in Europe, South Africa, South America, Japan, Australia and China. He holds weekly videoconferencing and one-to-one telephone conversations with each of his staff. There is also a quarterly virtual team meeting. He also visits each of the teams at least once a year: 'Technology can't replace the chemistry of personal contact and coaching. It's the personal touch of seeing me once or twice a year.'[6] Communicating a good flow of information is, he says, the most critical success factor.

Constructive conversations through structured dialogue

Communications vary widely in their degree of structure and codification (Figure 6.3). Whereas formal written communication may be highly structured, informal conversations may appear very unstructured wandering from topic to topic in an apparently haphazard way as the discourse unfolds. A useful discipline is that of structured dialogue, a halfway house between the two extremes. This puts purposeful conversations into a framework that helps knowledge exchange and codification.

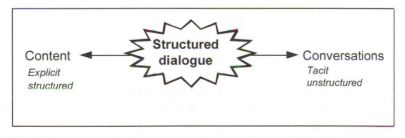

Figure 6.3 The communications spectrum according to knowledge

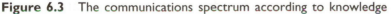

One model that adds a degree of structure to dialogue is the IBIS (Issues-Based Information System[7]) conversation model which is based around four primary conversational elements – questions, ideas, pros and cons. Jeff Conklin describes how a five-person software team used IBIS as the structure of their design meeting minutes. As a result they identified errors in the software specification at a much earlier stage than would otherwise have occurred, with an estimated savings of three to six times their investment in the lengthier dialogue.[7]

A more sophisticated method is that of Team Syntegrity, based on the cybernetics principles of Stafford Beer. It follows a precise structure and timetable over a three to five day period based around the geometry of a polyhedron. The thirty edges of the polyhedron represent individual stakeholders, the apexes represent topics for discussion, and the twelve surfaces represent dialogue teams. Following the geometry each individual is a participant in two dialogues, but they also act as critics on two others. Those who have participated in Team Syntegrity sessions attest to its effectiveness. According to Allenna Leonard, it results in: 'a high degree of emotional connection as well as shared information. The process is powerful; the topics chosen are close to the heart and the discussion is intense'.[9]

You don't need to go as far as this for more straightforward decision-making or problem-solving. An effective technique useful in almost any meeting is that of wall charting. A question is posed, individuals generate single phrase answers on cards or adhesive notes, which are then grouped onto a whiteboard for further exploration and discussion.

Trust – the linchpin

A team with trust is one that gives its members a high degree of autonomy to act on behalf of the team. In most team situations, and especially in virtual teams, trust builds up over time. However, there are many situations where trust needs to be more immediate. For example, you trust somebody who is a complete stranger, such as the pilot of your airline flight. Such 'swift' trust depends on context and on the reputation of the organization and the person. We tend to trust people as long as they fulfil our expectations. When they do not, trust can evaporate quickly and take much longer to rebuild.

Sirkka Jarvenpaa and Thomas Shaw, researchers of virtual teams, write on trust: 'In a virtual organization, trust is the heartbeat. Only trust can prevent geographical and organizational distances of team members from turning to unmanageable psychological distances. Only through trust can members be assured of others' willingness and ability to deliver on their obligations.'[10] Their research indicates that trust is initially built on personal referral or early disclosure of aspirations, but that it strengthens over time through communications and interaction, predictability and demonstrable capability. A key conclusion of her research with Dorothy Leidner was that high trust can be created in totally virtual teams even where people have no common past, as long as there is a focus on tasks, extensive and balanced communication and the ability to take initiative, manage uncertainty and expectations. Also, first impressions count: 'Trust might be imputed, but is more likely created via a communications behaviour established in the first few keystrokes'.[11]

Here are seven practical ways to hasten development of trust:

1   Clarify expectations. Be as explicit as you can.
2   When making important commitments, use face-to-face communications or videoconferencing to agree the commitment backed up by a hard record, e.g. on email.
3   Don't over commit. Make small commitments and meet them.
4   Communicate frequently and clearly. Remain alert for any possible misunderstandings.
5   Demonstrate interest and commitment to your team colleagues. Do things for them that will help them succeed. Address any negative emotions quickly.
6   Remind colleagues gently if they have not met their obligations or your trust, but do not make a big deal out of it.
7   Socialize – through informal emails if you can't meet face to face. Have conversations (via email if necessary) about shared interests beyond the immediate business tasks. This helps build closer personal bonds.

Activity 6.4: How good are your team processes?

List your processes in three groups – communications, core work processes, support processes. Make sure that there are clear linkages to the team roles you identified in Activity 6.3. Now go through each in turn, assigning a priority, saying what is good about each one, and what needs improving. Having gone through the list, pick out five process areas for improvement. Are there some common elements that suggest a new team development activity? Unless you already have a working list of core processes, this is likely to be a two to three hour team exercise. But the time spent will be rewarded many fold through increased performance.

Team technologies

16 Consider how various technologies could enhance team communications, work processes, meetings or team knowledge. Consider a wide range, from voice communications to groupware.

17 Agree on standards. Select a common core set of products and services – word processing, email, groupware, etc.

18 Go web-centric for important team documents. Create a team knowledge repository (on your intranet). Your documents can later be published for a wider internal or external audience.

19 Agree on content and usage standards when using the technologies, e.g. headings for emails, information structure in groupware databases, forwarding of messages.

20 Do not use technology just for the sake of it. Err on the side of proven rather than experimental technologies, but keep an open eye for opportunities to pilot technologies that could be beneficial.

As discussed in Chapter 3, there is a wide range of technologies that can enhance knowledge activities. From the team perspective, the important ones are those that help people communicate and collaborate. Table 6.2 shows a functional hierarchy of some of the commonly used technologies.

Every team should have access to a range of these, so that the functional spectrum is covered. More important than the choice of any specific technology, though, is how effectively they are used. The effective use of

Table 6.2 Functional hierarchy of team technologies

Function	Synchronous	Asynchronous	Comments
Collaboration	Electronic whiteboard	Document management Web pages	Shared knowledge sources
Conversation (structured)	Meeting support (GDSS)	Computer conferencing	More structured and explicit
Communication (basic)	Videoconferencing Telephone	Email Voicemail	Asynchronous communications can be retained as part of organizational memory

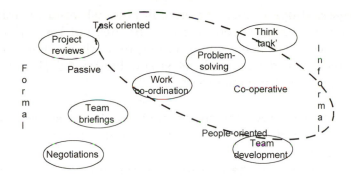

Figure 6.4 Types of meeting most appropriate for conferencing

email was covered in Chapter 5. Below, guidance is given on the effective use of two other contrasting technologies from Table 6.2 – computer conferencing and videoconferencing.

Computer conferencing – developing knowledge

As described in Chapter 3, computer conferencing performs several roles – facilitating communications, providing access to information and acting as a meeting substitute. The types of meeting where substitution by conferencing makes the most sense are shown within the dashed area of Figure 6.4.

Conferencing also helps teams interact better with their wider network, by testing new product ideas, posting solutions to customer problems and responding to suggestions. Many team conferences are restricted in membership so that confidential matters can be discussed. A problem in

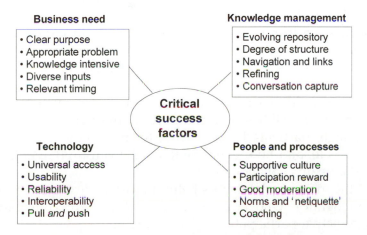

Figure 6.5 Critical success factors for a computer conference

many organizations is that conferences languish after an initial flush of enthusiasm. There are several reasons for this, not least of which is that the conference is not achieving anything more than what could be easily handled by other means such as email. Figure 6.5 shows factors that underpin a successful conference:

- A clear business need and an appropriate task that evolves over time and needs multiple inputs. Conferencing is not appropriate for urgent, single person tasks.
- The technology must be easy to access and use. Poor network access and reliability will discourage its use.
- Good information and knowledge management. The conference must be well structured so users can quickly find relevant information and contribute.
- The conference must take account of personal behaviour. If there are too many irrelevant contributions or people have to hunt for things that affect them, it will be discredited.

Ways to develop effective team conferences are:

- Actively solicit feedback – in a team you should be able to get frank feedback. A conference allows feedback to be structured according to specific topics.
- Recognize positive contributions – openly express appreciation.
- Be responsive – try and respond to most postings within a day. If you need time for a more informed comment, acknowledge receipt and say when you will respond more fully.
- Be more open about expressing concerns, although when criticizing always start positively with what you do like.
- In documents or reference information clearly identify the author, date, version and status.
- Regularly summarize conference conversations, so that you build up a valuable resource library, including such items as rationale for decisions, project histories, best practices, useful contacts, etc.

Conferences should have both private and public virtual workspaces. With appropriate facilities they can become the hub of a team's knowledge exchange, particularly for virtual teams. Lotus TeamRoom shows what is possible, and how good conferencing can fundamentally change the way that teams collaborate.

One of the most crucial factors behind most worthwhile conferences is a good moderator, who ensures a relevant flow of contributions and encourages active participation by all the team.

The role of moderator is discussed later in this chapter.

Lotus TeamRoom

Lotus TeamRoom was developed at the Lotus Institute, following research and experimentation with collaborative team technologies. It originated in a project to improve the performance and quality of work life at Lotus. Meetings were the primary means of group collaboration but proved difficult to organize because of people's locations and schedules. Therefore email was widely used for co-ordination and sharing information, the phone for one-to-one discussions and clarification of email messages, and Lotus Notes' discussion databases (conferences) and document libraries for communicating beyond the team. However, Lotus Notes was little used within the project team. TeamRoom added facilities that made this more practical:

- Users can modify the environment to suit their own preferences. Documents can be private or shared.
- There are team areas and personal workspace, which users can organize to suit their own preferences.
- There are links between discussion databases and email. Users can choose whether information is accessed by email or TeamRoom. They can be alerted by email if new information comes into specified areas of TeamRoom.
- TeamRoom allows them to assign categories to messages such as for discussion, action request, reference, meeting announcements.
- A structure for team co-ordination is provided through a mission page and linked user applications.

In common with many other groupware situations, the technology was merely an enabler, but not the driver of change. It was the encouragement and active coaching of users that changed the way the team worked. By changing their focus from email to the TeamRoom areas, they could see communications and information within its wider team structure.

Videoconferencing – enriching remote conversations

Videoconferencing is becoming as essential tool for many knowledge teams. While its use is not yet as natural as picking up the telephone, it is a commonly used tool in many organizations. As well as using it for scheduled meetings many knowledge teams use videoconferencing for ad hoc discussions when visual contact is helpful. A particularly useful feature is the 'joint viewing' of documents. Participants share a common view of a document on the screen, while discussing and amending it.

Using videoconferencing is quite straightforward, but there are a number of practical guidelines that catch out beginners, and will also help those familiar make better use of it:

- For multisite conferences, plan ahead – check availability and time restrictions; set an outline agenda.
- In a room setting, make sure one person is familiar with the camera operation and can zoom in on relevant people or objects; use camera presets to change the view and add interest.
- Be aware of technological limitations: use the 'mute' button to cut out background noise while others are speaking.
- Make yourself video friendly – wear pastel coloured clothes – avoid strong patterns, stripes and red. Look at the camera while speaking, avoid rapid movement. Pause frequently. Be natural.

Activity 6.5: Review your team technologies

List your team core processes and knowledge development activities. For each, consider what technologies could enhance them and how they might be introduced. For technologies you currently use, consider how they help or hinder key processes and knowledge development activities. Develop a plan that prioritizes technology improvements and how to learn to use them more effectively in team settings.

Managing team knowledge

21 Knowledge is an important team asset. Every team member should have some responsibility in their area of expertise for collating and distributing team knowledge. However, other knowledge roles, such as librarian, knowledge editor, gatekeeper and brokers should be specifically recognized and assigned.

22 Create a team knowledge repository organized according to one or more well understood structures. Business processes, domains of knowledge and categories of stakeholder are suitable categories.

23 Regard email exchanges and conference discussions as embryonic knowledge. In developing discussions, build on knowledge that exists or has been expressed. Archive them for future retrieval and knowledge 'refining'.

24 For each main task area or domain of expertise, appoint a knowledge editor. Their role is to take the best from this transitory information and compile it into a more structured document or web page for ongoing reference.

25 Be sure to capture lessons from team processes and projects. Over time this becomes team memory and a vital resource for future occasions and other part of the organization.

Teams generate so much informal knowledge in day-to-day work that they overlook the necessity to capture and store some of it in a more permanent knowledge repository. This is especially necessary as teams evolve and change. For example, continuity in a long project is helped when assumptions and rationale for decisions are recorded.

At first, some of the aspects of managing team knowledge may seem onerous. But the savings in time by having a well-organized team knowledge repository amply repay the initial investment. Many organizations will have knowledge centres to take care of these activities on an organization-wide basis. However, they rely on a good flow of knowledge to and from various teams. Therefore, teams need to be clear about what knowledge it wants to manage more effectively. This will be a mix of tacit and explicit, of formal and informal, and will almost certainly comprise key documents, selected emails and web pages intended for those outside the team.

Team knowledge development and innovation

High-performing teams usually exhibit higher than average creativity. Chapter 5 gave some pointers as to some of the many techniques used to enhance creativity. In a team setting ways to enhance creativity and develop team knowledge include:

*   having a stimulating and distraction free environment – often this means working in a location away from the main office
*   brainstorming – team members should suspend judgement however crazy an idea may seem
*   learning from recent past – asking a lot of 'what if' questions
*   repeated experimentation – learn by doing and take risks. Adopt an idea and move it forward. 3M did not get where they are by playing safe
*   making the team workplace conducive to thinking and stimulating discussion. Introduce soft furnishings, put up wall murals, have funny gadgets and sculptures – anything to create a talking point.

Virtual teams can introduce analogous practices, such as devoting a team discussion document to novel ideas, adding a 'thought for the day' on your email signature. Why not have the 'crazy but it might work idea of the month' award at team meetings?

Team memory

Team memory evolves from deliberations, decisions and actions. The knowledge generated needs capturing and managing. Computerized decision support systems that capture conversations can create useful both short- and long-term memory. Jeff Conklin cites an example of the use of QuestMap to capture key points in planning meetings for a utility company.[12] Three months after discussing pricing criteria, the group started to discuss this topic again. However, within a few seconds the facilitator had brought up the results of their previous deliberations, allowing the team to carry on from where they had previously left off. Rapid memory recall was also useful for an environmental scheme that had been discussed in detail but then shelved.

Teams should therefore give attention to the processes that develop team memory. They should regularly review and refine team knowledge bases, and convert their tacit knowledge into more explicit knowledge and map its flows to and from the team as part of their organization's wider knowledge network.

Activity 6.6: Enhance your team knowledge

What is your team's core knowledge? Where is it held? How could it be better packaged and made more readily available to other nodes in your team's knowledge network? What are the most important knowledge flows into and out of the team? How could they be better managed? Develop a plan and assign responsibilities for knowledge development roles.

Sustaining high performance

Teams face many challenges in creating and sustaining high performance. Frequently, members move and the demands placed on them change. Therefore, flexibility is paramount. Shared statements of principle are much better than detailed manuals of team processes. Teams must also work hard to maintain cohesion and avoid divisions. Members can help each other by being open on how they see each other's styles and behaviour, and expressing feelings more openly.

Global teams also face challenges of cultural differences. Although on-line culture tends to mask the differences, some nationalities rely much more on socialization and tacit knowledge rather than the written word. In his classic work on national differences Hofstede mapped national culture along four dimensions.[13] One dimension is individualism vs collectivism, which shows the USA having by far and being the highest individualist, followed by Australia, UK and Canada. In contrast, societies that work more cohesively include Latin America and some Far Eastern countries (though not Japan). On a competitive vs collaborative dimension, Scandinavian countries and the Netherlands are high in collaboration. Thus people from certain nationalities may gel more quickly into collaborative teams than others. In practice, corporate cultures and individual traits often matter more. Sensitivity to different national cultures is just another aspect of valuing diversity.

To keep achieving, teams must regularly celebrate success, and revisit their vision to keep it inspiring. To maintain enthusiasm, it must experiment, try out different formats for meetings and organize social events. In my experience the biggest causes of failures in teams are:

- not having a compelling shared vision
- not clearly identifying team roles
- having team missions and goals incompatible with individuals' aspirations
- having dominant personalities
- not communicating sufficiently and clearly enough
- devoting insufficient time and attention to team processes
- getting complacent.

Virtual teams face the additional challenge of separation. However, there is little evidence that a geographically dispersed team is any less effective than one based at a single location. On the contrary, there is some evidence that people put more effort into making remote linkages and communication work because there is less opportunity to meet face-to-face. One such team that puts several of the principles described in this chapter into practice is that of European Telework Development (ETD).

Virtual global collaboration: the ETD experience

European Telework Development (see page 111) is a project that consists of more than thirty organizations and individuals working in various virtual arrangements. Among its many teams are a management team, two teams of national co-ordinators and a media team. Most of its participants were already experienced teleworkers and extensive users of email before joining ETD. In reflecting on what makes these virtual teams effective, the team leaders drew the following lessons from their experience:

- Subdivide into smaller task teams for emergent tasks that are not obviously the remit of one team and are not high enough on their priority list.
- Allow time for relationships to develop and teams to gel; the occasional face-to-face meeting is an advantage, but with the right skill at electronic communications, is not essential for many tasks.
- Develop technical support mechanisms to help people with their

technical problems; the state of the Internet, service provision and quality of software is very variable across Europe (and the world).
- Develop 'standards' for communication; these include technical standards e.g. using MIME for email attachments, content standards, e.g. predefined templates for different document types, and procedures, e.g. not automatically copying every recipient when replying to an email.
- Structure information and messages well, using clear titles, identifying information type or status (e.g. draft, request for action etc.).
- Keep filing away those email contacts of people who conduct themselves well over networks; it's an essential skill for virtual knowledge transfer and such people are an extended team resource – they might even become a team member in future!

Knowledge communities

Teams interact with wider knowledge networks. Their members will frequently be members of communities of practice that span the organization. George Pór describes communities as 'connecting islands of knowledge into self-organizing, knowledge sharing networks'. While some communities focus on a particular profession or discipline, the most powerful communities are customer or problem focused. They transcend disciplines and bring in different perspectives. They exchange, develop and apply knowledge. Just as a knowledge team is more cohesive than a work group, a knowledge community is a more cohesive cluster within

Table 6.3 Knowledge communities contrasted with other groups

	Work group	Team	Knowledge network (CoI)	Knowledge community (CoP)
Typical size	3–30	5–8	30–300	15–150
Membership	Recruited for job	Recruited for team fit	Self-selecting	Self-selecting
Focus	Tasks	Output	Knowledge exchange	Applied knowledge
Goals	Explicit, given	Mutually agreed	Imprecise or implicit	Evolving and purposeful
Boundaries	Precise	Permeable	Fluid	Mutually adjusting

Note: CoI = community of interest; CoP = community of practice a diffuse knowledge network. Table 6.3 highlights the essential differences between groups, teams, networks and communities.

The main difference compared to a team in that the membership is self-selecting. Like a self-managed team they cannot be strongly directed or over directed. In fact the best management style for an in-house knowledge community is hands-off, but providing a climate in which they thrive. Communities are more social than structural. Etienne Wenger (an originator of communities of practice), and Bill Snyder list the following stages of community development:[14]

1   Latent: there is potential for such a community within the organization.
2   Coalescent: members come together and recognize their collective potential.
3   Active: engaged in developing a practice.
4   Legitimized: recognized as a valuable entity.
5   Strategic: central to the success of an organization.
6   Transformational: capable of redefining its environment.
7   In Diaspora: dispersed but still alive as a force.
8   Memorable: no longer very relevant, but still remembered as part of member's identities.

Compared to a knowledge team, the size of a community means that it loses some of the cohesiveness and commitment. However, good communities retain as many characteristics of effective knowledge teams as possible, including a shared sense of purpose, intensive external networking, effective knowledge management and trust. Many communities embody such considerations into their guiding principles.[15] The two most important parameters are a high flow of communications and passionate community leaders. In the virtual environment this role is performed by a person known as the conference host or moderator.

Virtual moderation for knowledge development

The role of a conference moderator is to stimulate virtual discussion and to guide the community forwards in its thinking and knowledge development. A good moderator has enthusiasm for their subject and likes networking. For most, moderating is not their primary job, but an important added daily activity. They activate knowledge development by:

*   Setting up conferences – admitting members, assigning privileges etc.
*   Defining the scope and agenda for discussion – posing key questions.
*   Defining the ground rules, e.g. no personal insults, no advertising.

- Keeping conversations developing – stimulating discussion, revisiting earlier topics.
- Summarizing – periodically reviewing progress and key contributions and maintaining a coherent structure.
- Cross-linking – connecting different conversational threads; this cross-fertilization often sparks new ideas and momentum.
- Managing inappropriate contributions or behaviour – defusing arguments (more of this is done behind the scenes with private emails or telephone conversations).
- Engaging people in conversation – actively seeking contributions from those they know have something worthwhile to contribute; visibly acknowledging good contributions.

Significant effort is needed in the early stages to gather momentum. Initially, it is usually better to organize conferences by broad topic areas, to get a critical mass for meaningful discussion. One can always subdivide later into more specific topics. Once up and running, Lisa Kimball suggests asking three simple questions to verify that a conference is progressing well:

1 Is the discussion moving forward?
2 Is it interesting?
3 Can new people find their way?[16]

Good conference leaders will identify important and challenging tasks that will benefit the whole community and keep the knowledge flowing, e.g. preparation of a best practice guidebook, a resources database, etc.

Sustaining communities

Those organizations that encourage communities as an integral part of corporate knowledge programmes will gain significant benefits. Good knowledge communities will be thought leaders, generating new product ideas and aggregating the collective thinking of a talented group of individuals to tackle difficult problems. They will significantly increase an organization's knowledge capital.

A potential threat to communities is that the very focus on knowledge management introduces a degree of formalization that could, if not dealt with sensitively, stifle them. How can organizations minimize this risk?

- Provide facilities that make it easy for these communities to meet and exchange: web space, internal newsgroups, mail lists; as well as physical meeting places where tacit knowledge conversion can take place.

- Offer facilitation to help them improve current processes – too often communities get bogged down in the content, not stepping back and seeing the effectiveness of their ongoing processes, e.g. when enrolling new members.
- Provide connection information – help others who share their interests apply to join, help them publicize their existence to the outside world, e.g. via community directories.
- Encourage note taking methods for meetings – have community members synthesize 'knowledge nuggets', that can be recalled and shared with those not at the meeting.
- Synthesize and edit email discussions – create 'knowledge editor' roles, people who respect their norms and values – some communities may want to remain small and intimate, and restrict membership.

Communities need a supportive organizational environment. An easy way to kill a community is to discourage people from spending time at it, or even, as some managers have tried, to suppress this 'non-essential work'. Reward systems and culture must support community participation. Endorsement, not enforcement, is the watchword. The whole ethos of a successful community is based much more on a knowledge ecology rather than a knowledge management emphasis (see Table 2.1). A good example of knowledge ecology in action is that of the Knowledge Ecology Fair.

The Knowledge Ecology Fair

Knowledge Ecology Fair 1998 was an on-line event that attracted over 300 virtual attendees and ran for three weeks.[17] The World Wide Web provided an entry point for the various activities of the conference:

- Keynote presentations – given by knowledge leaders such as Leif Edvinsson of Skandia, Karl Erik Sveiby, and Bipin Junnarkar of Monsanto.
- Workshops – led by subject experts, including Verna Allee[18] on 'Knowledge and self organization', Etienne Wenger 'Learning communities: the ecology of knowing', Arian Ward on futurizing and Michael Rey on creativity.
- Discussion groups such as workplace communities.
- Community Café – more informal discussion e.g. on shared interests, on books we love.
- The Open Space Circle – 'an open space for participant generated discussions; get first hand experience facilitating a learning conversation . . . explore questions of most interest to you'.

In the Open Space Circle forty-two discussion items were created, which covered topics as varied as organizational intelligence in family-owned businesses, knowledge artefacts and communities of practice in health care settings. As a result of discussion at the fair, new initiatives have evolved, such as KEN (Knowledge Ecology Network) and the Knowledge Ecology University.

Summary

This chapter has shown the importance of a team as a focal point for knowledge work, a node in an ever changing knowledge network. It has explored the dynamics of knowledge communities. Both teams and communities thrive through a shared sense of purpose and cohesion. High performance comes from integrating 'soft' factors such as building relationships and developing trust, alongside team processes and technology.

The twenty-five principles and additional guidelines just described have helped various virtual knowledge teams and communities collaborate more effectively. Are they appropriate for your teams? Yes and no. Yes – they are based on research and experience in teams that perform well and cover the key dimensions that need to be addressed. No – every team is different and will need to develop their own set of guiding principles according to their aims and circumstances.

Of the five groups, it is team processes that are usually the most important. Within team processes, it is the quality of conversations and structured dialogue that most frequently determines the difference between poor and well performing teams. In a virtual environment, moderators play an important role in stimulating this dialogue and thus adding to the knowledge capital of individuals, teams and the organization as a whole.

Action check list

Establishing teams

1   Have you identified the core teams of your business? Is there a directory or index of them?
2   Did Activity 6.2 identify the need for any changes in the organizational context? Develop a plan to make senior management aware of this need.

3   Develop a set of core principles for your team and have them printed and laminated.
4   Develop a set of team performance measures and success criteria that also take account of individual team member's needs. Review your operating plan against these indicators.
5   Identify your team's core knowledge inputs, processes and outputs. Ensure that you have assigned responsibilities for key knowledge processes and repositories.

Implementing good team practice
6   Develop a programme of liaison with those teams with which you have the greatest interdependence.
7   Develop a format for team meetings that ensure that sufficient time is devoted to review of processes and for team learning and development.
8   Identify a suitable facilitator external to your team, who can help the team throughout its ongoing development.
9   Identify which knowledge communities can contribute to your team's success. Ensure that appropriate team members are involved and that they share relevant knowledge within your team.
10   Periodically review your core principles and how well they are being followed.

Notes

1   Originally published as 'Virtual working', at http://www.skyrme. com/insights. More recently published in Lloyd, P. and Boyle, P. (eds) (1998). *Web Weaving: Intranets, Extranets and Strategic Alliances*. Butterworth-Heinemann.
2   Katzenbach, J. and Smith, D. (1992). *The Wisdom of Teams*. Harvard Business School Press.
3   Buchanan, D. A. and McCalman, J. (1989). *High Performance Work Systems: The Digital Experience*. Routledge.
4   Belbin M. (1993). *Team Roles at Work*. Butterworth-Heinemann.
5   Drexler, A. B. and Sibbert, D. L. (1993). *The Drexler/Sibbert Team Performance Model*. Graphic Guides; a good discussion of this with relevance to global virtual teams is found in O'Hara-Devereaux, M. and Johansen, R. (1994). *Globalwork: Bridging Distance, Culture and Time*, pp. 157–170. Jossey Bass.
6   Coles, M. (1998). Managers tackle world-wide teams. *Sunday Times*, 8 March, p 7.24.
7   Kuntz, W. and Rittel, H. (1972). Issues as elements of information systems. Working Paper No. 131, Institute of Urban and Regional Development, University of California at Berkeley.
8   Conklin, J. (1998). IBIS and organizational memory, at http://www. zilker.net/business/info/pubs/desom.

9   Beer, S. (1994). *Beyond Dispute: The Invention of Team Syntegrity*. John Wiley
     & Sons. A more recent write up including practical experiences is Lennard,
     A. D. (1997) at http://wwww.phrontis.com/TSBackgr.htm
10   Jarvenpaa, S. L. and Shaw, T. R. (1998). Global virtual teams: integrated
     models of trust. In: Sieber, P. and Griese, J. (eds.). *Organizational Virtualness*.
     Simowa Verlag, pp. 35-52.
11   Jarvenpaa, S. L. and Leidner, D. (1998). Communications and trust in virtual
     teams. *Journal of Computer Mediated Communications*, **3**(4), June 1998 at
     http://jcmc.huji.ac.il./vol3/issue4/jarvenpaa.html.
12   Conklin, J. (1998). IBIS and organizational memory, at http://www.
     zilker.net/business/info/pubs/desom.
13   Hofstede, G. (1991). *Cultures and Organizations*. McGraw Hill.
14   Wenger, E. and Snyder, W. (1998). *Learning Communities*, Workshop 5,
     KEFair 98. http://www.tmn.com
15   See for example, Community Intelligence Labs *Community Covenant*, at
     http://www.co-i-l.com/oil/iacenter/ccovenant.shtml
16   Lisa Kimball, *Moderator Guidelines*, at http://freenet.msp.mn.us/confdoc/
     modguide.htm
17   *Knowledge Ecology Fair 1998* at http://www.tmn.com/ksweb
18   Author of Allee, V. (1997). *The Knowledge Evolution: Expanding Organizational
     Intelligence*. Butterworth-Heinemann. Arian Ward was Leader of
     Collaboration, Knowledge and Learning for Hughes Space and
     Communication; Michael Ray Professor of Creativity and Innovation at
     Stanford Business School. Etienne Wenger coined the phrase 'communities
     of practice'.

Chapter 7

Toolkit for the knowledge-based enterprise

The most common question asked of me in my consulting role is 'how do you get people to share their knowledge?' Organizational culture is the main stumbling block facing many organizations trying to build a knowledge-based enterprise.

Human and behavioural factors therefore feature heavily throughout this chapter. The guiding framework used is derived from an analysis of factors that underscore the success of a knowledge-based business. Its elements include leadership, environment, culture and structure, processes for managing organizational knowledge, measures, and supporting infrastructures. The activities in this toolkit are sets of questions that preface discussion of each of ten success factors. These help you evaluate how well your organization is implementing the knowledge agenda. Guidance is then given on best practice for each element of the framework.

Leaders and laggards

In order to gain insights into what helps knowledge-based organizations succeed it is instructive to identify differences between leaders and laggards (Table 7.1).

Table 7.1 Leaders and laggards in knowledge initiatives

	Leaders	vs	Laggards
1	Clearly articulate a vision that incorporates knowledge.	vs	Knowledge is not viewed as a strategic lever, e.g. it is something just for the Information Services (IS) department.
2	Have enthusiastic knowledge champions who are supported by top management.	vs	Knowledge management activities take place in isolated pockets without strong senior management support.
3	A holistic perspective that embraces strategic, technological and organizational perspectives.	vs	A narrow process perspective, e.g. limited to knowledge sharing rather than embracing all processes including knowledge creation and innovation.
4	Use systematic processes and frameworks (the power of visualization).	vs	Follow a standard change process, e.g. BPR, without adding the associated knowledge dimension.
5	'Bet on knowledge', even when the cost-benefits cannot easily be measured.	vs	Downsize or outsource without realizing what vital knowledge might be lost.
6	Communicate effectively, both internally and externally.	vs	Disseminate knowledge that is most readily available rather than seek out that which is the most useful.
7	Interact extensively at all levels with customers and external experts.	vs	Think they 'know all the answers', i.e. they are not open to new ideas.
8	Demonstrate good teamwork, with knowledge team members drawn from many disciplines.	vs	View technology alone as the solution, e.g. 'it's in the database'.
9	A culture of openness and inquisitiveness that stimulates innovation and learning.	vs	Have cultural barriers, perhaps caused by a climate of 'knowledge is power'.
10	Incentives, sanctions and personal development programmes to change behaviours.	vs	Get impatient. View knowledge management as a 'quick fix', rather than allowing time for new systems and behaviours to become embedded.

Source: Skyrme, D. J. and Amidon, D. M. (1997). *Creating the Knowledge-Based Business*, ch. 9. Business Intelligence.

Similar success characteristics occur with innovation. More innovative companies: [1]

- make innovation a priority at board level
- continuously review where to focus innovation for maximum business benefit
- have well defined idea management processes that allow ideas and knowledge to be shared, stored and freely accessed
- have a working environment that encourages ideas to flow through the business
- reinforce (through reward systems) management behaviours that encourage innovation
- have a management style that is open, and not closely managed
- empower and trust individuals to initiate change and turn strategy into reality.

These characteristics indicate that success depends on simultaneously driving and aligning factors across several dimensions. These factors have been drawn together into an action-focused framework for this chapter's toolkit (Figure 7.1).

At the top layer of the framework are the enablers. Knowledge is seen as strategic and its contribution to the business is clearly articulated. The organization's structure, culture and environment encourage knowledge development and sharing. Without these enablers most knowledge initiatives drift or stall.

The second layer of the framework comprises a set of levers that amplify the contribution of knowledge. These include knowledge processes that facilitate knowledge flows, knowledge centres that provide faster access to explicit knowledge and better ways of handling tacit knowledge.

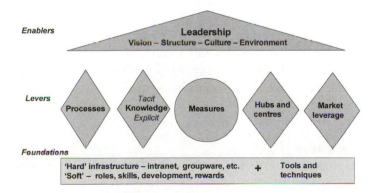

Figure 7.1 A knowledge initiative framework

Thirdly, the foundation layer provides the capacity and capability that embeds knowledge into the organization's infrastructure. It comprises two complementary strands – a 'hard' information and communications infrastructure that supports knowledge collaboration, and a 'soft' human and organization infrastructure that develops knowledge enhancing roles, skills and behaviours.

The following sections guide you through these layers in turn, covering ten groups of factors in all. Each section starts with a set of five assessment questions. Some have a clear yes or no answer, but you may prefer to grade your answers on a scale of 1–5, e.g.:

0 – Not at all
1 – Considering
2 – Recently introduced
3 – Progressing well
4 – Visible throughout the organization
5 – Making a strong business impact.

Use these individual answers to guide you in developing an overall rating on a scale of 0–10 for each group of five questions.

Knowledge leadership

1 Leadership

- Is there a compelling knowledge vision that is actively followed?
- Is the role of knowledge clearly articulated in organizational mission, objectives and plans?
- Are there clear responsibilities for knowledge strategy and activities, such as through a Chief Knowledge Officer?
- Are knowledge and information treated as vital resources and reviewed regularly at management meetings?
- Do your CEO and senior executives promote knowledge management within their team and to the outside world?

A vision for value

A knowledge-based enterprise needs a solid architecture around which to build its strategies. Most start with a simple effective model that acts as the focal point for its knowledge-enhancing activities. Skandia's Navigator, for example, uses a visual metaphor of its intellectual capital that guides objective settings. Monsanto's KMA (Knowledge Management Architecture) is based on a simple schematic that depicts internal and external knowledge, structured/unstructured. Others depict a cycle of knowledge processes, along the lines of Figure 2.6. The best knowledge models are visual, holistic, easily understood and actively promoted. A full architecture will contain many elements and layers, incorporating many of the factors discussed in this chapter. It should be your blueprint for action. But it must remain flexible, ready to accommodate new developments, either externally induced, such as technology, or internal management changes.

Knowledge champions

Knowledge champions promote the benefits of a knowledge-focused approach, and are at the forefront of experimentation. They may emerge from anywhere in the organization, and act as intrapreneurs. They will attract attention to their ideas and ultimately gain support to take them forward. Many knowledge programmes have evolved from the actions of such individuals.

Like any intrapreneur, the life of champions is made difficult in many organizations since they challenge the status quo. They may be unorthodox in their approach, as they seek novel ways of getting things done despite organizational reticence. Their success usually depends on a senior management sponsor or board-level support. Look around your organization and see how well it supports champions of innovation. If it squashes ideas, or reins in the innovators, it is destroying its future.

Knowledge initiatives and teams

The creation of a formal knowledge initiative is usually a starting point for giving an impetus to the knowledge agenda. Early projects within such initiatives are typically best practices databases, expertise profiling (creating so called Yellow Pages), development of a knowledge centre and the implementation of a corporate intranet. Most initiatives are co-ordinated by one or more knowledge teams. Successful teams draw together people from different backgrounds and disciplines including library science, information technology, human resources, marketing, as well as people with line management experience. Typically they will:

- help businesses formulate strategy for development and exploitation of knowledge – for example, using the seven levers of knowledge discussed in Chapter 2
- Support implementation by introducing knowledge management techniques, such as the processes described in Chapter 2 and later in this chapter

- provide co-ordination for knowledge specialists in various parts of the business
- oversee the development of a knowledge infrastructure, including the development of a knowledge inventory and standards for knowledge asset management
- facilitate and support knowledge communities.

They are the hubs of knowledge about knowledge, with links and nodes throughout the business. At Monsanto, for example, its knowledge team in 1995 had just four full-time staff at its hub, but an extended network of thirty to forty people in business units, who spent 20–30 per cent of their time working with the core team. Bipin Junnarkar, its leader, described the main role of the team as 'facilitators of the processes of knowledge creation and conversion, and also the cross-pollinating of knowledge across the organization'.

Do you need a Chief Knowledge Officer?
Many organizations are now appointing people with a title such as Chief Knowledge Officer (CKO), often a senior-level appointment, reporting directly to a top level strategy committee or the board of directors. Their role is to promulgate the knowledge agenda and oversee its implementation. They often directly manage the corporate knowledge team. Good CKOs 'walk the talk', paint the vision, tell anecdotes and stimulate new knowledge projects.

Is a CKO really necessary? Companies such as Hewlett-Packard have been very successful at knowledge management without one. Its Chief Executive, Lew Platt, actively promotes the strategic role of knowledge, while its decentralized structure and innovative culture allow knowledge initiatives to flourish. On the other hand, many CKOs argue that their appointment has legitimized knowledge management and sends a signal about its importance throughout the organization.

Britton Manasco reflects a growing view of the nature of knowledge leadership: 'The knowledge leader – or leaders – must become a vital and dynamic force in the organization rather than the figurehead(s) of yet another corporate change program. Eventually leadership must become dispersed and accountability for the success of knowledge initiatives widely held. As I see it, the CKO will have achieved real success when his or her position is no longer necessary.'[2]

Leading from the top
BP Amoco provides a good exemplar of knowledge leadership. John Browne, its Chief Executive, in an interview published in *Harvard Business Review* describes learning as 'at the heart of a company's ability to adapt

to a rapidly changing environment'. He cites learning from partners, contractors, suppliers and customers and of applying the knowledge gained: 'No matter where the knowledge comes from, the key to reaping a big return is to leverage that knowledge by replicating it throughout the company so that each unit is not learning in isolation and reinventing the wheel again and again'.[3]

His words are echoed by practical support. The pilot project on virtual teaming described in Chapter 4 was funded to the extent of $12 million, before the full extent of benefits were known. (In fact, it was later estimated that the benefits exceeded $30 million in its first year.) Browne challenges his managers to innovate and to seek breakthroughs. At one oil field five miles offshore, horizontal drilling was used instead of the more conventional artificial island. This saved BP $75 million. Throughout the interview Browne was enthusing about many of the practices described in this book, including learning communities, the free exchange of knowledge, peer groups and not hierarchies. He also stressed that leaders must demonstrate that they are active participants in the learning organization: 'learning is my job, too'.

Creating a knowledge-enriching environment

2 Culture/structure

> * Are project teams deliberately chosen to include people with a wide level of experience, different expertise and age ranges?
> * Do personal performance reviews assess and reward individuals for their knowledge contributions?
> * Is time for learning, thinking and reflection considered a good investment of time in your organization?
> * Do workplace settings encourage interaction and free flow of information, e.g. informal meeting areas, open plan offices, project rooms?
> * Are individual experts encouraged to contribute time and expertise to support other teams?

Culture has many definitions, and many facets. It consists of symbols and rituals, attitudes and behaviours, a set of values, yet is largely invisible. It is best described as: 'the way we do things around here'.[4] Throughout our research and consulting practice, culture stands out as the key factor that determines success or otherwise with knowledge management. A knowledge-enriching culture is characterized by:

- an organizational climate of openness
- empowered individuals
- active learning – from customers, from the results of individual's own actions
- a constant search for improvement and innovation
- intense communications, open and widespread
- organizational slack – time to experiment, reflect and learn
- boundary-crossing – individuals spend as much time interacting with those outside their team as those within it
- encouragement of experimentation, rather than blindly following rules
- aligned goals and performance measures, across departments, teams and individuals
- willingness to share knowledge widely among colleagues, even those in different groups.

3M exhibits the characteristics of such a culture. An important driver of behaviour is the goal that 30 per cent of revenues should be for products less than four years old. This makes people thirsty for knowledge. It aims to attract and keep the right people. According to 3M UK Project Manager, Adam Brand: 'We back people not projects; it's better to back good people with so-so projects rather than so-so people with good projects'. He describes 3M as a company of intrapreneurs – 'dreamers who do.' Individuals have 15 per cent of their time free to experiment as they please. 3M blends stretching goals, foresight and freedom. Its culture encourages tacit knowledge exchange through person-to-person connections.

In contrast, many organizational cultures put priority on following rules as opposed to acting in the right way. In these organizations 'knowledge is power'. A Reuters survey found that two out of three managers believe that their bosses and colleagues were 'information misers' who 'value information highly but are protective to the point of withholding it from others'.[5]

Why don't people share? Inherently, there is nothing an expert likes doing more than demonstrating their expertise and sharing it with others. Frequently organizations do not encourage them to do so. A culture of sharing can be engendered by creating the right attitudes and behaviours. You can change the style of meetings to encourage dialogue not monologue. You can formally recognize and reward good knowledge practice. Such changes also have to be reinforced by behaviours of senior managers. When British Airways moved to its new head office, Chief Executive, Bob Ayling, went through the same training programme as his staff. He shares the open space with others and has no office of his own.

Siemens's public networks division had a culture change programme as part of its transformation to a more global and competitive business. It had successive phases that mobilized more and more employees in change and organizational learning. An initial group of thirty-five people participated in an 'invent the future' workshop. Each participant then enrolled further people and so the change group grew from thirty-five to 220, then 1000 and then all 9000 in the organization. The programme introduced learning from mistakes, customer awards, friends and family days and communication corners.

Knowledge webs – structures for knowledge innovation

Culture and structure go hand in hand. One reinforces the other. If responsibilities and formal reporting is organized hierarchically, then communication patterns will reinforce it. To encourage lateral communications and boundary crossing, organizational structures must reinforce interdependence through knowledge teams and networks.

Examples of such structures are increasingly found. ABB has over 4000 business units working in a federation. Samsung describes itself as a network of alliances. In 1993 it changed its structure to a 'network of alliances'. It flattened its hierarchy from seven levels to three, increased teams and networking ('a clustered web'). In 1997 Monsanto Life Sciences created a 'honeycomb organization', where each business unit had two heads – a commercial and science head, and each management team had cross-representation with other teams.

Space – the last frontier?

Many conventional offices are not conducive to knowledge sharing. They have enclosed offices or cubicles that impede communications, or have poorly designed open areas that are distracting. Knowledge networking environments need a mix of 'caves' and 'commons', i.e. private workspace for intensive thinking or individual work and shared space that enhances interaction. Knowledge sharing is encouraged when offices have more shared space. Thus, 35 per cent of Sun's Menlo Park office is shared space with 225 different meeting places.[6] Better designed offices can reduce space needs by 30 per cent while simultaneously boosting productivity by 30 per cent or more. When Digital redesigned its 'office of the future' in Finland, it used a newsroom format with communication hubs and informal areas that had swing chairs. Ricoh's central research laboratories near Yokohama has its tree of imagination: 'Imaginative ideas don't grow on trees. But at the Ricoh Research and Development Centre, they often blossom around one. A giant, 250 year old keyaki tree carved into a star-shaped table, is the center's creative hub. Around it research staff from around the world meet to exchange ideas.'[7]

An office conducive for innovation and knowledge exchange is likely to have:

- 'talk rooms' or sitting out areas where people can meet informally and converse
- project rooms or 'whiteboard rooms' where information is displayed and annotated
- themed areas, such as a 'pit stop' or customer area
- easy access to senior executives, who also work in an open informal environment
- main 'streets', corridors or hubs that help increase the number of informal encounters.

Scandinavian architects are at the forefront of incorporating these ideas into building design. Waterside, British Airways' new headquarters near London's Heathrow Airport was designed by Norwegian Niels Torp to provide open informality and help 'management on the move'. The overall building is designed as six U-shaped blocks connected by a central street, 175 metres long. Away from the street are quieter, more private areas.[8] People can choose where they want to work and plug their portable computers and cordless phones into the telecommunications network. There are many informal meeting areas as well as shops, cafés and a gymnasium.

Managing organizational knowledge

Good organizational knowledge management requires effective mechanisms for each of the processes outlined in the knowledge cycles of Chapter 2. It requires effective sharing and development of integration of both internal and external, explicit and tacit knowledge.

3 The process perspective – systematic and chaordic

- Do you know what is vital knowledge – knowledge that underpins your core business processes?
- Is this knowledge readily accessible and naturally integrated in to the flow of work?
- Processes – does the organization have systematic processes for monitoring external knowledge sources and for gathering and classifying it?

- Are there clear policy guidelines on what is vital proprietary knowledge and needs to be protected?
- Does your organization benchmark its knowledge management activities against other firms and world-class best practice?

Knowledge is being continuously created in organizations. Explicit knowledge or information lends itself to systematic handling and widespread dissemination, using techniques of information resource management discussed shortly. On the other hand much organizational knowledge is tacit. One study found that managers garner some 70–80 per cent of the information they use in decision-making, not from formal sources but from informal activities, such as meetings and conversations.[9] Their decisions are as likely to be based on the opinions and reputation of the informant as they are on the information conveyed. How can such knowledge be better managed?

There are two general approaches to managing tacit knowledge:

1 Converting some of it into a more explicit form, through elicitation and articulation.
2 Creating mechanisms such that informal knowledge exchange can occur when needed.

Hence the challenge of managing organizational knowledge is twofold: that of systematic information management coupled to managing processes which to the outsider may seem chaotic but do have a certain order to them, i.e. they are chaordic (Figure 7.2).[10]

The first management task is to develop a set of guiding principles within which individual processes can operate. A suggested set is shown below.

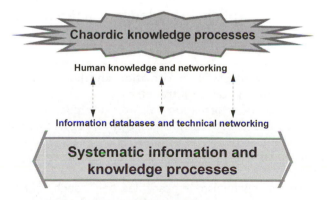

Figure 7.2 The knowledge management challenge

Ten principles for better knowledge management

1 *Develop clear policies.* There should be policies on ownership, maintaining and enhancing knowledge, quality, standards, the management of records and documents throughout their life cycle, and policies on safeguarding information and knowledge against misuse and loss.

2 *Conduct and maintain a knowledge inventory.* Identify core knowledge, its sources, its flows, it uses. Classify it by its key attributes. Gauge its quality and usefulness.

3 *Assign responsibilities.* Each important knowledge asset should have named individuals responsible for managing, developing and sharing it.

4 *Link knowledge to management processes and business objectives.* Make sure that key decision and business processes are supported by highly relevant knowledge.

5 *Integrate hard and soft, internal and external.* Such juxtaposition helps identify patterns and provide insights.

6 *Optimize acquisition and access.* Avoid fragmentation of purchasing and duplication of effort.

7 *Mine and refine.* Extract and synthesize core knowledge, combining the skills of information science, business analysis and editing.

8 *Understand the value of your knowledge* – both its asset value and value in use. What is its contribution to the bottom line? Consider also the cost of loss, such as key people or of reconstituting databases.

9 *Develop and exploit.* Continually examine each main knowledge asset and consider how its value could be increased, either for internal use, or external sale or licence.

10 *Balance access with security.* Protect proprietary knowledge, but not at the expense of inhibiting its development through overprotection.

4 Assessing your explicit knowledge – information resources management

- Is there a readily accessible information and knowledge inventory within your firm, e.g. on an intranet?
- Are the sources of information validated for quality?
- Are your databases, especially textual ones, regularly maintained?
- Are owners and experts regarding specific information databases clearly identified and held responsible for the integrity of the information?
- Do you have a mechanism, e.g. an idea bank, such that ideas not immediately used are not lost for future use?

The key discipline for managing explicit knowledge is information resources management (IRM), defined by ASLIB's IRM group as: 'the application of conventional management processes to information, with the aim of maximising its contribution to the achievement of organizational objectives'. A member of this group, Nick Willard, developed a framework for IRM, outlining the five key activities needed in any corporate IRM Programme (Table 7.2).[11]

Table 7.2 The Willard IRM model

Identification	What information is there? How is it identified and coded?
Ownership	Who is responsible for different information entities and co-ordination?
Cost and value	A basis for making judgements on purchase and use
Development	Increasing its value or stimulating demand
Exploitation	Proactive maximization of value for money

Good IRM underpins good knowledge management. We now consider some specific IRM activities involved in the knowledge cycles of Figure 2.6.

The knowledge inventory

This helps organizations know what they know. Within IRM the term information audit is frequently used, but this implies compliance. It does however suggest sampling rather than a complete inventory. You need to balance the cost of collating information about knowledge assets against likely benefits.

A typical method is described by Burk and Horton in their book *InfoMap*.[12] Whatever method is used, there are a few guidelines that will make the outcome more worthwhile:

- Start by focusing on business priorities and core processes.
- Sample a representative cross section of the user base – senior management, professionals, different types of job; brief them on the purpose of the inventory and how it will be conducted.
- Confirm the vital knowledge each use needs to perform their key tasks efficiently and effectively.
- Use a range of techniques – surveys, interviews, usage analysis. Intranet search statistics and library access information provide useful hard data.
- Develop lists of knowledge entities. For each entity record its key attributes such as form, subject, content, owner, location, quality, exploitability and where it is used.
- Analyse the flows of knowledge between creators, gatherers and users.

The result of such information gathering can be portrayed as a set of knowledge flows or maps. Matrixes or network diagrams can be used to identify crucial links in the chains of knowledge. Usually what emerge are areas of duplication and gaps. For example, an information audit at one financial institution found twelve different versions of one type of information.

Innovation – the creativity conundrum

The confusion between innovation and creativity was discussed in Chapter 2. The real problem is that organizations do not manage their creative ideas well. What happens to the ninety-nine out of a hundred new product ideas that do not make it through the typical stage gate process to a successful product launch? Mostly they are lost. Yet the ideas might not be bad. It may simply be that *at the time* they were not technically feasible, there were insufficient investment funds, or market conditions were not appropriate. But conditions change. Therefore a good innovation process will make sure that such ideas are available for future use.

Schlumberger's ClientLink, for example, matches two databases – an idea bank and a problem bank. Its researchers actively identify client needs and record them on an intranet database in three categories:

1   A solution exists, and there is best practice that can be transferred.
2   There is partial solutions with opportunities and capabilities for tailoring and/or joint development.
3   There is no known solution.

This is then periodically compared with ideas and solutions that other researchers add to the evolving idea bank. Another organization actively encourages individuals throughout the organization to have their ideas more widely exposed. 'Don't tell your boss, tell us' goes the slogan for its idea bank.

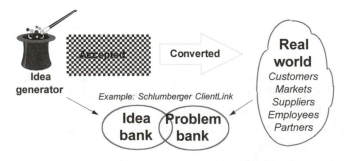

Figure 7.3   Capturing creative ideas in an innovation process

5 Tacit knowledge

- Do you know who are your best experts for different knowledge areas?
- Do your knowledge repositories have information that will lead to better tacit knowledge exchange?
- Are important meetings videoed or recorded for later reference and sharing of knowledge?
- Is knowledge captured at the customer interface, e.g. call centres, visits, fed back and used in service improvement?
- Are experts encouraged to convert their tacit knowledge into explicit, e.g. via seminars (videoed), 'how to' guides etc.?

Tacit knowledge is difficult to access, since by definition it is in people's heads. However, you can record explicitly knowledge about where it exists, for example through expertise profiling.

Expertise profiling

Expertise profiling captures information about the expertise and responsibilities of individuals. Most useful are expertise databases that blend some degree of formal structure, such as competencies in defined categories, alongside informal entries kept up to date by the individual. Often referred to as 'Yellow Pages', users search by category of knowledge to find relevant individuals and their contact details. Novartis has taken the concept a stage further in its 'Blue Pages' which has details of external experts and consultants with whom it has worked. The most difficult challenge is keeping these entries up to date, for example with current projects and activities, since without appropriate culture and rewards, many individuals will rightly ask 'what's in it for me?'

Enriching the knowledge repository

As soon as knowledge is expressed explicitly, some of the key features of tacit knowledge are filtered out. It loses contextual richness, the human cognitive dimension and intuitive understanding. That's why many so-called knowledge bases are really misnamed, since they are databases about knowledge. They can, however, go some way to matching up to their name by adding some element of tacit richness:

- Contextual information – why is this information here? How is it used? What factors need to be considered when using it? Where is it applicable and not applicable?
- Pointers to people – contact details of originators, and links to other experts, e.g. via email hypertext links.
- Addition of multimedia material, e.g. sound clips, extracts of meetings and presentations, a visual demonstration of an entry, such as a team at work. Desktop conferencing also means that information in a database can be used as the object of a tacit knowledge-sharing discussion.
- Associated discussion databases and knowledge communities – places where dialogue can continue.

Knowledge transfer mechanisms

The key to better tacit knowledge transfer is to orchestrate a range of mechanisms that allow personal interaction to take place, in a range of settings. Figure 7.4 shows a range of such mechanisms for both explicit and tacit knowledge.

	Same place	Different place
Same time	***Settings*** Workshops Meeting support 'Share fairs' Structured dialogue	***Remote access*** Videoconferencing Audioconferencing Desktop conferencing
Different time	***Information objects*** Document mgmt Whiteboards Project rooms Log books	***Asynchronous*** Email lists Intranets Web conferencing Voicemail

Figure 7.4   Knowledge transfer mechanisms

Most are self-explanatory. Knowledge 'share fairs' however are worth a mention. They act like a marketplace of ideas, bringing those with knowledge into contact with people from business units, or even outside companies, who are potential investors in the much more lengthy process of converting the ideas into prototypes and products. Knowledge providers have posters and 'stands' at an exhibition-like setting. They may be accompanied by workshops and other forums for knowledge exchange. They are a good way of bringing researchers into contact with those people who might benefit from it. Hoechst Celanese, for example, has used 'share fairs' successfully to find business sponsors for its innovative researchers.

6 Knowledge hubs and centres

- Does your organization have knowledge centres or hubs, where you can find out the best sources of knowledge?
- Can users find what knowledge they need quickly?
- Are your physical holdings – books, periodicals, reports – easily accessible and their key contents searchable on-line?
- Is there systematic monitoring, gathering and classifying of external sources?
- Is your key knowledge indexed and mapped using a clear common taxonomy and classification scheme?

Many organizations are now creating, or rather re-creating, knowledge centres. These are a reinvention and updating of the corporate library, many of which were disbanded or evolved into business units in the early 1990s. A typical knowledge centre:

- knows where to find knowledge, both inside and outside the organization
- catalogues and indexes all types of knowledge asset to aid efficient retrieval
- maintains and sustains the knowledge repository
- integrates hard-copy and on-line information
- provides a one stop shop for multiple knowledge needs
- runs a client advisory service – offering expertise on sources, their availability, relevance, quality and overall usefulness to the business
- helps individuals connect with each other
- offers skills and advice in knowledge management practices
- maintains content standards and provides high level knowledge maps for navigating the corporate intranet.

They are thus a focal point for collection, structuring and disseminating knowledge. This does not mean they do it all themselves. They set the framework and structures, develop guidance and provide information management expertise. A centralized approach offers certain advantages in the handling of information. It offers economies of scale, the pooling of expertise and helps minimize duplication. By acting as a knowledge hub, it also learns how the organization uses knowledge. It can apply this learning by alerting users to new knowledge, connecting people who have problems with those who have potential solutions.

A centre aggregates knowledge that would otherwise be dispersed and lack critical mass. On the other hand, individuals and teams in different locations need rapid access to knowledge. There is, therefore, a case for local knowledge hubs. These can be part of a virtual knowledge centre or network, where each hub specializes and has a physical presence, that provides an access point to the network.

Codifying – the power of taxonomy

Of all the other processes in the knowledge cycle, classification is one of the most powerful, yet the least valued. Even today's highly sophisticated search and retrieval mechanisms are no match for knowledge structured in a well-designed classification system or taxonomy. Knowledge domains are organized into hierarchies of concepts and related terms. These thesauri help organizations develop a common language and build bridges across disciplines. However, classifying in the context of knowledge management requires a new slant. One primary classification should be by type of use. A division of Siemens, for example, classifies its documents according to a hierarchical problem tree. Users seeking problem diagnosis can therefore systematically work through the symptoms to retrieve relevant information.

Price Waterhouse has used taxonomy to good effect. To contrast best practices across industries, it developed The International Business Language[SM] that maps industry-specific terms against generic business processes in several languages. Users in a given industry can gain new insights by looking at best practice for comparable processes in other

---

Knowledge hubs at American Management Systems

American Management Systems (AMS), a systems consultancy firm, has fifty-three offices worldwide. Susan Hanley, its knowledge manager, says: 'my job is to help 7000 consultants leverage their knowledge'. It runs a network of six knowledge centres. The centre acts as a virtual community of expert practitioners throughout AMS. There are seventeen leaders from six core disciplines, 300 associates and eighty support staff whose role is to make a tangible contribution to AMS's 3000 knowledge bases. There are also video-conferencing facilities at twenty-five different sites. Hanley emphasizes that the centres offer more than a collection of information: 'they actively and creatively link people'. They provide 'virtual communities of experts who find and deliver information to client teams'. They operate a 'hotline' that consultants call to get access to the centre's knowledge. It is estimated that the centre saved AMS $5 million in its first year of operation, mainly through faster query handling. On average, the information specialists at the centres can find relevant information and answer questions eight times faster than the typical consultant!

industries. Likewise Teltech (page 55) finds its thesaurus invaluable in solving customer problems. In one example, an artificial heart pump manufacturer had spent months trying to solve a leakage problem in a valve. Teltech found an expert from submarine engineering who solved the problem in two weeks. The common connection, achieved through their taxonomy, was pump seals in saline solutions![13]

A key ingredient of the success of a centre is that it markets its capabilities well. It should inform and educate potential users. Its staff should get out and meet users. It should host stands at customers' key internal events such as sales meetings or the in-house annual research conference. It is also important to evaluate the use of the centre and its resources and gain feedback on how it contributes to the business bottom line.

7 Market leverage

> - Is information and knowledge readily available in a form that enhances your services to your customers?
> - Have you considered reselling your core expertise in ways that will generate new revenue streams?
> - Are your services 'smart', i.e. customizable and adaptable e.g. by aggregating knowledge from disparate sources?
> - Are you known among your clients and peers as exemplars of good knowledge management practice?
> - Does your publicity and marketing messages convey the importance and depth of your know-how?

Ultimately, to benefit the organization, knowledge must be exploited externally. This can be in the form of improved products and services or knowledge-based products and services in their own right. Examples were given in Chapter 2. Key methods include publications, on-line information services, adding consulting services, as well as knowledge-enriching existing services.

In every activity where information and knowledge is processed, individuals should be conscious of exploitation opportunities and the need of users. Knowledge is more diffusable and usable in the external world when:

- tacit knowledge is converted to explicit knowledge
- common formats and document templates are used, so that users know where to look for specific items

- it is linked to associated knowledge, e.g. through personal contact details
- it is 'packaged' with 'wrappers' that define the contents of the package
- it is part of a familiar system or process, such as a customer advisory service
- knowledge carriers, especially people, are easily accessible to explain it.

Thus, even if the marketable knowledge is tacit, it has to be explicitly described to aid marketability. The following list suggests ten ways in which the value of explicit knowledge can be enhanced.

Ten ways to add value to knowledge

1   *Timeliness*: knowledge is perishable. Different knowledge has different half-lives ('sell by dates'). Some degrades rapidly.

2   *Accessibility*: easy to find and retrieve – no long-winded searches, good 'hits'.

3   *Quality and utility*: it is accurate, reliable, credible, validated. It is easy to use and can be manipulated to suit specific users and applications.

4   *Customized*: filtered, targeted, appropriate style and format; needs minimum processing for specified application.

5   *Contextualized*: Ways of using it are explained. It is enriched by adding some tacit richness (see page 192).

6   *Connected*: there are many links to related documents and sources.

7   *Medium and packaging*: the medium is appropriate for portability and ongoing use. It can be reconfigured easily in different packages and reused in different ways.

8   *Refined*: continually refined by knowledge editors based on feedback from users.

9   *Marketed*: marketing helps to create demand, thus increasing exposure and use that feeds back into higher quality and additional knowledge.

10 *Meta-knowledge*: knowledge about knowledge. It is mapped, categorized and its key attributes recorded.

Any knowledge initiative, whether internally or externally focused, can benefit through external publicity. It demonstrates their organization's seriousness about knowledge to existing and potential customers. Skandia widely publicizes its work on intellectual capital measurement in the form of brochures and CD-ROMs.[14] Other organizations find that marketing led campaigns also draw attention internally, and provide a spur for the organization to live up to its external image. Amidon has traced the growing use of marketing slogans that exploit knowledge concepts to gain market leverage.[15] More recent examples include:

- 'With AOL you have the knowledge of 20 million people' (London Underground poster).
- 'Them: We hold the knowledge. Deloitte Consulting: We hand over the knowledge' (*Business Week*, 7 December 1998).
- 'With M&G, investment knowledge doesn't come cheap. It's free' (*Money Observer*, February 1999).
- 'Making knowledge work' (University of Bradford advertisement, June 1998).

The value of knowledge

8 Assessing your measures

> - Are the bottom line benefits of knowledge management clearly articulated in terms that all your managers understand?
> - Does your organization measure and manage its intellectual capital in a systematic way?
> - Do your performance measurement systems explicitly include intangible and knowledge-based measures e.g. customers?
> - Do you report regularly on your knowledge assets, such as in supplements to your annual reports?
> - Is your measurement system used as a focus for dialogue and learning?

One aspect of measurement that attracts attention is that of justifying investment in knowledge initiatives. Searching for simplistic return on investment (ROI) measures is fraught with difficulties. IDC, for example, cites an ROI of 1000 per cent and more for investment in corporate intranets.[16] Eighty per cent of the investment goes on training, content generation and database maintenance, with the remainder on hardware and software. The returns are based on savings in photocopying, document distribution and time spent seeking information. In a series of studies, it found payback periods of just six to eight weeks! In reality these benefits are only realized if time saved by knowledge users is put to good use, which may be hard to prove in the typical case of just 10 minutes a day. The real benefits, though, are not measurable in such simplistic terms. They come through better information, better knowledge connections, better insights and better 'peripheral vision', and how they contribute to better decisions and better business performance.

The value proposition

As with many other infrastructure investments, such as email, many of the benefits of knowledge management were not initially anticipated. Few organizations, for example, realize in advance how new communications patterns lead to identification of new business opportunities. Knowledge leaders act first and measure later. They build teams and attract investment without detailed cost-benefit analyses or justification. They have a 'gut feel' and are willing to experiment. That does not mean that they do not measure. They do, but retrospectively, once they understand the real impact of knowledge in their business and can articulate the benefits. Their value propositions fall into several groups:

* Knowledge efficiency – e.g. faster access and reuse of knowledge, minimal duplication.
* Business efficiency – e.g. sharing of best practices.
* Business leverage – e.g. better customer service, new product development, innovation.
* Cost and risk avoidance – e.g. reduced rework, fewer loss-making contracts, less risk of knowledge loss or theft.
* Value in intangibles – e.g. improved skills, know-how databases, patents, intellectual property.

Even so, the relationship between cause and effect is complex and often difficult to unravel. For an enlightened knowledge-based enterprise, getting a strategic lead takes priority over worrying too much about detailed justification.

Measuring intellectual capital

While most organizations carry out detailed financial measurement and reporting, few do the same for their intellectual and knowledge assets that are much more valuable. This has led in part to the introduction of non-financial performance measurement systems to guide day to day management actions. Examples are the Balanced Business Scorecard (BBS) and the EFQM (European Foundation for Quality Management) Excellence Model. While these systems give some attention to knowledge related items, such as innovation and learning, they do not explicitly capture knowledge measures. Nor do they help managers identify the underlying cause of different outcomes. The last few years has therefore seen the development of several new measurement systems directly focused on intellectual capital including:[17]

* The Skandia Navigator (a kind of balanced scorecard) and its underlying value creation model.

- Karl Erik Sveiby's Intangible Assets Monitor (IAM) – that divides intangible assets into external structure, internal structure and competence of people.
- The Intellectual Capital Index (IC Index™), of Intellectual Capital Services. A special feature of this system is that it considers flows of knowledge, e.g. from human capital into structural capital.
- The Inclusive Value Methodology (IVM™) of Professor Philip M'Pherson. This combines financial and non-financial hierarchies of value. It uses combinatorial mathematics.

The starting point of each of these systems is the identification of the different components that constitute intellectual capital, such as human capital, structural capital and customer capital (see page 58). The number of individual indicators in these categories can be quite high. Edvinsson and Malone list ninety different measures in the five groups of the Skandia Navigator, although in any one unit, only a fraction of these will be used. Measures are of different types – absolute, relative, percentages, ratios, etc. It is also important to distinguish inputs, outputs or outcomes (see Chapter 5). Thus while R&D and IT spend feature as measures in Skandia's Navigator, better measures may be the actual results of this spending, e.g. number of patents granted, reliability of email service. Sveiby's IAM is particularly interesting since alongside its main categories of competence, internal structure (processes, systems, etc.) and external structure (customer and stakeholder measures) are subdivisions of stability, efficiency, growth and renewal (Table 7.3).

Even with these measurement systems, it is difficult to give precise numbers that value knowledge. This is because the value of knowledge

Table 7.3 Sample indicators in the Intangible Assets Monitor

	External structure	Internal structure	Competence
Growth/renewal	Profit/customer; growth in market share; satisfied customer index	IT investments; R&D investment	No. years education; share of sales from competence-enhancing customers
Efficiency	sales per professional; profit per customer	Support staff %; values	Value added/employee
Stability	% large companies; devoted customers (repeat orders)	Turnover; 'rookie' ratio*	Professional turnover; relative pay

Note: * percentage of new employees

is context dependent and subjective. Thus IC measurement systems tend to focus on broad measures and direction (e.g. improvement) rather than absolute values. Practical steps to develop and use an IC management system are shown below.

Ten steps to intellectual capital measurement

1   Root the language of knowledge and intellectual capital in the business strategy.
2   Review existing performance measurement systems to see how well they address the intangibles of intellectual capital and knowledge.
3   Develop an appropriate model of intellectual capital, using categories that give balance, and reflect the needs of the organization.
4   Within each unit or team, develop measures within these categories linked to team goals. There should be about three to five per category, say ten to fifteen overall. Involve everybody.
5   Good measures are understandable, practical and predictive. Be approximately right rather than precisely wrong.
6   Integrate these indicators into management goal setting and reporting.
7   Look for some common measures that can be used for comparison across business units.
8   As experience is gained, introduced measures of flow, to help understand time lags, cause and effect, and conversion of human capital into structural capital.
9   Regularly review the measures so that they become part of the learning process of how knowledge supports business strategies.
10 When confidence is gained, start reporting these to external bodies. Drug companies, for example, give details of progress of their R&D pipelines in analysts' briefings.

Human factors

9 Assessing your 'soft' infrastructure

• Have specific knowledge roles been identified and assigned, e.g. knowledge editor, knowledge analyst?
• Is knowledge management considered a core management skill in which every manager and professional has some familiarity?

- Are there individuals in each main group who are responsible for demonstrating good knowledge practice within their group and acting as a coach to others?
- Is your training approach learner centred and does it mesh with the day-to-day activities of the organization?
- Are acquisition of knowledge management competencies and knowledge-sharing behaviours recognized and rewarded?

The human resources function should play a key role in establishing the 'soft' infrastructure. In particular, it must:

- Recognize new knowledge roles and skills (see panel), profiling them and integrating them into career structures and plans.
- Create hybrid career paths – legitimate promotion paths that encourage cross-functional moves, job rotation and secondment.
- Develop appropriate recruitment and induction processes, focusing less on jobs and more on transferable knowledge skills and behaviours.
- Enhance learning and development opportunities, so that individuals and teams can continually increase their knowledge.
- Develop appropriate reward and recognition systems, e.g. including knowledge sharing behaviours in performance appraisal and recognizing knowledge skills in skill-based pay arrangements.

Additionally, human resources personnel are usually very prominent as team facilitators and putting in place some key aspects of culture change.

Knowledge roles and skills

- *Knowledge analyst* – interprets new knowledge in its business and organizational context or translates user needs into knowledge requirements.
- *Knowledge broker or connector* – links people who need knowledge with those who have it.
- *Knowledge editor or synthesizer* – reformats conversations, emails and other unstructured knowledge into more structured information.
- *Knowledge steward* – nurtures and manages knowledge resources; custodian of the knowledge repository.
- *Knowledge messenger or gatekeeper* – senses the external world, and routes knowledge to where it might be useful; more proactive than the broker who handles specific user requests.
- *Knowledge creator* – an ideas person, inventor, someone who adds to the organization's knowledge pool.

Learning organization

Continuous learning is a key component of a knowledge-based organization. Learning is closely related to knowledge. As you learn more, you gain knowledge, which can be applied to gain more learning. A learning organization is one that is committed to learning, both for personal development and the organization as a whole. Learning is recognized and rewarded. Time devoted to thinking and learning is not viewed as wasted time. Organizational learning involves learning from both successes and failures. Practices that are prevalent in a learning organization are:

*   Individual learning contracts, based around the needs of the individual and linked to performance and business goals.
*   Individuals receive top-up learning budgets to spend as they choose.
*   Time is built into meetings to allow for reflection and review.
*   Learning takes place on-the-job and when it is needed rather than dictated around course schedules.
*   Experienced people coach the less experienced; people new in post are mentored by peers.
*   Leadership development: structured learning assignments based on business needs, perhaps in conjunction with external facilitators and institutions.
*   Learning is captured as part of organization memory, for example decision diaries that record the results of earlier decisions.

A growing number of organizations are formalizing such practices through a corporate university. Many started by offering courses in conjunction with academic institutions, but are now becoming the focal point for various kinds of learning activity. Anglian Water's *Aqua Universitas*, for example, offers participants The Journey, an action-centred learning process. It consists of three parts – orientation, an expedition and review. A typical expedition involves work in the community or installing water supplies in a third world village.

Another facet of the learning organization is reflected in the shift from more formal classroom settings, whether real or virtual, to informal learning networks such as knowledge communities. The networks can also provide virtual classrooms where tutors and students, and student groups do assignments and learn together on-line.

Rewards and recognition

A frequent barrier to better knowledge sharing is an inappropriate reward system. Employees must be motivated to spend time in developing and sharing their knowledge. Many consultancies are now making knowledge contributions part of each person's annual appraisal and pay award. They review how many 'thought leadership' papers were produced, or how many knowledge base entries were created and how well they were used. As was noted in Chapter 5 many knowledge workers value intrinsic rewards as much as monetary ones.

Therefore, various forms of recognition are needed, day in and day out. These include complimenting and praising individuals for their contributions, and giving them opportunities for external visibility and recognition, such as through presentations and publications. Annual awards for knowledge achievement are also motivators.

A more tangible incentive is a stake in the future prosperity of the business. Silicon Valley companies are well known for awarding key employees, but many established organizations seem slow in adjusting to this route. Only recently has IBM opened its stock options beyond a small group of senior executives, thus increasing the number sixfold in two years from 1997.[18]

Technology, tools and techniques

10 Technology infrastructure

> • Can all important information be quickly found by new users on your organization's intranet?
> • Do you use intelligent agents/filters to sift, find and sort key external information that might not normally be available?
> • Can people readily share documents and multimedia objects (e.g. video clips) over the internal network?
> • Are there discussion forums that support learning networks or communities of practice?
> • Is videoconferencing used to connect dispersed locations into regular meetings?

Information and communications technologies can significantly enhance knowledge activities, as demonstrated in Chapter 3. These technologies have maximum benefit when part of a viable collaborative infrastructure that acts as a conduit for knowledge sharing and development. Document management systems, groupware and the intranet are the most commonly found components of such an infrastructure.

An essential element is a collaborative knowledge partnership between the IS function and user departments. Jointly they should investigate the potential of emerging technologies, for example through a technology watch and assessment programme. They should jointly develop a viable knowledge management technical architecture and introduce user-centred applications. They should also act as an exemplar of knowledge management in practice, for example by creating a knowledge base and associated discussion forums to keep the business informed about the practical aspects of choosing and applying the various knowledge technologies.

A viable knowledge information technology architecture

A viable knowledge architecture will cover all aspects of the human–computer interface and supporting services, from physical connectivity to collaborative solutions. Figure 7.5 depicts these in the form of a multilayered architecture, each layer building on the foundation of the ones below.

The base level provides the facilities to connect people whenever and wherever they are – in the office, at remote sites, on the move etc. The next level is provision of basic communications. In many organizations, email has been the technology that has been most significant in enhancing knowledge sharing. The conversation level adds richness and structure to communications. One way is through 'threading' messages to show how a dialogue has developed. Co-ordination is provided through facilities such as workflow software or shared information bases. The highest level provides facilities for close collaboration including joint development of documents and the development of knowledge communities through virtual conferencing.

Any architecture must be flexible enough to accommodate the needs of different groups, and to allow for continuous improvement and innovation. This may be achieved by centrally supporting common core elements, while allowing experimentation and local support. Most organizations already have an IT architecture, but many were developed before knowledge management became a strategic priority. It will therefore need to be adapted to accommodate these new needs, which if it was

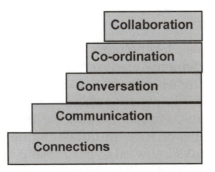

Collaboration	*Documents; GDSS; conferencing*
Co-ordination	*Workflow; shared information*
Conversation	*Threaded discussion; refining*
Communication	*Email; telephone; voicemail; videoconferencing.*
Connections	*Networks; voice/data; mobile; Internet; intranet.*

Figure 7.5   A layered knowledge infrastructure

originally designed as flexible, scaleable architecture that takes account of knowledge work and the needs of knowledge workers, should pose few problems. However, this is frequently not the case.

Collaborative knowledge development

Most organizations are only operating effectively at the lower levels of the architecture. They are only scratching the surface at the higher levels. Organizations that have developed their intranets to a fully effective knowledge-sharing and development tool have typically evolved through several phases like those for the Internet (see page 18).

A rich collaborative environment will meld as conversation space and content space (relationships and repositories). Web conferencing tools and knowledge management suites (page 91) are helping this integration. Consideration needs to be given to the interplay between these two spaces (Figure 7.6).

Many companies find that encouragement of personal and informal web pages is one of the fastest ways to grow content and to build knowledge networks. After all, if the individuals are already networking, they will build corresponding links into their personal pages to create dense knowledge webs, thus making it easier for others to enter specialized parts of the network.

Figure 7.6 Collaborative workspaces
Source: George Pór, Community Intelligence Labs (reproduced with permission)

Ten guidelines for creating an effective intranet

1   Link your intranet to key business objectives and processes. Be clear about its purpose and what kind of activities you want it to support.
2   Focus on the user and content. Too many intranet pages are 'producer-centric' with pages organized by department. Put in plenty of contact links.
3   Do not focus exclusively on the Web. Use it in conjunction with other tools and applications, including email and computer conferencing and web front-ends to other applications and databases.
4   Provide well-organized information – develop a clear information structure, using a consistent classification system. Provide a map and signposts.
5   Use a clear simple design. Avoid Java and frames unless they really add user value. Don't overburden with graphics or technical wizardry. Design for maintainability and scalability. This means giving special attention to clusters of information and hierarchies.
6   Make it easy for users to publish. Provide simple to use editors, e.g. exporting from word processors. Provide templates for standard types of information, e.g. expertise profiles, best practice examples, etc.
7   Increase the density of links between different clusters of information – develop reinforcing 'webs'. Readers will value pointers to other locations with complementary information.
8   Generate opportunities for interaction. Each group of information pages should have an associated discussion database where people can pool their knowledge and further develop the ideas.
9   Employ knowledge editors to continually review and refine information, from other pages and from discussion, and from non-computer based sources.
10 Maintain and sustain it. A programme of systematic updating, based on life expectancy of information, should be part of the organization's IRM framework.

Such repositories help to being new people up to speed quickly. Schlumberger's R&D efforts combine technology watch, vision and road maps, portfolio analysis and concurrent engineering. Its ClientLink system (mentioned earlier) connects customer needs to technological solutions. Following the success of its intranet, Schlumberger is using its network to nurture existing communities of practice. It is also borrowing ideas from journalism to improve the communication of knowledge better. However, the essential ingredient on which its distributed R&D

Schlumberger – an evolving R&D knowledge network

Schlumberger's Information Network – SINet – provides a crucial infrastructure for knowledge sharing and development among its many virtual teams. It connects around 25 000 users at 500 locations in over fifty-five countries. One feature that helps knowledge sharing is the large number of shared information repositories, e.g. client and supplier information, site information, project databases, personnel, marketing, clients and business. Project archives are an example of an evolving knowledge repository with project histories, discussion and decisions:

- Plan synopsis – What are we doing? Why are we doing it? Who is the customer?
- Current status – progress reports, milestones, real-time activity, documents
- Future – vision, roadmap, plan
- What we have learned – historical records, reports, results, of which distillation is a key component.

---

effort is built is a solid IT infrastructure, giving instant access from anywhere around the world with high reliability.

From knowledge management to knowledge leadership

The ten dimensions and fifty assessment questions covered in this chapter provide a useful starting point for evaluating and planning knowledge initiatives. They can easily be adapted to suit specific organizations. Thus, for those selling knowledge services, I tend to expand market leverage into two dimensions – services and promotion, and combine tacit and explicit knowledge into one.

Whichever you use, make sure it is a rounded set that covers hard and soft factors, processes and content, business outcomes and knowledge. Information is typically gathered as a result of a series of workshops or surveys, perhaps as part of a formal review. By plotting your results on a radar chart, you can quickly identify opportunities for improvement (Figure 7.7).

Other starting points for an initiative are to include:

- Make knowledge a key dimension of the annual strategic plan.

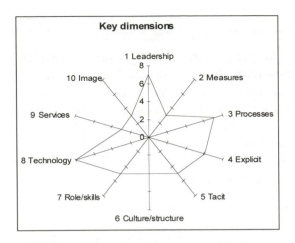

Figure 7.7   A completed knowledge assessment

- Start with customers – find out how you learn about their current and anticipated needs.
- Perform a strategic review. Create a strategy for knowledge exploitation. Integrate knowledge into business strategies.
- Start with a chronic problem – always a good place to get the thinking caps on.
- Initiate a task force – a common response, but they will need drive and vision.
- Make recording of knowledge needs and sources a step in the business process redesign.

Wherever you start, you will quickly find that knowledge management is not a stand-alone initiative. It is but one node in a web of strategic activities. It therefore makes sense to identify related initiatives, into which knowledge can be added as a further strand.

Throughout this chapter we have deliberately referred to a knowledge initiative rather than a knowledge management initiative. This is because the term knowledge management is something of an oxymoron, especially where knowledge in people's heads is concerned. The word 'management' suggests custodianship, even control, and a concentration on managing resources that already exist. A better term is knowledge leadership. In contrast to management, 'leadership' is about continual development and innovation – of information resources, of individual skills (an important part of the knowledge resource) and of knowledge and learning networks. It embraces both the sharing of what is known, and the innovation of the new – the two thrusts of a knowledge-enhanced strategy.

Summary

The toolkit is an integration of knowledge activities in ten dimensions that cover strategic, technological, human and organizational information and knowledge management factors. In the course of this and preceding chapters a number of practices commonly found in knowledge initiatives have been discussed (Table 7.4).

Table 7.4 Principal practices used in knowledge management

Creating and discovering	Sharing and learning	Organizing and managing
Creativity techniques	Communities of practice	Expertise profiling
Data mining	Learning networks	Knowledge mapping
Text mining	Sharing best practice	Information audits/inventory
Environment scanning	After action reviews	IRM (information resources
Knowledge elicitation	Structured dialogue	management)
Business simulation	Share fairs	Classifying
Content analysis	Cross-functional teams	Intranets/groupware
	Decision diaries	Measuring intellectual capital

This list will evolve as new tools and techniques become more widely accepted. Whatever methods are used, a successful enterprise initiative depends on a balanced approach that:

- focuses on knowledge that is important and used widely throughout the organization
- integrates knowledge as a dimension in existing processes
- integrates and aligns both human and technological systems
- uses a range of mechanisms and technologies, for different types of knowledge transfer
- modifies workplace settings to create opportunities for interaction
- applies IRM skills, so that knowledge is properly classified and mapped
- creates conditions in which knowledge communities can thrive
- ensures that the organization's culture and human resource policies are supportive of knowledge creation and transfer.

This last point, the cultural challenge, is usually the most difficult. It is best not to be too ambitious. Start a small pilot project and evolve – learning and adding to your knowledge base as you do so.

Agenda for action

1   Apply the diagnostic tool kit in a structured workshop with delegates from different business units.
2   Review your corporate vision and strategic plan to see how knowledge can contribute.
3   Identify the knowledge champions in your organization.
4   Ask each of your senior executives to list four to six specific items of knowledge they need to succeed in their jobs.
5   Review each of your core business processes. What knowledge inputs do they need to be effective? What knowledge do they generate?
6   Print out and display a high-level knowledge map of your company's intranet. Invite key professionals to identify what they use, and what is missing.
7   Review your senior management's performance measures. What proportion are aimed at growing the organization's intellectual capital?
8   Review your organization's information management policy. Are there policies for ownership, development, exploitation and protection?
9   Do you have a knowledge centre? If so, what are its demonstrable benefits to the business. If you don't have one, why not?
10 Does your culture support innovation and knowledge sharing? List specific activities that do so and those that inhibit it.

Notes

1   Innovation Research Centre (1998). *Annual Innovation Survey*. Henley Management College and Coopers & Lybrand.
2   Manasco, B. (1997). Should your company appoint a chief knowledge officer? *Knowledge Inc.*, **2**(7), July, 12.
3   Prokesch, S. E. (1997). 'Unleashing the power of learning': an interview with John Browne. *Harvard Business Review*, September–October, p. 147–68.
4   Over 164 definitions were cited in Kroeber, A. L. and Kluckhohn, C. (1952). *Culture: A Critical Review of Concepts and Definitions*. Vintage Books. The definition cited here comes from M. Bower, cited in Deal, T. E. and Kennedy, A. A. (1982). *Corporate Cultures: The Rites and Rituals of Corporate Life*. Addison-Wesley. For a down to earth guide on culture read Williams, A., Dobson, P. and Walters, M. (1989). *Changing Culture*. Institute of Personnel Management.
5   Reuters Business Information (1996). *Dying for Information: A Report on the Effects of Information Overload in the UK and Worldwide*. Reuters.
6   Verespej, M. A. (1996). The idea is to talk. *Industry Week*, 15 April, 28.
7   Advertisement, Ricoh Corporation (1995).
8   *The Times* (1998). The workplace revolution. Special Supplement, 20 July.

9   McKinnon, S. M. and Bruns, W. J. (1992).*The Information Mosaic*. Harvard Business School Press.

10 The term chaordic was coined by Dee Hock, founder of Visa, to describe a system that had creative tension between the chaotic and the ordered. There is a Chaordic Alliance website at http://www.chaordic.org

11 Willard, N. (1993). Information resources management. *Aslib Information*, **21**(5), May. The definition comes from Aslib (1993). Working paper - Definitions Task Force. Aslib IRM Network.

12 Burk, C. F. and Horton, F. W. (1998). *InfoMap: A Complete Guide to Discovering Corporate Information Resources*. Prentice Hall.

13 Michuda, A. (1998). Building a practical framework for knowledge and idea sharing success. Teltech Resources, at *Facilitating Corporate Innovation via Knowledge Management* conference, ICM, New York, April.

14 It has produced Intellectual Capital Report Supplements to its company reports since 1994. Titles include *Visualizing Intellectual Captial, Customer Value* and *Intelligent Interprising*.

15 Amidon, D. M. (1997). *Innovation Strategy for the Knowledge Economy: The Ken Awakening*. Butterworth-Heinemann.

16 Campbell, I. (1997). *The Intranet: Slashing the Cost of Business*. IDC.

17 A review of these and other methods will be found in Skyrme, D. (1998). *Measuring the Value of Knowledge*. Business Intelligence. The Skandia Navigator is described in Edvinsson, L. and Malone, M. S. (1997). *Intellectual Capital*. HarperBusiness. IC Index is described in Roos, J., Roos, G., Edvinsson, L. and Dragonetti, N. (1997). *Intellectual Capital: Navigating in the New Business Landscape*. Macmillan. The Intangible Assets Monitor is described in Sveiby, K. E. (1997). *The New Organizational Wealth: Managing and Measuring Knowledge-Based Assets*. Berrett Koehler.

18 Sanger, I. (1998). Stock options: Lou takes a cue from Silicon Valley. *Business Week*, 30 March, p. 34.

Chapter 8

The interprise toolkit

No enterprise is an island. It depends on the active support of customers, suppliers, employees and many other stakeholders for its continued success. Collaboration is inevitable. It is needed to bolster innovation and meet diverse needs. Collaboration with competitors is also frequently needed. Thus, many embryonic markets will remain small and fragmented until manufacturers agree common standards. Collaboration takes many forms such as supplier–customer partnerships, strategic alliances, informal co-operative marketing and, of course, virtual corporations.

What does it take to create a successful interprise – a collaborative venture comprising several enterprises? Who makes suitable partners? How can inter-enterprise knowledge networks be created and sustained? Whether your enterprise is large or small, this chapter takes you through a series of steps that addresses these challenges.

Collaboration knowledges

Before you can start to build a successful collaborative interprise, you need a set of basic knowledges – the know-why, know-what, know-who and know-how of interprising.

Know-why: the interprising advantage

There are many reasons to seek collaboration and partnership with other organizations, such as those listed in Table 8.1.

Table 8.1 Benefits of inter-enterprise collaboration

Resource efficiency	Market development
Economies of scale – sharing resources	Innovation
Reduced investment costs through sharing	Faster time to market
Flexibility of resource allocation	Flexibility of response
Access to specialist skills	Addressing needs of larger customers
Better deployment of your own skills and assets	Meeting more complex requirements
Access to technical resources, licences	Broadening product portfolio
Reduction of risk for investment	Access to non-traditional markets
	Access to new channels
	Denying unique resources to a competitor
	Increased geographic coverage

The first group of benefits involves pooling of resources to increase efficiency and reduce duplication. An example of this is the LearnShare alliance, a consortium of non-competing technology organizations (including 3M, Deere, Motorola, Owens-Illinois and Warner-Lambert), who pool their training materials and resources. It was found that 76 per cent of their internal training needs were identical and that they were duplicating effort.

The second group of benefits increases market leverage, and is particularly beneficial for smaller organizations and the self-employed who by themselves do not have a complete range of skills to meet customer needs. By creating a virtual organization, they can combine competencies and other resources, to meet specific customer needs. SciNet is a virtual

Activity 8.1: Examine your motives for collaboration

- Are you facing an external threat e.g. regulatory or a dominant competitor, where several players in the industry need to develop a concerted strategy?
- Do your customers have needs that are not being met? Are they demanding more than you alone can deliver, quicker?
- Do you have unrealized ambitions that you cannot fulfil due to lack of resources and skills?
- Is there over-capacity in your market that is resulting in duplication of effort?
- Are there investments you would like to make but are too large or risky?

biotech company, based in Brauschweig, Northern Germany. It develops, manufactures and markets bioactive proteins to speciality chemical and pharmaceutical companies. Its network of 300 members includes scientists, engineering, project management, industry experts and lawyers. SciNet manages projects by bringing together the necessary expertise from its membership network.

In seeking collaboration, your main aim is to address situations and create new opportunities that would be impossible to do by yourself.

Know-what: structures and forms

There are many types of collaboration. They may be formal or informal, stable or dynamic, close or loose, involve two parties or many. In the multiple-partner situation there may be a co-ordinating hub, such as a trade association or network broker, or a network of equals. Table 8.2 identifies some of these forms. The various forms are not mutually exclusive. Many large companies enter many different arrangements, each for a specific purpose.

Interactions between enterprises range from a straightforward trading relationship to complex knowledge networking. Knowledge relationships are also very varied. Some are based around pooled knowledge sharing. A trade association, for example, may co-ordinate members' sales statistics, providing aggregated information and making individual submissions anonymous. More in-depth relationships involve collaborative knowledge development. Here, interactions are unstructured, evolving, and depend on high levels of communications and trust.

Activity 8.2: Knowledge of structures

Review the various types of collaboration (Table 8.2) in which your enterprise is already participating. Which are the more and less successful? Can you explain why? What are their advantages and disadvantages for your organization, bearing in mind its strategic intent?

When considering a new collaboration:

1   What knowledge will be exchanged?
2   What will be jointly developed?
3   How can it be exploited?
4   Who owns the collaborative knowledge?
5   What are the ownership and exploitation rights?

Table 8.2 Different types of interorganizational structures

Structural arrangement	Types of collaboration	Typical characteristics – knowledge considerations
One to one	Joint venture; strategic alliance; cross licensing; co-operative marketing; subcontracting	Bipartite interactions. Often explicit agreements about resource exchange and ownership of jointly developed intellectual property.
Multiple – central co-ordination	Supply chain network; trade association; trusted third party*; business network with broker; expert networks; special interest forums	Some have a dominant partner, who dictates the rules for participants. Others have steering bodies and committees that represent the interests of all members. The co-ordinating authority acts like a knowledge hub, and may well have a knowledge advantage over individual participants.
Multiple – self-managed	Consortium; co-operative; dynamic business networks; virtual corporation	A network of peers offering complementary resources and knowledge. May start with less formality than other arrangements that could lead to disputes over intellectual capital, unless addressed in a timely fashion.

Note: * Trusted third parties are found in electronic commerce networks, where an intermediary, such as a bank holds confidential information that neither party wants to reveal to the other.

Another overlay is that many knowledge networks, such as professional associations, straddle enterprise boundaries. So while enterprise boundaries delineate formal commercial and legal entities, they are permeable to knowledge. This creates challenges in a knowledge networking environment, where new forms of boundary are constantly being drawn and redrawn.

What kind of arrangements should you enter? The short answer is as many as you need to achieve your aims, bearing in mind that each and every collaboration will take valuable management time to work successfully.

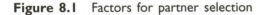

Knowledge collaboration

Figure 8.1   Factors for partner selection

Know-who: selecting partners

Selecting the right business partner is as much about culture and personality as about other attributes. Sometimes you may appear to have little choice of partner – they are trading with you as customers or are a unique and critical cog in your value system. However, you should consider how closely you want to work with them in the long term and whether other partners are, or could emerge, as more suitable.

Successful partners share mutual interests, offer complementary competencies, and have compatible (though not necessarily identical) cultures (Figure 8.1). Good collaborative partnerships create something new for each party. They harmonize different organizational perspectives and have balanced relationships where no single partner is dominant.

Activity 8.3: Finding suitable partners

- Are there organizations with whom you already have good working relationships?
- Are there organizations in other fields, but who have competencies you need, that you secretly admire?
- Are there natural partners in your supply chains (e.g. suppliers, customers) offering complementary products or services?
- For each potential partner: do you know their key competencies, their motivation and key strengths and weaknesses?
- Consider developing a knowledge base, which holds such information on potential partners.

Various business networks offer a pre-qualification stage before more formal partnering. Typically, their member organizations have demonstrated their credentials and distinctive competencies. The network promotes the members, and they promote the network.

A common characteristic among collaborating companies is that they are simultaneously customers and competitors. This does not matter, as long as individuals working in each enterprise know which role applies when and where. It may be necessary to create so-called Chinese walls, where knowledge from one part of the business is deliberately withheld from another part playing a different role.

Know-how: a framework for collaboration

There are several models of collaboration development, most based on finding strategic fit and cultural compatibility.[1] The marriage metaphor is frequently used. Larraine Segil lists elements that make for harmony in both regimes – compatibility, commitment, sharing. She reminds us that in both domestic life and strategic alliances the failure rate is high – as much as 60 per cent in the first five years. This is one reason why some of the best collaborations prepare plans for an orderly dissolution, akin to a prenuptial divorce settlement. She describes an approach based on check lists and guidelines for diagnosing your enterprise personality, the stage of the enterprise life cycle, and the relative importance of each enterprising joint venture.[2]

Our perspective here extends to virtual collaboration to generate opportunities based on knowledge. There are two good sources of such

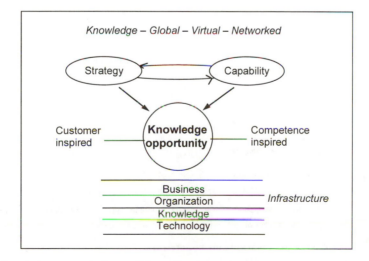

Figure 8.2 A framework for collaboration

an opportunity – the customer interface and combinations of distinctive competencies, which are themselves influenced by collective strategies and capabilities (Figure 8.2). Also essential to any long-term collaboration is a set of infrastructures to sustain the jointly developed intellectual capital. These elements provide a framework to guide us through the rest of the chapter.

Knowledge collaboration

Innovating with customers

Despite its importance customer knowledge is only superficially tapped by most organizations. Debra Amidon, who has explored customer knowledge in some depth writes about *Innovating with Customers*[SM]:

> Customers have always been integral to the innovation process. What else is the purpose of productization and commercialization? However, current global business conditions have shed a new light on the value of customer interaction and the scope and structure of the innovation process itself. Moreover, what good are your customers if they are satisfied, and not successful?[3]

She explains that the biggest opportunity lies in the development of new products and services to fulfil unarticulated customer needs and

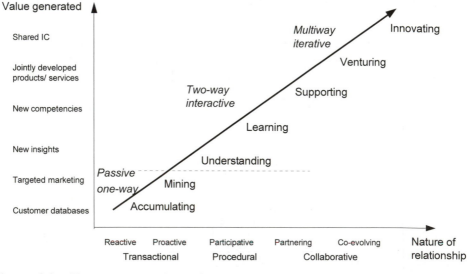

Figure 8.3 The customer relationship spectrum
Source: Adapted from Amidon (1997)[4]

unserved markets. Developing a relationship that achieves this means moving beyond a purely transactional relationship to intense dialogue and full partnering (Figure 8.3). As the relationship progresses through these transitions deeper levels of knowledge are shared and created, resulting in new and larger sources of value.

The higher levels of partnering represent the development of two-way customer knowledge channels that go way beyond market research. The classic example is that of the Sony Walkman. Sony's market research implied that the innovative combination of personal headphones and portable tape recorders would not sell. But Akio Morita, head of Sony, sensed there was a need: 'In New York, even in Tokyo, I had seen people with big players and radios perched on their shoulders blaring out music'.[5] Tools and techniques to deploy along the customer relationship spectrum include:

- Data mining and business modelling – are there correlations with purchasing patterns that give new insights into your customers' behaviour?
- Individual customer interviews and visits – finding out about your company and products in the customer's context. Product managers and engineers can often develop a rapport with customers that is not normally possible with a salesperson merely intent on selling products.
- Focus groups – representatives from several customer groups explore in some depth a particular issue.
- Inviting customers into your in-house marketing or product development meetings. This means overcoming the psychological hurdle of 'washing your dirty linen in public before getting your act together'. But if you can do this you have got past barriers of creating more openness.
- Creating joint development teams. This allows true collaboration in pursuit of product improvement or tackling a difficult customer problem.

Activity 8.4: Deepening your customer knowledge

How well do you know the business plan of your key customers? How can your products or service help them pursue new opportunities?
- How well do you know your customers' customers?
- What are your standards of customer performance? How well do they mesh with your customers. Can you integrate them more closely?
- What are your customers' core competencies and technologies? Is there a joint opportunity for exploitation?
- What learning environments do you share? Can more be done together to broaden the range of knowledge sharing?

Your focus must be on your customer's success. At its simplest this means customizing your standard product to specific needs. More in depth collaboration will go further and address the needs of the customer's customer. Steelcase, a supplier of office furniture, is a good example of this. It works with a network that includes architects, end-users and hotel operators. Typical results of this in-depth dialogue are new opportunities with a hotel chain to meet the needs of the peripatetic professional that also involved computer manufacturers and telecommunication service providers to make it successful.

Collaborative knowledge venturing

The second main source of knowledge opportunity comes through combining complementary competencies. Here, organizations collaborate without at first knowing in detail what outcomes they are seeking. Nevertheless, they will have some mutually compatible high level objectives such as developing products for an emerging new market.

The initial reason for networking and collaborating may arise from a specific need, but after that need has been met, ongoing collaboration may generate new opportunities unforeseen by any party at the outset. For example, Du Pont has several collaborations with universities. The main reason for collaborating is to mix expertise and capabilities within a broad programme of work. One such collaboration, initially instigated to develop a CFC replacement in aerosols, resulted in a new line of polymers. This outcome was never expected or designed in at the outset. It emerged from an idea by a university researcher that was later refined through continual dialogue with Du Pont as an existing collaborative partner.

Activity 8.5: Creating collaborative networks

- Explore your supply chain – from suppliers to ultimate consumer. Are there organizations within it whose competencies and culture would make natural innovation partners?
- Are there events or forums you have attended that included people from outside your industry, where you would like to continue exploring opportunities?
- Are there existing collaboration partners with whom you have good rapport, but which are narrowly focused, where a day or two of brainstorming might identify some new co-operative activities?

Such collaboration calls for teams from different organizations to network together regularly in various knowledge-sharing projects and forums, such as innovation workshops. As with teams, diversity is important. An ideal collaborative network would include companies close to consumers and those further back in the supply chain. It would include product, project and service companies, and relate to a particular type of consumer need. Thus a food chain cluster might include a retailer, a food manufacturer, an agrochemical company, as well as an airline, a hotel, a telecommunications provider and a bank. As specific projects emerge, virtual organizations are formed and the network evolves to provide a rounded set of competencies needed.

Exploiting virtual knowledge space

Many of today's innovative organizations exploit the advantages of the Internet. Chapters 2 and 4 give several such examples. One framework for exploring the possibilities more systematically is Albert Angehrn's ICDT model. The ICDT model portrays four virtual spaces (Information, Communications, Distribution, Transaction) in which to develop new opportunities from traditional markets (bottom segment of diagram). To this basic model, two spaces representing new information and knowledge markets have been added to provide a more complete framework (Figure 8.4).

Angehrn cites the strategic value of the Internet as its ability to enhance linkages over distance. Core competencies in this environment include the ability to move and integrate information and knowledge quickly. Speed is of the essence: 'Speed in detecting markets, in the first place. Speed in finding out which are the required resources and where they lie.

Figure 8.4   Sources of virtual knowledge opportunities
Source: Adapted from the ICDT Model of Albert Angehrn[6]

Speed in internalising them and combining them with existing compe-tencies. And ultimately, speed in exploiting markets before competitors acquire similar competencies. Here again, the Internet promises to be a powerful weapon.'[7] His language reflects the competitive paradigm, and as written applies to a single enterprise. However, we can extend his ideas and apply the model of Figure 8.4 to collaborative opportunities:

- *Virtual transaction space* (VTS) – where transactions take place. Look for collaborative opportunities with providers of payment services, or virtual locations, which have the pull to attract your potential customers.
- *Virtual distribution space* (VDS) – channels for distribution of digitally encoded goods. Look for co-operation with high-volume or specialist distributors of software, books, information bases etc. Can they help you expand your markets by offering samples?
- *Virtual communications space* (VCS) – where interaction takes place. Are there natural communities that attract your target customers? Can you identify opportunities for collaboration to meet unmet needs expressed in these communities? Network with potential collaborators in closed user groups to discuss trends, opportunities and common issues.
- *Virtual information space* (VIS) – the place for visibility. Are there relationships you can develop with those who organize information, such as directory providers or on-line magazines? Consider a specialized portal site that adds value through aggregation and customization. Seek collaborators who can contribute and do local language or national variants.
- *Virtual information markets* (VIM) – integrated spaces where all phases of an information purchase are addressed. Work with database providers, media and software companies to collaborate with you and industry peers in creating niche markets based around unique information resources.
- *Virtual knowledge markets* (VKM). These extend beyond information to fully interactive knowledge sharing. Expert networks are an example of this. Look for collaborators with complementary expertise that could offer on-line advice or services for knowledge communities. There are also opportunities for market makers who connect providers of knowledge with users.

Each space is a hotbed of entrepreneurial activity with new players emerging who act as intermediaries to a large number of different compa-nies and industries. What they often lack is content. Thus, there are many unexploited opportunities in working with others to provide a virtual 'one stop shop' of information and knowledge for a cluster of related customer needs. Throughout virtual space, there are opportunities for collaboration, mutual linking and web building that are impossible in physical space. As electronic commerce in traditional goods grows, virtual knowledge markets are the new wave of collaborative opportunity.

Activity 8.6: Collaborative exploitation of virtual knowledge space

- What customer knowledge can be extracted from existing or new virtual spaces? Can you create a community that draws in your customers to share knowledge of your product applications?
- Are there established or emerging players who provide global virtual spaces for your industry and customer groups? If so, how can you collaborate with them? If not, who are the natural collaborators to develop such information and knowledge spaces?

Organizing collaboration

Strategic fit

The starting point of a successful collaboration is strategic fit – how complementary the business strategies of the two organizations are. A useful way of assessing this is by mapping the strategic dimensions of your industry. Figure 8.5 shows a generic template from which industry or market specific templates can be derived.

By comparing your own coverage and that of your potential collaborators, the degree of strategic fit can be determined. Generally you are looking for complementarity. However, the closer the relationship is

Customers	Consumers	Small business	Medium business	Large enterprise	Public sector
Industries	Primary	Manufacturing	Distribution	Services	Utilities
Geographies	Regional	National		Global	
	Europe	North America	Central and South America	Asia	Africa
Channels	Direct	Dealers/agents	Retail	Mail order	On-line
Applications	Built-in	Industrial	Commercial	Consumer	Leisure
Services	Installation	Maintenance	Pre-sales	Advisory	Project management
Products	Small/portable	Small/fixed	Group/medium	Industrial	Industrial/project
Technologies	Mechanical	Process	Electronic	Engineering	Materials

Figure 8.5 Strategic fit template

expected to develop, some overlap is desirable, especially in terms of customer groups served. This will generate efficiency savings. Your overall aim should be to cover the strategically important parts of the chart that are beyond your own immediate capabilities. It is also important to consider the wider business context. How are political, regulatory, economic and social trends affecting your industry and potential collaborators? Will they affect certain combinations differently to others?

Activity 8.7: Determining strategic fit

Draw up a specific template for your key businesses, using the language of your industry. Add or subtract dimensions (rows) as appropriate. Using separate acetate overlays for your own firm and potential collaborators, colour individual blocks according to the level of coverage or market penetration. Use different shades for intensity and different colours for different firms. See which combinations of collaboration make the most strategic sense.

Competence matching

Complementary competencies are an integral part of knowledge-based collaboration. As well as knowledge of the different strategic domains, consider also each partner's contribution in terms of:

- age profiles – does the combination produce a balanced age range?
- key tasks – knowledge and skills for the key activities of the interprise
- process expertise – what key process knowledge does each party contribute?
- core functions – who provides strength in research, manufacturing, marketing, sales, service etc.?
- support functions – who will provide services such as IT, human resources, legal?
- core competencies – what are the unique skills of each partner? What and who will be contributed?
- key assets and resources – offices, equipment, intellectual property etc.

The strengths and weaknesses in each of these areas should be reviewed. Each party has to be clear what is in the organization as a whole, and what is accessible to the network or collaborative relationship. Compatibility is more than just complementarity. It involves some commonality in approach and outlook. Alliances of very similar or totally unrelated competencies are unlikely to succeed. In addition to general competence matching, Lorange and Roos[8] identify three critical competencies needed in alliance building and development. The first is political, managing the interprise's different stakeholders. The second is entrepreneurial, knowing how to enable people from different organizations to work together effectively. The third is analytical, the ability to carry out specific investigations, such as those suggested in these activities.

Activity 8.8: Mapping alliance competency profiles

• Map the competencies of collaborators in your existing alliances. (Use bubble charts or templates.) Is there a pattern in those that are successful and those that are not?
• Develop a map of the key competencies needed in your planned new interprise. Show the relative strengths of each potential partner. List them and show how they contribute to the combined vision and strategy. Identify differences and determine how they can be worked through or overcome.

Cultural compatibility

Cultural incompatibility between partners is a primary reason why many collaborations fail. Cultural differences do not necessarily mean failure. In general cultures that are organic, achievement or person oriented and outward looking are more mutually compatible, but clash with cultures that are mechanistic, rule bound, bureaucratic or hierarchical. In cross-border partnerships, the power–distance dimension of Hofstede is the one that needs to be most compatible.

A useful diagnostic tool has been developed as part of the EU's Innovation Programme.[9] This programme encourages collaboration across both organizational and national boundaries, where overcoming cultural problems is a major consideration. The tool helps project participants understand the key dimensions of their own culture and management styles and draws out orientations in eight dimensions (Figure 8.6).

More important that any particular cultural differences is cultural rigidity. Use of such a diagnostic tool allows interprise participants to explore their differences and consider ways of adapting to mutually accepting working norms. The interprise culture can either be a fused new culture, a transition from one to the other or separate team cultures that know

Focus on the individual	Focus on the group
Formal rules	Context and strategies
Status	Achievement
Hierarchical authority	Participative orientation
Past	Future
Pragmatic	Conceptual
Explicit communication	Implicit
Conflictual	Consensual

Figure 8.6 Dimensions of culture (from EU Innovation Culture Diagnostic)

how to work with each other. Perhaps the most important cultural trait is the willingness to co-operate and wholeheartedly support the collaborative venture.

> **Activity 8.9: Exploring culture compatibility**
>
> Share with your partners your key values and elements of your organization's culture. If possible, use a common diagnostic instrument and compare differences. Discuss the values and kind of culture that you feel would be appropriate for your collaborative venture. Use principles 6–15 of Chapter 6 to help you define your values.

Building the virtual organization

Any collaborative venture will need to go through many of the activities described for teams in Chapter 6. Here we consider the particular case of building a virtual organization, a joint venture of several organizations, typically geographically dispersed. A starting point of a growing number of virtual organizations is a loosely connected business network from which different virtual organizations can be formed as needed.

Business networks

A key feature of networks is that they constantly change. Today's clusters and close connections may not be tomorrow's. A network offers a more fluid arrangement than formal long-term alliances. Individual members can readjust their position in the network as their interests and those of the network as a whole evolve.

Business networking is most developed in Denmark, as a result of a national enterprise initiative in the late 1980s to help smaller enterprises collaborate.[10] The programme has three main elements – a network support infrastructure, network brokers and the creation of individual networks or virtual organizations. The programme is described more fully in Chapter 9. The evolution phases in the Danish model are:[11]

1 A business network creates awareness of its capabilities and network broker competencies for a specific business sector. It analyses its members competencies and identifies potential joint opportunities. Potential partners who can plug competency gaps are also identified.
2 Validation of core idea and network competence. A strategic analysis and a feasibility study of network opportunities are carried out. At this stage, confidentiality agreements are drawn up between members and the broker.
3 A network business plan. This determines funding for network activities and assigns responsibilities. The terms of co-operation are finalized, and the necessary legal entities created.
4 The network process of building and launch. This puts in place core processes and necessary infrastructures.

A key feature of the Danish model is the network broker. A broker acts as a facilitator to bring network members together. An example of the Danish model in the UK is that of the Campbell, Hare and Jenkins network. This combined the competencies of a printing shop, a translation service and a computer graphic house in south-west England. The partners did not previously know each other and were brought together by a network broker in 1994. In combination they were able to offer clients a complete service in producing technical product publications in foreign languages.

Perhaps more common than the formal broker role is the natural evolution of informal business networks. Members may meet occasionally to exchange information, while clusters of members form closer associations where interests and opportunities coincide. However, they can still benefit by explicitly carrying out brokering tasks, such as defining capabilities. This provides pre-qualification and can save valuable time when setting up an individual virtual project or organization.

Activity 8.10: Know your business network

List enterprises with which you have developed more than a casual relationship. Now provide an overview of their competencies, their strategic intent and what constitutes an ideal opportunity to work together. Is this information kept as organizational knowledge and regularly updated when individuals from the two enterprises meet?

Network analysis

Network analysis techniques provide more sophisticated ways of tracking emerging clusters in your industry and those organizations who may or may not make potential virtual organization partners. A good example of this is an analysis by Valdis Krebs of alliance activity for the main actors in the Internet marketplace. Two primary measures were used – level of activity and reach, i.e. the number of steps to reach others. Using the network analysis package Xsite, he found that Netscape and Microsoft were two key relationship hubs. They each had joint agreements with a third of other Internet participants.[12] Krebs also found that of fifty-nine linkages, just five organizations had links to both Netscape and Microsoft, the two cluster hubs. These 'boundary spanners' have a unique view of both clusters, and are pivotal knowledge points. As Krebs notes they are 'the shortest path between two arch competitors', and thus care is needed as to what knowledge flows through them.

Another form of analysis is that used by the Agility Forum. It uses Dooley graphs to show the interactions and process loops between different members in a virtual organization. Some are one-to-one interactions, while others involve interactions that ripple through the network.[13] Factors analysed in a process are the number of nodes and loops, the lengths of paths and time delays. This analysis determines the time it takes to make decisions or modify inter-enterprise processes.

Such analyses can reveal the nature of knowledge flows and provide insights into critical knowledge areas that depend on high degrees of trust or high degrees of responsiveness.

Collaboration contracts

At some stage, usually when resources are committed or confidential knowledge is exchanged, formal contracts are needed. However, collaborating partners can do much useful preparation before involving lawyers by thinking through the topics that such an agreement will cover.

There are several other legal and regulatory matters that may fall outside the scope of formal agreements but should nevertheless be addressed. One is that of labour agreements for the interprise, especially if the working conditions and pay scales of each partner are different. Irrespective of formal agreements, the ultimate success of collaboration depends on trust and working well together. Those who focus too early on contractual arrangements will miss out on relationship building and opportunity development.

Topics for a virtual organization agreement

- Purpose – the reason why each partner is entering the contract.
- Exchange – what is exchanged, what each partner gives and expects in return; obligations and rights.
- Identity – how the virtual organization is represented to the outside world.
- Key personnel – roles and responsibilities in the venture; named people where critical.
- Key working processes – budgeting, planning, work allocation, execution of projects.
- Information and knowledge exchange – ownership, intellectual proprietary rights, ownership of new knowledge.
- Commercial arrangements – valuing contributions and assets, sharing of costs and revenues, responsibilities for liabilities.
- Monitoring and enforcement – changing priorities, adjustment, adjudication.
- Dispute resolution – procedures, independent arbitrators.
- Dissolution or restructuring – how members can leave and others join. Sharing of assets on dissolution.

Implementing the infrastructure

Sustaining an interprise over any length of time requires the implementation of an interprise infrastructure, independent of its members, although shared by them. The infrastructure supports the *modus operandi* of the interprise along four key dimensions – business processes, organizational arrangements, knowledge and technology.

Business infrastructure

The business processes of most virtual organizations include a mix of routine development activities, such as planning, product development, sales and marketing, production and delivery. Each will evolve into a set of agreed methods, systems and procedures, which in turn become part of the infrastructure and hence intellectual capital of the interprise.

Knowledge networking is enhanced if key processes are the joint responsibility of more than one member, one acting as a lead partner and others supporting. This forces dialogue and co-operation. Interprise outputs such as the results of market and business research should be widely disseminated. The more knowledge and information collected, shared and discussed, the more the opportunities and risks are clarified. For all activities, each participant should ask themselves: 'How can I contribute to the success of my fellow partners?' – that is true collaborative working.

Activity 8.11: Core business processes

Are key processes identified and joint responsibilities allocated? Which are the critical processes on which the joint venture depends? Have these processes sufficient breadth of knowledge and commitment of resources? What processes are predefined, what is determined by joint negotiation? How are new business opportunities allocated?

One of the most difficult challenges in a virtual organization is agreeing how to share costs and benefits. Where a separate joint venture company has been formed, this is taken care of through allocation of share capital and formal accounting, just as in a traditional organization. But when a virtual organization is building, individual members are investing time and money to make it successful. The value of such contributions is difficult to value. Should it be based on normal labour and overhead rates for that organization? Should it be the same for all contributors? Should it be based on the commercial rate for the specific task? Some networks use a notional development rate that is used as network members perform such tasks. These notional credits and debits are put on account and settled when revenue is generated. By balancing development work across the network, settling accounts is less of an issue.

The situation is easier for client projects with definitive revenues. The Phrontis consulting network allocates its revenues broadly as follows:[14]

- 50 per cent of the overall project value goes directly to those delivering services
- 25 per cent is for marketing and sales: 10 per cent to the lead creator and 15 per cent for closing the sale
- 5 per cent is for quality checking, by a network member not directly involved
- 5 per cent is for administration, order processing, etc.
- 15 per cent is for development activities.

The responsibilities and detailed percentages are agreed up front on a project-by-project basis, as is the ownership of any intellectual property generated.

Organizational infrastructure

An organizational infrastructure is built along similar lines to that of a team as described in Chapter 6. This requires articulation of shared purpose and principles, and a summary of how each partner can enhance the success of each of the others. Developing an 'offer'–'needs' matrix for each contributor is a useful tool for identifying gaps and highlighting interdependencies. As with a virtual team the essential 'glue' of a virtual organization is regular and extensive communications.

A good basis around which to develop plans and gauge progress is through tracking the performance of the interprise. Define success metrics for the enterprise as a whole as well as for key development projects. Develop a system of information collection and progress monitoring. Use network members not directly involved as reviewers and arbiters.

Virtual organizations vary in their degree of formalism. A small network just starting is likely to develop its operating principles and contractual arrangements as its goes along. Over time these can be formalized in a collaboration agreement (page 229). Most importantly, every interprise must consider how to retain flexibility to change its configuration and membership. This is a healthy process that recognizes that partners' interests and market conditions change. There are three general situations:

1   Mutual acceptance of the need to change, e.g. one member wants to leave to pursue other ambitions. By updating regularly the list of individual interests, needs and offers, potential changes are anticipated.

2   One member wants to leave, but would leave the interprise with a void. To minimize such occurrences, work out the degree of interdependency at the start and attempt to reduce over-dependency on one member or individual through allocation of tasks.

3   The majority of the network wants to force another member out, perhaps because they are not pulling their weight or failing to meet commitments, or because of other conflicting business relationships. Agreed processes and peer performance review should ease this painful situation.

In all these cases, forward planning helps. Your statement of principles should address changing membership and dispute resolution. Agile Web offers a good example of a virtual organization infrastructure.

Agile Web

Agile Web describes itself as: 'a new corporate entity that brings together diverse capabilities, complementary skills and entrepreneurial inventiveness from an array of well-established companies to provide a totally integrated capability for fast-response product design and manufacturing'.

Although incorporated as a separate legal entity, the main work is carried out by its twenty-one members, although certain activities are carried out centrally:

- strategic market planning
- the screening and pursuit of specific business opportunities
- the compilation of a core competency data base of its members
- providing a single point of contact for customers
- customizing core competencies to each opportunity (by creating a virtual organization)
- searching for potential members to augment existing competencies.

It has a fourteen-point process for generating opportunities, qualifying customers and building temporary virtual organizations to carry out the tasks required. A neutral team qualifies the opportunity and shares their findings with Agile Web members. For opportunities considered worthy of follow up, members are invited to come together and form a response team. They create a memorandum of agreement with each other as well as with the customer. If the response team makes a recommendation not to proceed, individual members can pursue the opportunity by themselves. For each project revenues are distributed according to the direct (not indirect) costs of every participant, and profits shared according to an agreed formula based on contributions. This methodology, the nuts and bolts of building a successful virtual corporation, is a vital knowledge resource of Agile Web.

The governance of Agile Web is carried out by three committees. The Entity Committee addresses entry and exit policies, limits on competition, dispute resolution and contract liabilities. The Marketing Committee considers product definition, competencies including deficiencies and verification. The Operations Committee develops monitoring procedures and quality control.

The twenty-one participants in Agile Web place trust at a premium – if one member lets down the Web (or Agile Web) the rest suffer. They therefore monitor their own standards and behaviours of each other. Agile Web has therefore developed a set of ethics statements, to which they all subscribe and sign. These include statements about trustworthiness, keeping promises, valuing people and committing to continuous improvement.

Sources: The fourteen-step methodology can be found in *Cybercorp* by James Martin.[15] The full ethics statement can be found at http://www.lehigh.edu/~inbft/ethics.html

> ## Activity 8.12: Develop your intraprise principles
>
> What does the intraprise need to organize to be successful?
>
> *   What are basic operating principles for the enterprise?
> *   Who is responsible for each core development task?
> *   Prepare an offers/needs chart and agree the process for updating.

Knowledge infrastructure

Knowledge is frequently the interprise's most important resource and may also be one of its key outputs. Just as within an enterprise, the virtual organization will need to manage its own knowledge – in databases on web pages, holding records of assignments and expertise, working documents and so on.

The interprise is also a rich source of knowledge that is often not systematically captured. There are several strategies that a participating enterprise should pursue to maximize the benefits of this collaboratively generated knowledge (Figure 8.7):

1   Control the flow of your proprietary knowledge into the interprise. Determine what knowledge should be made available to the interprise and under what conditions. It could represent a significant commitment, yet be undervalued. Make sure your employees understand which knowledge falls into which category.
2   Extract as much knowledge and experience from collaboration as you can, and disseminate it around your organization. Too often, an interprise has an arm's length relationship so that the knowledge resides only with those people who have been seconded to it. The Japanese view joint ventures as great sources of learning, something many Western companies have yet to grasp.

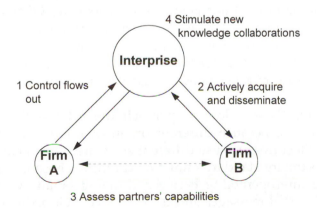

Figure 8.7   Strategies for a participating enterprise to exploit interprise knowledge

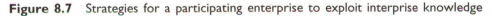

3   Continually assess the competency and the capacity of network partners.
     What knowledge do they have that could be of value to both the
     interprise and to yourselves?
4   Stimulate new collaborations as ideas emerge. These may be with
     subgroups within the existing virtual organization or newly constituted
     intraprises.

Therefore, put in place mechanisms to help knowledge flows between the
enterprise and interprise. This may be through gatekeepers or regular
liaison by participants as a key organizational responsibility.

The technological infrastructure

For many virtual organizations an intranet, or some other form of groupware, provides the basis of the technology infrastructure. Ideally the
interprise should have its own intranet which can simply be provided
though password protected access to servers in the different enterprises.
Depending on what information access has been agreed, different
members should be part of their partner's extranet and vice versa. In
other words they can access specified areas of that firm's own intranet.
A typical set up might be:

*   Email, using agreed conventions. The interprise may set up its own domain
    name with alias addresses (such as info@interprise.com,
    sales@interprise.com) that are routed to specific enterprise addresses
    according to roles and responsibilities.
*   Interprise website, divided into three broad areas: public (Internet
    accessible); restricted (enterprise members and partners – various
    grouping) and closed (for interprise workers only). Often individual
    projects and teams will have their own private areas.
*   A conferencing system, such as Lotus Notes or web conferencing. This is
    useful for the creative development activities of the interprise.
*   An agreed set of applications and database formats.

The rules for these follow very much the rules within an enterprise.
Difficulties arise because different organizations have different technological architectures and use different software. This means that messaging and document standards must be carefully chosen. Fortunately there
is growing interoperability between different email systems and word
processors so that messages and documents developed in one system can
be read in another. Where this is not true or where specialist applications

or databases are involved, the interprise should standardize on one. Do not spend too much time arguing about technology. Use the best that is readily available. After all, it is merely a carrier and interface to the interprise knowledge infrastructure.

Sustaining success

Virtual organizations pose unfamiliar challenges for those used to working in conventional organization settings. The key ingredients for developing a successful virtual corporation are:

1 Each partner must offer some distinctive added value.
2 There should be sufficient members that a viable mix of competencies is provided, but not too many that co-ordination and interfacing becomes difficult.
3 Relationships must be balanced. Dominant partners or high dependency on any one or two makes the virtual organization fragile.
4 Members must develop a high degree of mutual understanding and commitment.
5 Projects and processes should be the focus of co-operation. Usually they will be for clients but some, e.g. marketing product development, can be done by a few members on behalf of the virtual organization as a whole.
6 Key principles or 'rules of engagement' need to be defined fairly broadly at the outset, covering areas like responsibilities and reward expectations, sharing of risk and returns. However, momentum is lost if too much is formalized too soon.
7 Members should recognize the need for brokering and co-ordination activities, and either commit time to them or pay for them to be undertaken.
8 A virtual organization needs a clear identity and interface to the outside world. One approach is to complement your individual identity with an addition such as 'a member of the XYZ federation'. Contracts may either be with one firm acting as prime contractor, or a legally constituted organization 'the XYZ Federation'.
9 Developing trust is crucial, especially in the early stages of formation, or where there is no shared past, or where virtuality means little face-to-face contact.
10 Plan for reconfiguration or dissolution. Agree how to replace non-performing members with new ones. Continually reaffirm each member's interests, commitment, competencies and capacity.

The Trust Group

The Trust Group is an example of a virtual network whose members are individual contractors, but who gain from being part of a larger skills pool.[16] It was formed in 1996 as an evolution of shared interests communicated in a CompuServe forum. It is a voluntary network of IT specialists – programmers, systems analysts and project managers – who make themselves available for short-term contract work. The attraction for individuals is that it helps find them opportunities through shared marketing, while allowing them to remain independent. The Trust Group has developed its business through being able to offer large corporations a highly skilled resource, committed to standards and quality. It may seem like a typical contract agency, but it is run as a club by its members for its members. Its clients do not pay agency fees, and deal direct with individuals after the introductions have been made. A modest subscription covers administration and marketing costs, which include both conventional publicity and a World Wide Web site. Client opportunities are referred to appropriate people with the specialist skills. Teams are assembled for larger projects, by posting requirements on a private Internet newsgroup and website.

Robert Pearson, one of its founders, attributes its success to its members' level of competence but, more fundamentally, on what its name suggests – *trust*.

The reality is that many collaborative ventures end in failure. Business networks or electronic communities that start with good intentions fail to move forward. There is nothing as good as a funded project or customer contract to crystallize action, but even then a collaboration champion is needed. Building an interprise is not unlike building a new enterprise from scratch. It therefore needs entrepreneurial zeal and commitment, which may be difficult if individuals already have their time committed to their main employer. Therefore, the more interprising can be made a natural part of the routine work of an enterprise, and a significant time commitment for key employees, the easier it is to develop and sustain. Common reasons why interprises stall, and how the risk can be minimized are:

- Over-optimism – develop a better understanding of partners, especially their competencies, motives and top management commitment.
- No obvious strategic necessity or fit – there is no clear benefit for an individual organization.
- Assigning inappropriate individuals to the interprise – it should have some of your most competent people, not those who just happen to be free.

- Conflicting, neglected or unbalanced interests – motives must be clearly understood; the offers/needs approach helps.
- Cultural or management style incompatibility – early use of a diagnostic tool will help identify potential issues to see if they are insurmountable.
- Changing business context – anticipate the affects of changing regulatory, market conditions and how they affect each enterprise and the interprise as whole.
- Poor marketing both internally and externally – the benefits, core competencies and products need to be sold to attract ongoing revenues and investment.
- Inadequate infrastructure – explicitly address the technical, business, knowledge and organizational infrastructures.
- Unclear or unfair sharing of risks and rewards – develop principles for valuing contributions and sharing of revenues and rewards.
- Festering disputes and unmet commitments – instigate good performance monitoring and methods of dispute resolution.
- Partners abscond or breaks ranks, taking unfair advantage of the others – build in legal safeguards or network surveillance.

Overall, many of these situations can be avoided through constant communications and reinforcing trust, rather than having to resort to legal measures. A little early planning and discussion of key principles can prevent anguish later. Address and resolve small annoyances before they become festering sores.

Summary

This chapter has considered some whys and wherefores of collaborative interprising. Specific attention has been given to creating and sustaining virtual organizations. The diversity of structures and working arrangements is huge, ranging from loosely formed business networks, as in the Danish model, to tightly knit formal virtual organization structures like Agile Web.

Creating a successful interprise extends many of the principles already discussed in earlier chapters in this part of the book, such as the need for an integrated perspective that includes business, organizational, knowledge and technical dimensions. In particular, many of the facets that apply to virtual knowledge teams, discussed in Chapter 6, also apply in the virtual organization. Of these, extensive communications and trust are the core foundations.

Agenda for action

Developing collaboration knowledge

1   Review any existing collaborative arrangements. Draw lessons from their success or failure. Are there organizing principles you can carry over?
2   Identify knowledge and experience of collaborations that exist, either within your organization or in already proven external examples, such as Agile Web.
3   Develop a strategic map, specific for your business, highlighting areas of strategic intent i.e. future strategic moves.
4   Create a potential partners' database, mapping their key competencies into your strategic map.
5   Review any business networks or virtual organizations that address similar customer needs. Do any of them represent an expanded opportunity for you? Are there practices that can be emulated?

Creating collaboration infrastructures and practices

6   Review your existing technological, business and knowledge infrastructures. How easy is it to modify or extend these to collaborating partners?
7   List your top ten customers. To what extent have you developed deep relationships, knowledge sharing and dialogue for innovation?
8   Review your innovation process. Consider how more external input can be integrated into the process, such as customers, suppliers or external experts.
9   Review your key knowledge databases. Do they include records of collaborative activities? To what extent can they be enriched by direct collaborator involvement?
10 Review various intellectual property contracts you have. Do they inhibit or help future collaboration?

Notes

1   Most interorganizational models are based on exchange theory i.e. each party exchanges some resource or economic 'good' for another resource or benefit. Typical of such academic models is that described in Ring, P. S. and Van den Ven, A. H. (1992). Structuring interorganizational relationships. *Strategic Management Journal*, **13**(2), pp. 483–98.
2   Segil, L. (1998). *Intelligent Business Alliances*. Century Business Books.
3   Amidon, D. M. (1997). Customer innovation: a function of knowledge. *Journal of Customer Relationships* (5), pp. 28–35.

4   Amidon, D. M. (1997). Customer innovation: a function of knowledge. *Journal of Customer Relationships* (5), pp. 28–35.

5   Morita, A. (1986). *Made in Japan*. E. P. Dutton.

6   Angehrn, A. (1997). Designing mature Internet business strategies: the ICDT model. *European Management Journal*, **15**(5), August, pp. 361-369.

7   Angehrn, A. (1998). The strategic implications of the Internet. INSEAD Working Paper at http://www.insead.fr/CALT/Publication/ICDT/strategicImplication.htm.

8   Lorange, P. and Roos, J. (1992). *Strategic Alliances: Formation, Implementation and Evolution*. Blackwell.

9   EU Innovation Programme 'Innovation across cultural borders'. The web page http://www.cordis.lu/innovation/src/culture1.htm describes the approach. Associated web pages give six case studies of culture clash and a downloadable software tool based on the diagnostic.

10 Chaston, I. (1995). Danish Technological Institute SME sector network model: implementing broker competencies. *Journal of European Industrial Training*, **19**(1), pp. 10–17.

11 Martinussen, J. and Jantzen, O. (1994). Business networking – a transferable model for a European SME support structure. *TII/Focus*, August.

12 Krebs, V. (1997). Patterns in the Net. http://www.orgnet.com/netpatterns1.htm

13 The Agility Forum at http://www.agilityforum.org/Ex_proj/MAVE/1.htm.

14 Phrontis Consulting at http://www.phrontis.com

15 Martin, J. (1998). *Cybercorp: The New Business Revolution*, p. 130, Amacom.

16 The Trust Group at http://www.trustgroup.com.

Pathways to Prosperity

The knowledge economy is significantly different to that for which most managers and policy-makers were educated and trained. Around the world various institutions and organizations are trying to get to grips with new ways of working that will create frameworks for future prosperity. This is not easy as the new economy and its activities rubs shoulders with the old. There are tensions between established businesses and institutions and the 'new kids on the block'. A concern of many commentators is the gap between the haves and the have nots – those individuals and societies that participate in the new economy and prosper, and those that do not. This problem is potentially caused in part by unequal access to necessary support services and infrastructures, such as education, Internet access and business finance. For everyone to share in the prosperity brought about by the knowledge revolution new agendas are needed.

The developments described in Part B of this book create an unrivalled opportunity for creating this prosperity. However, the very interdependence that these developments create, call for a greater degree of coherence between businesses, governments and a wide range of other agencies. All are part of an evolving interdependent knowledge ecosystem.

This part of the book looks at the wider ecosystem and how it might develop. Chapter 9 reviews the contribution of public policy and programmes at several levels – community, national, and supranational including groupings such as the European Union and G7 nations. It calls for more cross sector collaboration and initiatives that stimulate entrepreneurship and innovation. Chapter 10 ponders the future. While it does make some forecasts, it suggests that more emphasis should be put on developing alternative scenarios, five of which are postulated. Whatever the scenario, it is likely to be 'all change' from the way we do things today. We need more extensive knowledge networking and global collaboration to develop our own prosperous futures.

Chapter 9

The public policy agenda

Public policy plays an important part in shaping the environment in which individuals and organizations can create wealth and contribute to society's prosperity. As the knowledge economy takes hold, significant changes are needed in many areas of public policy to stimulate, and not stifle, the right kind of entrepreneurial activity.

The global and pervasive nature of knowledge activities means that national governments can no longer act in isolation on such matters. Before discussing specific aspects of the policy agenda, this chapter considers what factors underpin a successful knowledge economy. Policy areas that need addressing include the global infrastructures for telecommunications, the legal and regulatory environment, and international agreements on electronic commerce. As well as a regulatory role, policymakers must also collaborate in initiatives that stimulate innovation in knowledge based enterprise. Examples are given of pioneering initiatives that are building the foundations for a prosperous knowledge society.

Knowledge for posterity

Knowledge has always underpinned mankind's prosperity. Scientific and technical knowledge has helped us lead better and longer lives. Management knowledge has helped us to organize resources and produce products and service more efficiently. As we enter the new millennium deeper knowledge about man's interaction with the natural environment will help us build a sustainable future. The World Bank, whose investment is predominantly targeted at development of poorer countries, chose *Knowledge for Development* as the title of its 1998–9 *World Development Report*.[1] Its preface reads:

> This year's World Development Report, the twenty first in this annual series, examines the role of knowledge in advancing economic and social well being. Because knowledge matters, understanding how people and societies acquire and use knowledge – and why they sometimes fail to do so – is essential to improving people's lives, especially the lives of the poorest among us ... by recognising that knowledge is at the core of our development effort, unexpected solutions to seemingly intractable problems will be discovered.

New measures of success

Success in today's world is frequently measured in financial terms. We measure a country's prosperity by its GDP. But is this really a meaningful measure in the knowledge economy? Prosperity in the twenty-first century is not about financial wealth. It is about personal well-being and fulfilment, and living in a sustainable environment. A forward thinking country like Sweden has quality of life (QoL) of its citizens as one of its public policy goals.

Two institutions that now examine more deeply the factors behind wealth creation are the World Economic Forum (WEF) of Geneva and IMD (the International Institute for Management Development) of Lausanne. They prepare annual reports that rank national 'competitiveness', a country's ability to generate wealth. A large number of factors are

Table 9.1 Categories of national competitiveness indicators

World Competitiveness Yearbook (IMD)	Global Competitiveness Report (WEF)
Management	Quality of business management
Domestic economy	Openness to international trade
Science and technology	Quality of technology
People	Labour market flexibility
Government	Role of government budget and regulation
Internationalization	Quality of political/judicial institutions
Infrastructure	Quality of infrastructure
Finance	Development of financial markets

involved – 223 in the case of IMD and 155 for WEF.[2] Both organizations group them into eight categories that show remarkable similarities (Table 9.1).

Many of these indicators are intangible and related to knowledge. The importance of knowledge and innovation to competitiveness is recognized by the Massachusetts Technology Forum, a consortium of businesses, government and academia. Its Innovation Index is a set of economic indicators that 'more clearly identify and better explain the essential ingredients, dynamics and comparative values of the innovation economy'.[3] The index comprises thirty-three indicators in three categories – critical inputs, processes and results (Table 9.2).

Table 9.2 The Massachusetts Innovation Index (sample indicators)

Inputs (16 indicators)	Processes (9)	Results (8)
Human resources:	Business innovation:	Job growth
population growth	industry value added	Average wages
education level	value of intangible assets	Income distribution
assessment scores	Commercialization:	Export sales
Technology:	licence royalties	Business climate
per capita R&D	FDA drug approval rates	New industry clusters
corporate R&D	Entrepreneurship:	
Investment:	innovation awards	
venture capital	no. of 'gazelle' companies	
research tax credit use	initial public offerings (IPOs)	
Infrastructure:	Idea generation:	
ISDN availability	patents filed	
Internet connectivity		
classroom Internet access		
international airline routes		

Foundations for the future

These approaches give us insights into the key factors behind wealth creation in a knowledge economy (Figure 9.1).

The policy agenda, like those in previous chapters, must integrate technology, economic and social factors. It must cohesively integrate policy at local, national regional and international levels. It must provide a legal and regulatory framework, stimulate initiative, and create suitable infrastructures for innovation and knowledge development.

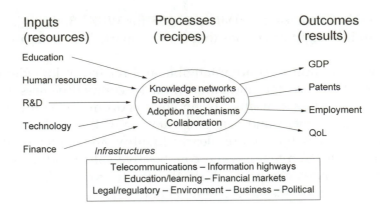

Figure 9.1 A simplified model of the global knowledge economy

The elements of such an infrastructure are portrayed in the model in Figure 9.2. This has been derived from the work of George Kozmetsky and colleagues at Austin, Texas, a good exemplar of a region whose infrastructures have stimulated innovation and wealth creation.

Kotzmetsky highlights the importance of both technological infrastructure and entrepreneurial networks as key ingredients: 'The promotion of technology activities requires working links, or relationships, not only among and between individuals, but also among and between a variety of institutions. The more extensive, complex and diverse the webs of relationships, the more likely a region is to accelerate industrial and

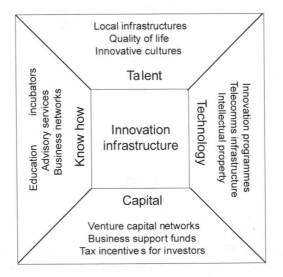

Figure 9.2 Elements of a typical innovation infrastructure
Source: Adapted from Kozmetsky, G. (1994). *Technology Transfer in a Global Context.* Working Paper No. 294-04-01, IC², University of Texas at Austin

technological development.'[4] Based on his own successful experiences, he explains that the networks should include:

- Universities to provide quality of initial and continuing education, as well as research facilities and programmes of benefit to potential entrepreneurs.
- Established and other growing businesses, who can provide links to suppliers and customers, peer support and role models.
- Business support services such as accountants, lawyers, financiers.
- Regional and national government agencies to provide funding and other forms of support.
- A range of individual experts and consultants, social and civic groups.

Many of the US high-technology wealth-creating regions, such as Silicon Valley, Austin, and Route 128 near Boston, can be traced to this diversity of networks.

Technological infrastructure

The Internet today is just the first step towards a universal technology infrastructure. The next five years will see a quantum leap in bandwidth and access speed. Broadband multimedia, cabled into homes and offices, will bring live broadcast quality video and interactive three-dimensional applications. Infrastructure investment is stimulated by the development of services that have widespread business and consumer appeal. Several national governments have recognized their role in stimulating such developments.

The USA's National Information Infrastructure (NII), was proposed by Al Gore as 'a seamless web of communications networks, computers, databases and consumer electronics that will put vast amounts of information at users' fingertips'.[5] Today this vision has moved on to the Global Information Infrastructure (GII), where electronic commerce will take place on a global scale.[6] A related initiative is the Next Generation Internet Initiative (NGII) which has funds of $110 million allocated to build a research network that is 1000 times faster than today's Internet.

The EU's Advanced Communications Technology and Services (ACTS) programme is concerned with the deployment of advanced communications infrastructures and services aimed at businesses and consumers. Over its lifetime from 1994 to 1999, the work in ACTS has shifted progressively from fundamental research to demonstrator applications, with user trials being a key feature of most projects. Development areas include interactive digital media services, such as telework and teleshopping, high-speed networking using ATM, and the integration of fixed and mobile networks. The EU regards cross-border broadband communications services as 'an essential infrastructure for competitiveness and the basis for trade, provision of services, production, transport, education and entertainment'.[7]

Perhaps the most ambitious national initiative is that of Singapore.

Singapore – the wired island

Ranked first in the 1998 WEF World Competitiveness report, Singapore has developed its infrastructure in several areas, not least in the area of broadband communications. A city-state, no larger than London and with no physical resources, it is the archetypal knowledge community, relying on the talents of its populace. The National Computer Board has played a leading role in furthering the broader societal benefits of computerization, for example with its National IT plan in 1986. In 1992 its 'IT2000 Vision of a Wired Island' was launched. Its aims are to become a regional hub, boost the economy and improve quality of life. Its education system has created over 20 000 IT professionals. Foreign companies have put their regional headquarters in Singapore and used it as a centre for software development, data hubs and network management. Government is advanced in its use of computers with intense interaction between departments. For example, licences for exports that need approval from several government departments and previously took weeks, can now be completed in hours following an exporter's email request.

Singapore's main ambition is to become completely wired for broadband by 2007, linking every home, school and business premises. Construction started in mid-1996 on building the infrastructure based on an ATM backbone network. In 1997 fourteen leading multinational corporations signed up as application and service providers, and a pilot service, Singapore ONE was launched. The trial of this 'network for everybody' rapidly expanded to provide 123 services to over 10 000 consumers in its first year of operation. As well as over thirty television channels, there are interactive multimedia services in education, entertainment, information and teleshopping. Children can even look after their own virtual pet!

The examples of the USA, EU and Singapore, show how appropriate public-private partnerships can stimulate progress toward creating high-speed infrastructures and value-added services. One general concern is that access to such services should be both universal and affordable. The problems of taking high-speed networks to remote areas with low population densities may in the end call for public subsidies, although advances in satellite communications may alleviate the problem.

Awareness and education

The knowledge society needs new competencies, in using technology, managing information and in entrepreneurship. Furthermore, the pace of change and future uncertainty means that basic education needs to change in four fundamental ways:

1 A shift from an emphasis on imparting knowledge into one of developing thinking and learning skills.
2 A shift from a one off activity in childhood into lifelong learning.
3 Making IT literacy an evolving skill from an early age.
4 Bringing the world of business into the classroom.

Education systems are often slow to change. Specialists in existing subjects are reluctant to give up curriculum time as pressure grows to add new subjects. While many national governments, such as that of Denmark, have for many years made IT in schools a high priority, the pace of development and the need for equipment and training has often outstripped pubic resources. Active partnership with the private sector and other organizations is crucial. Many education establishments achieve this through closer community involvement, such as providing access to their facilities and hosting collaborative education programmes.

Corporate universities, distance education and virtual learning networks are other examples of collaboration between businesses and education. One example of such collaboration at community level is that of the South Bristol Learning Network (see panel overleaf).

At the national level more needs to be done in co-ordinating such activities and setting the framework for national competence development. As in many other areas, Denmark is taking a lead with its National Council for Competency, created as the nation's 'advisory institution for competence development in the knowledge society'. Initiated by a leading socioeconomic think-tank, Strategic Forum, it brings together in a network public institutions, leading Danish companies and local governmental agencies.

Finance for innovation

A third vital infrastructure is that of financing innovation and knowledge-based enterprises. Financial institutions are notoriously fickle in their

South Bristol Learning Network

The South Bristol Learning Network (SBLN) was established in 1993 to create opportunities for local individuals and organizations to learn at home, in school, at work or in the community. It is now a leading exemplar of community driven learning enhanced by ICT. Under the slogan 'Business – Education – Community' it represents a broad community enterprise which should eventually involve over 400 agencies.

Its first emphasis was to provide retraining opportunities for fifty-five unemployed people to learn about emerging information and communications technologies. As a result, most subsequently gained employment. The network has enlisted the help of many companies both local and further afield, including the local cable company, a media design company and a leading national computer company. A couple of years after its launch the programme gained a boost of £750 000 from winning a national competition sponsored by the Department of Employment.

Facilities include a local bulletin board system and access to the Internet. The portfolio of services continues to grow and involves all sections of the community:

*   An InfoCentre offering on-line city wide access to local information.
*   'Workstore' – state-of-the-art media production multimedia workshops, aimed at the inner city ethnic minority community.
*   A technology roadshow, introducing new technologies to neighbourhoods, schools and business areas.
*   Increasing awareness in the education community: explaining the value of ICT to not only teachers but also school heads and administrators.
*   Videoconference training and suite hire.
*   'Internet for Education'.
*   Public access local cable television.

One of the most successful ventures has been a 'Cyberskills Training' programme. With the focus 'people first, technology second', it uses a workshop setting where participants apply different ICT technologies to tasks of their own choosing. One outcome is that 75 per cent of companies that have attended these workshops now use the Internet for their business, a much higher proportion than the UK national average. This workshop has now been made available nationally through ICL.

The SBLN is an active participant in other national and international programmes, such as the UK's IT for All programme, and Schoolnet. Schoolnet is an EU-supported educational network that involves over 700 secondary school teachers across Europe. Teachers and pupils have collaboratively created via the Internet some seventy educational projects in a wide range of subjects. There are similar initiatives in Canada (SchoolNet), USA (Link2Learn) and Japan (KONET).

lending, with wild gyrations according to economic cycles. They also tend to back traditional investments in tangible assets rather than creating the infrastructures for tomorrow's knowledge businesses.

What is needed are financial networks and mechanisms that make it easier for the genuine wealth-creating knowledge-based businesses to get appropriate levels of finance. NASDAQ, the US-based stock exchange specializing in initial public offerings for high-technology companies, is one example. But a local financial network linked to other infrastructure dimensions fills other needs. Silicon Valley and Austin have vibrant venture capital networks, many of the investors being individual business angels whose wealth has come from their own business ventures. The public sector can stimulate the formation of such networks, but it also has a wider role. It needs to create a favourable climate for this kind of investment, through tax breaks on start-up companies and their investors. It must also minimize the bureaucracy needed to create and run start-up companies. However, in countries like France small companies face bureaucratic burdens not significantly different from a large company, which has a higher disproportionate impact on them.

Legal and regulatory frameworks

The knowledge economy is rapidly developing without the necessary legal and regulatory framework. The pace of legislation usually significantly lags that of technology. Much legislation affecting knowledge industries evolves on a national basis. This leads to wide variations in law in key areas such as intellectual property, personal data privacy and freedom of information. Yet the Internet transcends national boundaries.

A spokesman for the Transatlantic Business Club, an influential group comprising over 100 chief executives from major businesses in Europe and the USA describes the current situation as 'inadequate' and 'a patchwork of laws, and in some cases, contradictory'. They are arguing for a high degree of self-regulation with a minimal, globally harmonized, technological neutral.[8] An example of such an anomaly is that the US Freedom of Information Act allows UK citizens to access information in US government databases concerning the UK that is not published in the UK. In the USA 150 Internet-related bills were introduced in state and federal legislatures during 1998. For example, there was a proposal in Texas to tax any electronic traffic that passes through the state, even if the server and client are located elsewhere. Taxation anomalies also exist. In many countries, goods purchased over the Internet are free from taxes, yet the same goods bought locally are not.

Table 9.3 Summary of rights and responsibilities for electronic publishing

Rights	Responsibilities
Integrity – accuracy of author's work maintained	Accuracy – factual and not libellous; integrity is maintained
Identification – of author, publisher and distributor visible to user	Signature – to show origination and publisher
Conditions – terms of use can be imposed and are clear to the user	Terms – specify any special condition of use and reuse
Remuneration – right to establish a price for value each party adds that is also fair to user	Value – quality work worthy of publication whose value is maintained throughout the distribution system
Attribution – acknowledgement of source	Attribution – of sources cited, of author and of publisher
Permissions – requests promptly dealt with	Permission – is sought to incorporate other's works or to use in ways beyond terms of use
Privacy – rights to monitor usage while respecting individual privacy	
Security – to prevent misuse and respect privacy of users	

Source: The National Federation of Abstracting and Information Services (1997). *The Rights and Responsibilities of Content Creators, Providers and Users: A White Paper*, NFAIS.

Intellectual property is another area of knowledge based activity that suffers from lack of harmonization of legislation as new technologies create a legal minefield. The ease with which information can be copied and transmitted means that without some protection, the incentive for producers to create new information may be reduced. However, too much protection may restrict the flow of knowledge and stifle innovation.

A fair balance has to be struck between providers and users. A White Paper by the National Federation of Abstracting and Information Services proposes a set of rights and responsibilities for content creators (authors), providers (publishers, database producers, distributors) and users (Table 9.3).

Knowledge society initiatives

Around the world there are initiatives to stimulate moves towards an information or knowledge society. The EU started on this path in 1993 with a White Paper *Growth, Competitiveness, Employment*.[9] This was quickly followed by the Bangemann Report, named after the European Commissioner for Industry, Martin Bangemann, who chaired the group of IT industry leaders that developed it. Anxious to emulate the lead of the USA, their report *Europe and the Global Information Society* urged action by the EU 'to put its faith in market mechanisms as the motive power to carry us into the information age'. It called for actions to foster an entrepreneurial spirit, developing a common regulatory approach and warned against public subsidies and protectionism.[10] It sought the development

---

Ten key information society applications – the Bangemann Report

1   *Teleworking*: 'more jobs, new jobs for a mobile society' – to improve flexibility, increase productivity and reduce commuting.
2   *Distance learning*: 'life long learning for a changing society' – to provide easier access and to optimize the use of scarce training resources.
3   A network for universities and research centres: 'networking Europe's brain power' – to make research more productive through greater collaboration and access to information.
4   *Electronic data transmission for SMEs*: 'relaunching a main engine for growth and employment in Europe' – promoting the use of EDI, e mail, videoconferencing, etc., so that SMEs will become more competitive, grow faster and create more jobs.
5   *Road traffic management*: 'electronic roads for better quality of life' – advanced systems for driver information, route guidance and road pricing to reduce traffic congestion and save energy.
6   *Air traffic control*: 'an electronic airway for Europe' – creating a pan-European communications system to create safer, less congested air travel.
7   *Healthcare networks*: 'less costly and more effective healthcare systems for Europe's citizens' – to link general practitioners, medical specialists and community centres for better on-line diagnosis, faster analysis of tests, and speedier administration.
8   *Electronic tendering*: 'more effective administration at lower cost' – a network for public procurement linking public sector buyers with suppliers.
9   *Trans-European public administration network*: 'better government, cheaper government' – linking public authorities for information exchange, and ultimately the citizen.
10 *City information highways*: 'bringing the information society into the home' – connecting households to a range of multimedia services, such as teleshopping and on-line education.

of a high bandwidth of networks and a set of application services, so that a critical mass of users could be achieved and thus stimulate further invest-ment. Ten transnational applications were proposed (see panel on page 253).

As a result many programmes in the EU's Fourth Framework research programme have supported these developments. But the EU's view of what they call 'the information society' goes beyond technology. Its 1994 policy and action agenda balances services, application and content with social, societal and cultural aspects.[11] It envisages a pragmatic bottom-up approach, with the private sector implementing projects, while the Union acts as a catalyst and provides some financial support where necessary. The 1998 updated 'Rolling Action Plan' identifies five priorities:[12]

1   Improving the business environment, including promoting the uptake of electronic commerce, especially by SMEs.
2   Investing in the future – starting with classroom education but extending into lifelong learning.
3   Supporting European technology, especially substantial investment at a relatively early stage of market development in key emerging technologies.
4   Putting people at the centre, e.g. improving employment opportunities and quality of life.
5   A focus on the global context, recognizing that Europea must participate in global frameworks.

G7

The G7 group of countries – (Canada, France, the USA, the UK, Germany, Japan and Italy) also has a set of co-operative information society projects. Eleven pilot projects were initiated in 1995 to set the groundwork for ongoing co-operation, and to identify obstacles in creating practical global applications (Table 9.4).[13]

UK national initiatives

The UK offers a good example of a series of initiatives addressing the development of a knowledge society. Its Information Society Initiative (ISI), launched in 1996 aims to stimulate the overall uptake of informa-tion systems, through three major programmes:

1   *IT for All* – making IT accessible and used by the average person; some 2000 access centres are planned where members of the public can see IT in action.

Table 9.4 G7 information society projects (1995–9)

1 Global Inventory of Applications	A one-stop shop for information on 2000 projects, whose visibility will create 'alliance-building opportunities'.[14]
2 Global Interoperability of Broadband Networks	19 major applications projects including education and medical networks.
3 Cross Cultural Education and Training: (Tel*Lingua)	An international network for language education connecting teachers, trainers and users.
4 Electronic Libraries: (Bibliotheca Universalis)	Co-operation between national libraries to establish the framework for a global electronic library system.
5 Multimedia Access to World Cultural Heritage	Electronic museums and art galleries.
6 Environment and Natural Resources Management	Agreeing standards for a virtual library of environment and natural resources management information.
7 Global Emergency Management (Gemini)	28 demonstration projects from seven countries covering networks, communications, support functions and specific hazards.
8 Global Healthcare Applications	Projects dealing with cancer, cardiovascular disease etc. that have demonstrated interoperability of medical images and health cards so patients can be treated irrespective of location.
9 Government On-Line	Disseminating information about best practice by governments in providing and promoting on-line services.
10 Global Marketplace for SMEs	Over 30 projects demonstrating various applications and services, resulting in electronic commerce policy development, and a best practice guide.
11 Maritime Information Society: (MARIS)	Links existing systems to create global maritime networks, e.g. for fishing (MARSOURCE), for information on vessel movements (MARTRANS).

2 *ISI Programme for Business* – especially targeted at small businesses. Projects include support centres and a series of basic but helpful booklets, such as 'How electronic mail can work for you'.
3 *IT for Schools* – gives children and teachers access to the Internet.

The UK government sees itself as having a fourfold role:

1 Providing leadership – the creation of a vision of the future; encouraging wider participation.

2   Providing an appropriate regulatory framework that encourages effective competition, and inspires innovation.
3   Raising awareness – among users and suppliers, in public and private sectors, firms and individuals.
4   Acting as an intelligent user – of the Internet, email, videoconferencing and other technologies.

One way of furthering these goals is for the government itself to go on-line. It has pledged to put more public information on-line and has set a target for 35 per cent of government services to be available on-line by 2002. Wider access to government is planned through computers in libraries and on-line kiosks in public places such as shopping centres and railway stations.

Other initiatives include a National Grid for Learning, connecting schools to the Internet, and a twenty-four hour telephone support line for medical advice staffed by trained nurses. In December 1998 the Department of Trade and Industry published a White Paper *Our Competitive Future: Building the Knowledge Driven Economy* (at http://www.dti.gov.uk). In it the government commits to 'build capabilities, catalyze collaboration and promote competition'. Specific programmes include rewarding universities for increasing interaction with business, developing entrepreneurial skills in students and sharing best practice. The White Paper is said to have been heavily influenced by the entrepreneurial climate in the USA and especially in Silicon Valley.

On-line trading and working

Electronic commerce

The potential of electronic commerce has already been outlined in Chapter 4. Realization of this potential, though, depends on collaborative initiatives at local, national and international level. Perhaps the best known local initiative, whose influence has extended globally, is that of CommerceNet, which started in 1994 as a not-for-profit initiative in Silicon Valley with a mission 'Working Together to Make Electronic Commerce Easy, Trusted and Ubiquitous'.[15]

At national level various governments are now setting down principles and policies as a framework for global electronic commerce. In 1997, the US administration set down five principles and made recommendations for international action:

Principles for electronic commerce (USA)

1   The private sector should lead. The Internet should be market driven and not a regulated industry.
2   Governments should avoid undue restrictions on electronic commerce. Buyers and sellers should be able to trade with minimal regulations, and without new taxes or tariffs.
3   Where government and legislative involvement is needed, it should be predictable, minimalist, consistent and simple. It should ensure competition, protect intellectual property and privacy, prevent fraud, foster transparency and facilitate dispute resolution.
4   Governments should recognize the unique qualities of the Internet, its decentralized nature and its tradition of bottom-up governance, unlike the regulatory frameworks for telecommunications or broadcasting. Existing laws and regulations that may hinder electronic commerce should be revised or eliminated to reflect the needs of the media.
5   Electronic commerce on the Internet should be facilitated globally. The legal framework should be consistent and predictable regardless of the jurisdiction in which buyers and sellers live.

The EU launched its corresponding initiative in mid-1997.[16] While it recognized the US lead in electronic commerce, it noted how Europe could build on some of its unique strengths in content creation, linguistic and cultural diversity, and the European single currency. Specific areas of action include telecommunications deregulation, creating a favourable regulatory framework and promoting a favourable business environment. In May 1998 the EU issued a directive on electronic signatures. Electronic information is accompanied by an encrypted certificate issued by an accredited certification agency that validates the authenticity of the sender. The directive specifies minimum requirements for a signature, for providers and rules on liability. However, implementation is not planned until January 2001.

Comparison of the US and European public positions shows a high level of commonality but some significant differences. The USA is strong on self-regulation, while Europe has a predilection to back up self-regulation with legislative powers. The OECD is behind moves to draw together different national perspectives into a coherent international framework. At a ministerial conference on electronic commerce in Ottawa in October 1998, representatives of its twenty-nine member countries agreed a vision of 'a borderless world, realizing the potential of global E-commerce'. It issued declarations on privacy, consumer protection and authentication. It agreed a structural, simple and fair tax system with no new discriminatory taxes on electronic commerce and the application of the traditional principle of taxing goods where they are consumed. The agenda will now be developed in small working groups.[17] Whether they will work fast enough to exert significant influence on a market that is evolving so quickly remains to be seen. The pace of technological change means that policy-makers must legislate with a light touch and resist temptation to interfere in markets that are largely supplier and user driven.

Teleworking

Teleworking is mostly stimulated by enterprise and community initiatives. At a national level, efforts are needed to make telework a more natural way of working. Governments can take a lead by demonstrating their own use of telework, and by removing legal barriers, such as anomalies in employment law. The Italian government passed laws in 1998 aimed at stimulating teleworking in public administration by making more flexible patterns of work permissible.

One of the most sustained public programmes has been that of the European Commission who over the last five years has had a number of initiatives to create awareness, conduct studies and promote pilot projects. The projects have included comparative reviews of laws in each country, projects to enable disabled people to gain employment through telework and projects to train SMEs in virtual working. Awareness has improved through a series of telework weeks, taking place each November. Since the first European Telework Week (ETW) in 1995, the scale has grown from thirty to over 300 events, with a corresponding growth in press and media coverage. Typical events are conferences, telecentre open days with videoconference links across countries and the launch of new community networks. In Holland there are national telework prizes culminating with an award ceremony on television. European-wide activities include an annual telework congress, on-line activities and the European Telework Awards, recognizing achievements such as teleworking's contribution to competitiveness and to sustainability, and the most original teleworking scheme. ETW emphasizes that telework, like electronic commerce, should be an integral strategy for achieving business competitiveness.

Another EU-supported telework initiative is European Telework Development (see page 111). It supports initiatives in many countries based on needs identified from its annual status reports. It works closely with suppliers, government agencies and local agencies. Its website provides comprehensive information about initiatives in twenty-five countries in fifteen languages.

Stimulating innovation

Governments have a long tradition of investing in research and development. However, as was discussed in Chapter 2, this is only the starting point of innovation and wealth creation. Attention needs to shift to R&D exploitation, and the creation of conditions for the complete innovation cycle to work well. This section indicates the types of initiative that are needed.

Updated industrial policies

Many developed Western countries have witnessed the decline of their traditional manufacturing base, such as steel-making, shipbuilding and car-making. Unfortunately industrial policy has often been geared to protecting and creating jobs in manufacturing. But this is a futile short-term expedient. Even high-tech computer factories in Ireland and semiconductor plants in north-east England have closed, some within ten years of opening.

In the global knowledge economy, countries must develop their own niches based on specialized knowledge. Even in a wired world, location does count. London hosts more international banks than any other city. High-speed networks are complemented by strong personal networks and a wide range of supporting service companies. Switzerland supports a unique niche in precision engineering, and Israel in defence-related software.

Industrial policy must therefore shift to creating knowledge hubs, and embedding the capabilities into local infrastructures, to minimize the possibility of wealth migration.

European framework programmes

The EU's five-year research and technology framework programmes have already been mentioned. From broad policy objectives, specific programmes and 'calls for proposal' are developed, against which interested consortia make bids for projects of their choosing. Many consortia contain a mix of university researchers and commercial companies, thus encouraging transfer of research knowledge into commercial activity, although commercialization as such is beyond the scope of EU funding. One of Europe's successes has undoubtedly been its leadership in mobile communications. Manufacturers have benefited from the strong stance taken on adopting the pan-European GSM standard. Companies such as

Ericsson, Siemens and Nokia have been active participants in framework projects.

The Fifth Framework programme starts in 1999 with funding of 14 billion ECU, and clearly shifts the emphasis to 'research at the service of the citizen and European competitiveness in a global framework'. Projects will be judged according to how well they meet economic and social objectives. Activities within the programme are grouped into three themes:

*   unlocking the resources of the living world and the ecosystems
*   creating a user-friendly information society
*   promoting competitive and sustainable growth.

Typical projects will address services for the citizen, new ways of working, electronic commerce, multimedia content and tools. A worthwhile feature of the latest programme is that it specifically encourages multidisciplinary activities, and puts socioeconomic considerations on a par with technology. However, critics still see such programmes as not attracting a sufficient number of entrepreneurial SMEs, the very companies who are at the forefront of innovation. Another EU programme, the innovation programme, may be more successful at this.

The EU innovation programme

Europe's innovation paradox is that it invests considerably in R&D, without commensurate returns. Whereas the USA and Japan have a trade surplus in high-technology goods of $150 billion, Europe's deficit is $25 billion. Patents, too, are much lower than would be expected from R&D spend. As a result the EU, under the direction of Commissioner Edith Cresson, launched its innovation programme in 1997.[18]

While the Commission notes that action for innovation 'is in the first instance the responsibility of citizens, of industry and of national, regional and local authorities', it identifies three central areas for action:

1   Fostering an innovation culture, through education, mobility for researchers, and propagation of best management practice.
2   Establishing a framework conducive for innovation, by simplifying the European patent system, access to a new finance and reducing the formalities for business start-ups.
3   Linking research more closely to innovation, by encouraging more intense co-operation between public, and private sectors, through campus companies, spin-offs etc.

By mid-1998 300 projects were under way, of which seventy had reached implementation. Examples include the marketing of a silent exhaust pipe and the development of a bio-monitoring instrument for assessing lake-water quality. Various innovation tools have also been developed, such as GOAL (Goal Oriented Project Planning) and BETTI (a benchmarking tool). In finance, EASDAQ, a European stock exchange backed by sixty financial institutions and modelled on NASDAQ, listed its first companies in November 1996.

While the programme is to be welcomed for some good plans and the closer involvement between technologists and users, it remains to be seen how much of an impact it will really have. In particular, will it create a truly entrepreneurial mindset amongst politicians and European businesses? The programme uses language strongly rooted in Industrial Age logic: 'technology transfer', 'benchmarking', 'best practices', etc. It needs to shift focus:

- from technology transfer to the innovation system as a whole
- from information society to the knowledge economy
- from the language of competitiveness to the practice of collaboration
- from training approaches to learning networks.

Innovation needs knowledge networks that cross sector boundaries. It needs an environment that motivates individuals to innovate, and where start-up entrepreneurs can access finance and incubate new businesses. Let's look at two types of programme that illustrate the above shifts and which more policy-makers should emulate.

Technopoles and incubators

Silicon Valley is perhaps the best known example of an innovation region. What supports innovative and entrepreneurial activities is a local infrastructure that draws together education, finance and business networks. It is not uncommon to discuss an idea with a venture capitalist at breakfast, create a new company by lunchtime, and have venture capital secured later the same day. Silicon Valley is an example of a technopole, a high-technology region which creates opportunities through collaboration between companies, research centres and technological support agencies. Another example is that of the Austin area of Texas (see page 262).

Business networks

Collaborative business networks are another source of innovation and economic development. One of the best examples is that of Denmark's

Austin: From backwater to technopolis

Once an industrial backwater, the state capital of Texas is now one of the high-tech regions of the world.[19] It hosts Dell's headquarters, Motorola's advanced semiconductor plant, key facilities for IBM and Hewlett-Packard, and is home to over 300 software companies. An early landmark in its transformation was the arrival of research consortium MCC in 1983. It selected Austin ahead of three other locations because of:

1   The university and the quality of its teaching.
2   The quality of life, including education, affordable housing, cultural and recreational amenities.
3   Airline connections to the major cities where MCC companies were located.
4   State and local government support.[20]

The development of Austin is a truly collaborative effort between the state university, leading industrialists, the state government and the entrepreneurial vision of George Kotzmetsky. The Institute of Creativity and Capital (IC^2) is a centre of expertise in technology transfer and business creation. It carries out research and runs masters degree courses in science and technology commercialization. The Centre for Commercialization and Enterprise (C^2E) was spun off in 1989 as part of a model to develop an infrastructure to launch globally successful high-technology firms. Help for new companies is provided through new educational programmes and the Austin Technology Incubator. By December 1992, it had created 350 new technology jobs at an investment of only $2000 a job, and raised over $60 million in external capital. Budding entrepreneurs can access a wide range of know-how, and have access to a thriving business capital network. The incubator has now spawned over fifty new companies generating annual revenues in excess of $185 million. Its knowledge of the commercialization of technology has been transferred through several collaborative partnerships including one with the Technology Transfer and Innovation Centre in Moscow. More recent local collaborative initiatives are the Austin Multimedia Incubator, the Entrepreneurs Association, and the Austin Software Council.

Business Networks. What started as a government initiative in 1988, rapidly evolved so that by the mid-1990s more than 25 000 of Denmark's small and mid-size firms were active in over 1000 networks. A key feature is a network centre that stimulates the formation of an individual network. These centres provide various co-ordinating activities, such as providing a network broker who brings together firms with complementary competencies. They also offer development and marketing services, and help networks and member firms gain access to funding. What has also been found to be important is the value of a broker support infra-structure. It is also recognized that there needs to be better sharing of best practice amongst brokers, and more performance monitoring and quality control. Since the introduction of these networks, Denmark's position in comparative league tables of national competitiveness has jumped from low in the tables to fifth position.

The Danish model has also been taken, with some success, elsewhere. The Avon Network Centre in south-west England is one example. It markets and promotes business networking, and provides business advis-ers and network brokers. Within two years of starting Avon had eight networks in place involving forty enterprises, with twenty potential networks involving a further 100.

Actors and roles

The largest impediment to progress towards creating a prosperous knowledge economy is the networking between various actors. Inadequate knowledge results in lack of mutual understanding and in inadequate pooling of the competencies needed to innovate. There are several groups of actors who should be collaborating much more.

The contribution of enterprise

The primary focus of commercial organizations is generally considered to be wealth creation for their shareholders. However, organizations of all types have great reservoirs of knowledge that should be made more widely available for societal benefits. Enterprises should pool their knowledge through partnership with other stakeholders through:

- Contributing to education – encouraging employees to spend time helping local schools; contributing expertise to new curriculum materials; providing work experience opportunities; participating in policy forums to shape the future of education.
- Community involvement – many companies do not do this until they are of a certain size, or need the help of a community, such as support for locating a new office. However, their inputs are valuable in building community knowledge infrastructures (see below).
- Participating in policy bodies, public agencies and forums – many policy bodies can benefit from professional business input. Two-way benefits are

achieved when individuals provide expertise on a regular basis and gain
personal development opportunities in return.
- Secondments and exchange – encouraging employees to spend time in
  government departments, education establishments, and vice versa. This
  may take the form of a period for exchange, say six months, or regular
  involvement on a part-time basis.

Many organizations are already doing these things to some extent. But,
they need to happen more extensively and with a wider range of employees, including young professionals. Many growing companies feel they
cannot afford to divert key people to such activities. Therefore, tax incentives might help.

Government roles

Governments have three main roles:

1 Regulator – providing a legal and regulatory framework that is neither
   too restrictive that it stifles innovation, nor too *laissez-faire* that it allows
   dominant forces to prevail.
2 Actor – stimulating the development of knowledge markets and
   enterprises, including the Internet, teleworking, electronic commerce and
   innovation.
3 Intelligent user – being a good provider, customer, and partner in
   knowledge initiatives.

This is the order in which many governments concentrate their efforts
when confronting new situations. However, it needs reversing. Many
senior policy-makers are woefully ignorant of the dramatic changes
taking place around them. They need personal hands-on experience of
tools such as the Internet. Each level of government has its part to play.

Local government
Community initiatives, like those of the SBLN described earlier in this
chapter, are where much innovation is taking place. Local government
must be actively involved in creating the knowledge infrastructure –
high-speed telecommunications, a range of education institutions and the
development of community networks. They can often be the stimulus for
bringing actors together and in identifying gaps, such as lack of continuing education in new knowledge-based skills. They should also participate actively in various international initiatives, such as Manchester has
done in the Digital Cities programme.

Manchester – a digital city

For nearly a decade, Manchester has promoted itself as 'the information city'. An earlier initiative, the Manchester HOST, stimulated inner city economic development through access to IT services. A disused warehouse was the location for computer-based bulletin boards and support services. The project reached out to suburbs through its electronic village halls, and catered for minority groups such as women's groups and the ethnic Bangladeshi community. One initiative to emerge from these early efforts was the Manchester Asian Trading Information network. It has improved the viability of trading links between the Asian community in Manchester and corresponding communities in South Asia, as well as initiating social and cultural links. Companies in Bangladesh that use these links are in textiles, graphic design, chemicals telecommunications and handicrafts. One problem encountered was poor access to telecommunications. This prompted their Manchester-based partners to expedite the provision of local dial-up lines and Internet nodes in Bangladesh.

Manchester is not alone in promoting such environments. Throughout Europe there is now a thriving Digital Cities programme that started in 1995. A similar initiative in New York transformed a former bank building into a powerful local technological and business infrastructure, involving all sections of the community. The Mayor of Stockholm has been instrumental in stimulating and giving visibility to such initiatives, through the Bangemann challenge,[21] now an annual competition to find the best city exemplars of the information society in action.

National governments

Though few national governments will admit it, power in the knowledge economy diffuses both upwards and downwards – to supranational bodies and local communities. However, they have an important role as a knowledge hub. They should provide on-line services to citizens and businesses, and develop on-line democracy. Almost every policy area needs updating to take account of the new realities. Education needs to combine IT literacy, new knowledge networks and lifelong learning. Economic development policies must change from attracting inward investment of jobs, to creating sustainable knowledge infrastructures that attract innovative knowledge-based companies. They must start measuring the economy with the new indicators. Nova Scotia, for example, has developed knowledge quotients for its economy. Governments must support international moves towards legislative harmonization in key areas such as intellectual property and electronic commerce.

International government and agencies
The role of the EU in various information society initiatives has already
been noted. Other regions, with their unique characteristics, could also
benefit from similar concerted actions. The main developments, though,
are likely to come through international agencies that have the broad
support of many governments. These include the International
Telecommunications Union, the World Trade Organization, the OECD
and the World Bank.

Community initiatives

It is appropriate to finish coverage on public policy with this topic. For
it is communities, both local communities based on geography, and global
communities based on domains of knowledge, that are likely to be the
main shapers of our future society. The Web and other virtual environments create the spaces for knowledge communities to form. However, if
they are to reach their full potential they must go beyond mere knowledge exchange and develop collaborative agendas. Examples have been
noted earlier – KEN, CommerceNet, SBLN, etc. All demonstrate how
knowledge networking creates benefits for their participants and those
with whom they interact. Successful communities follow the principles
described in Chapters 6 and 8. They need a compelling vision, effective
structures and processes, a good knowledge infrastructure and, above all,
leadership.

Communities which make the most impact in the wider world will
engage contributors from all walks of life – business, academia, government and the ordinary citizen. They need enrichment from all generations, all cultures and all regions of the world. They are knowledge
networks within larger knowledge networks. They are a microcosm of
the way that many of tomorrow's institutions will be formed and operate.
A crucial part of their agenda is that they therefore share their knowledge
about creating sustainable communities.

Summary

The prosperity of individuals, enterprises and whole nations in the
knowledge economy, depends on creating the conditions in which knowledge-based enterprises and entrepreneurial individuals can thrive. Too
frequently the focus of policy-makers is on regulation and legislation.
However, this chapter has given examples, from business networks in

Denmark to high-tech regions such as Austin, Texas, where policy-makers have been active partners in stimulating knowledge-based initiatives that help create wealth. There are several prerequisites for creating the right conditions:

- *Recognition of today's realities* – that the knowledge economy is different and that policies that worked in the past are unlikely to do so in the future.
- *All sectors must be involved* – creating prosperity requires closer collaboration between business, government, academic and research institutions.
- *Initiatives at all levels* – top down and bottom up; high levels of leadership to provide vision and inspiration must be complemented by ground level activity by committed individuals working through personal, business and community networks.
- *Transnational collaboration* – most opportunities and problems are not unique to a given locality.

The challenge facing anyone involved with policy-making is to develop appropriate transnational institutions which, while providing an overall global framework, do not enmesh themselves too closely with detailed regulation that stifles ground-level entrepreneurial activities.

Notes

1 World Bank (1998). *World Development Report 1998/99: Knowledge*. Oxford University Press.
2 World Economic Forum (1998). *Global Competitiveness Report, 1998*. WEF, May; IMD (1998). *World Competitiveness Yearbook, 1998*. IMD, Lausanne, June.
3 Massachusetts Technology Collaborative (1997). *New Index of the Massachusetts Innovation Economy* at htpp://www.mtpc.org (October).
4 Kozmetsky, G. (1994). *Technology Transfer in a Global Context*. Working Paper No. 294-04-01, Institute of Creativity and Capital, University of Texas at Austin.
5 Gore, A. (1993). *The National Information Infrastructure: Agenda for Action*. National Telecommunications and Information Administration, Washington.
6 Hof, R. D. (1998). The 21st century economy: keeping growth strong. Special Feature, *Business Week*, 31 August, pp. 108–109.
7 European Commission (1997). *ACTS 97 Overview*. DG XIII-B, EC, August. Information and project descriptions can be obtained from the ACTS Information Window (INFOWIN) website http://www.uk.infowin.org/acts/
8 Moran, N. (1998). Tensions rise between governments and the world of business. *Financial Times*, FT-IT, 1 April, XII.

9   European Commission (1993). *Growth, Competitiveness, Employment: The Challenges and Way Forward into the 21st Century.*

10 European Commission (1994). *Europe and the Global Information Society: Recommendations to the European Council.* EC, 26 May, p. 3. On line at http://www.ispo.cec.be/infosoc/backg/bangeman.html.

11 European Commission (1994). *Europe's Way to the Information Society: An Action Plan.* COM(94) 347 final, July.

12 European Commission (1997). *Europe at the Forefront of the Global Information Society: Rolling Action Plan.* EC.

13 An index of projects are at http://www.g7.fed.us/. Details of progress can be found at http://www.ispo.be/

14 G7 Inventory of Projects at http://www.gip.int

15 Commercenet at http://www.commercenet.com/

16 European Commission (1997). *A European Initiative on Electronic Commerce.* Communication to the European Parliament, COM(97)157.

17 Various reports and working papers are available at http://www.ottawa-conference.org. Included are 'Activities and initiatives in E-commerce' and 'Global action plan for e-commerce', with business recommendations for governments.

18 European Commission (1997). *Towards the 5th Framework Programme: Scientific and Technological Objectives.* European Commission Working Paper COM(97)47, CEC, Brussels, February. Online at http://www.cordis.lu/fifth/src/47-en-1.htm

19 Texas surpassed New York in 1997, to become second only to California in the number of high-tech jobs – 313 000 (*Wall Street Journal*, 5 March 1997).

20 Gibson, D. V. (1994). *R&D Collaboration on Trial: The Microelectronic and Computer Technology Corporation.* Harvard Business School Press.

21 Global Bangemann Challenge at http://www.challenge.stockholme.se

Chapter 10

Forward to the future

The future is full of uncertainties. During the course of writing this book, the Asian economic miracle has taken a battering, the whiz kids of Wall Street took a hedge too far, and some commentators are questioning whether the new knowledge economy is really any different from the old. While some of these changes may seem remote to our daily lives, various interdependencies mean that they are ultimately likely to affect us one way or another. Thus, we may find more Western jobs migrate to Asia or we may find it more difficult to borrow money from our bank. So what can we say with certainty about the future of the knowledge agenda?

I spend much of my time analysing developments in technologies and business practice and am regularly asked to make forecasts of their impact. This chapter is no exception. It will give some of my personal projections of how the knowledge agenda will unfold. But this is only one person's perspective and viewpoint at a particular moment. Therefore the forecasts are prefaced with some general views on how to plan for the future. The book concludes with a review of the challenges facing us, and how we might work collaboratively together to create a future that is prosperous for us all, whatever our desires and values.

Forecasting the future

Forecasting is a huge business. Organizations spend millions of dollars annually with analysts, researchers and consultants for economic and market forecasts. Some of the most expensive are the predictions of sizes

Table 10.1 Examples of two divergent Internet scenarios

150 million users (year end 2000)	500 million users
Service providers or key telecommunications services have Y2K problems that disrupt traffic	Digital TVs offer Internet access as a standard feature, so more consumers access it
A better method of estimating users is developed, indicating that the 7:1 algorithm (host:users) was wrong all along	Kanji-like editors become affordable so the Chinese and Japanese markets expand rapidly
The Internet is replaced by an alternative broadband technology and networks	Internet use is mandated as part of the curriculum in China's schools
Congestion at routers makes it so slow that serious users abandon it	On-line shopping by consumers rises dramatically as retailers go on-line
There are battles between interconnection providers, so that the current free exchange of messages at hubs does not take place	Retailers install Internet terminals at sales counters to check on-line catalogues
Consumer interest wanes; people find more important things to do with their time	Far East on-line shopping hubs attract many regular shoppers
Governments start to impose taxes on data transmission.	Micropayment mechanisms boost electronic markets
	Internet access is built into household appliances and automatic vending machines

and values of different product markets. Research companies are happy to comply, and provide apparently authoritative tables of data neatly presented to two-decimal figure accuracy. When pushed many of them admit that the data is merely an aggregation of what each supplier expects to sell. Some do have more sophisticated models that take into account consumer demand and behaviour, but in the event, and with the advantage of hindsight, many of these forecasts are wildly wrong. Few customers of such data seriously analyse in retrospect the accuracy of what they bought. My own experience is that in boom times forecasters overestimate, and in leaner times underestimate. In other words there is a great human tendency to extrapolate into the future the world as we see it today.

Let me give a recent example. An industry analyst forecast in mid-1998 that 327 million people are expected to be accessing the Internet by the end of the year 2000. If you take the estimated number of Internet users in 1995 and project an annual compound growth of 50 per cent (which had been the growth rate in the preceding few years), you would arrive at something pretty close. My two quick calculations using slightly different starting figures came to 300 million and 337 million. What would be more interesting, and gives real insight, is to devise different scenarios as to why it might be only 150 million or as high as 500 million, each of which has rational explanations (Table 10.1).

Thus, the 327 million scenario implies that many of the changes suggested in each column of Table 10.1 do not happen, or that there are counterbalancing factors that boost or dampen demand beyond today's smooth trend line. This approach of developing alternative scenarios is a technique that Shell has been using for more than two decades. At a time when industry forecasters were projecting an inevitable rise in oil prices, planners at Shell devised a plausible scenario for a significantly reduced oil price. This actually happened with the collapse of consensus among the oil producers in the Organization of Petroleum Exporting Countries (OPEC).[1] More important than the scenario prediction was the process of scenario-building, since it forced a dialogue between external experts and Shell managers that gave them greater understanding of the different factors influencing the price of oil. As Dwight D. Eisenhower is said to have remarked: 'plans are nothing; planning is everything'. In the same vein, despite some problems, Shell today is widely recognized as a good exemplar of the learning organization and is heavily involved in knowledge communities. In contrast, those organizations that take forecasts at face value without exploring the factors and assumptions beneath them are not developing the knowledge they need to use them effectively.

Flexibility

Responsiveness, adaptability and flexibility are characteristics that have been echoed at several places in this book. Having detailed reliable forecasts or intelligence on which to base your plans matters less if you have the flexibility to adapt as the outcomes change. A useful planning grid to help determine your intelligence needs is shown in Figure 10.1. Your overall investment in external intelligence gathering or in buying ever more refined market data depends on the overall level of business impact of a bad forecast and your ability to respond to changes. If, once an external change is detected, it takes too long to respond relative to the impact of the change, then contingency planning and early warning signals are needed to minimize the risk of error. On the other hand if you can respond quickly, then a systematic external monitoring system

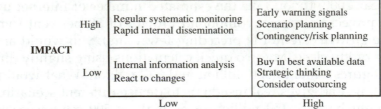

		Low	High
IMPACT	High	Regular systematic monitoring Rapid internal dissemination	Early warning signals Scenario planning Contingency/risk planning
	Low	Internal information analysis React to changes	Buy in best available data Strategic thinking Consider outsourcing

Low   High
TIME TO RESPOND

Figure 10.1   Intelligence needs grid

coupled with effective analysis and good internal knowledge flows may be all that is necessary. Whatever part of the grid you are in, it pays to invest in appropriate knowledge sharing and refining processes, so that the external information is knowledgeably analysed. However, your best investment may be in creating more organizational flexibility, through increased networking and virtualization.

Futurizing

Where do forecasts go wrong? In a classic paper Michel Godet puts it down to people not reacting or behaving as expected: 'The inadequacy of "classical" forecasting techniques can be exemplified by their downplaying, or outright ignoring, of the role played by creative human actions in determining the future.'[2]

He then goes on to say that there are multiple possible futures, and that the resulting outcome is shaped by human action. In 'la prospective' approach, the future is actively created and not forecast. By using scenarios as a tool to create alternative futures, people and organizations can determine which ones they want to help bring about through the involvement of the influential actors.

It is this perspective that Skandia has adopted in an approach it calls 'futurizing'. Its innovations are not only shaping its own future but are influencing the whole insurance industry and beyond. In May 1996 the first Skandia Future Centre (SFC) was opened at Vaxholm on the Stockholm archipelago: 'And despite its location on the periphery – geographically speaking – in terms of the global flow of ideas it is right in the centre. Through SFC – eventually also in other locations in the world – Skandia aims to advance its position in the market and innovatively create its future instead of being surprised by it.'[3]

Futurizing involves bringing together futures teams, that comprise individuals drawn from different groups in Skandia and who represent the 3Gs (three generation age groups of twenties, thirties and forty-plus), different competencies and geographic perspectives. They view the future as 'an ocean of unexploited opportunity' and think creatively of how Skandia might innovate in it. They also involve external 'competence partners' in this innovation process which starts, not from Skandia's existing products, but from a perspective of different future worlds and the life stages of its customers. A visitor to the centre enters through a door that resembles the bow of a ship. Inside is a layout designed for thinking and knowledge exchange. Furniture is comfortable, room layout is flexible, and there are high-tech facilities to record the structured dialogue that is steered by experienced facilitators. All help to create an informal yet purposeful atmosphere where participants are committed to creating the future. The challenge I pose to all readers of this book is, how can we collaboratively futurize a prosperous future enhanced by knowledge?

Scenario development

A technique that can play a useful role in futurizing is that of scenario planning. Typically it involves a number of iterative phases such as the following:

1   Analysis of trends and anticipation of potential discontinuities in the wider environment – economic, political, regulatory, technology, social and demographic, environmental. A discontinuity is something dramatic, such as a major earthquake in California or a collapse in financial markets.
2   Determining the inter-relationship between different variables. This depends on the relative strength and direction of different drivers and inhibitors, and the actions of key influencers. Techniques such as cross-impact analysis can be used to identify clusters of reinforcing trends.
3   Development of alternative scenarios that combine different sets of trends and discontinuities. Mostly these will result in a point of divergence along a trend line, e.g. oil prices continue to increase vs a collapse in oil prices.
4   Creation of event strings. These are pathways through time with the occurrence of events that cause the scenarios to unfold.
5   Drawing together the different strands into a cohesive story. Story-telling is a powerful method of conveying and discussing scenarios. They can either describe a future state or how we go from here to there.

Although scenarios are backed up by hard data and forecasts, their richness comes from the creative thinking of participants and constructive dialogue. In the Open University's MBA course on the external environment, students develop scenarios in groups, using on-line computer conferencing as a tool. Over the years some very instructive scenarios of the wider global business environment have been developed.[4] Let us now consider some trends in the knowledge movement and what scenarios might result.

Knowledge futures

Many developments in knowledge management have been driven by technological advances. However, its current relevance in most organizations is largely due to the way that good knowledge management can contribute to topical business issues, such as the need for efficiency and the drive for improved products and services. It is part of many important management activities – managing information (explicit/recorded knowledge), managing processes (embedded knowledge), managing people (tacit knowledge), managing innovation (knowledge conversion), managing assets (intellectual capital). Each can benefit by more explicit consideration of the knowledge dimension. Its pivotal role is leading to a convergence of different developments that are in turn leading to some discernible trends.

Ten trends in knowledge management

1   *From a dimension of other disciplines to a recognized discipline in its own right.* Since knowledge offers a unifying perspective over many different management disciplines we can expect to see knowledge management emerge as a subject in its own right. Already modules are being developed in degree and MBA courses and professors of knowledge Management are being appointed.

2   *From strategic initiative to routine practice.* The CKOs of the future (if they exist) will embrace some of the functions of today's human resource managers and chief information officers. Not only will there be specialist knowledge roles, such as knowledge editors or knowledge brokers, every professional and manager will need some essential knowledge skills to be proficient in their job.

3   *From an inward focus on knowledge sharing to an external focus on creating value.* As organizations gain efficiency through better sharing of best practice and other knowledge, their focus will shift to creating value. They will better understand the contribution of knowledge to business performance and apply and repackage it in creative ways for customer

---

benefit. They will spawn entirely new lines of businesses based predominantly on knowledge. For example, a manufacturer of engineered products might create an engineering consultancy business.

4 *From best practices to breakthrough practices.* Sharing best practice gives incremental improvements in performance, usually of the order of 10–30 per cent per year. Copying what others are doing is a prescription for mediocrity. True market leadership comes through innovating with breakthrough practices that achieve improvements of tenfold or more in key areas, such as time to market, and functionality per unit cost. This is what every organization should strive for, as such achievements are not uncommon.

5 *From knowledge processes to knowledge objects.* Computer applications are moving to object orientation, where the focus is on entities and how their state is changed, rather than on procedures. Expect more packaging of knowledge as objects that might include a chunk of information record, a multimedia clip and personal contact hyperlinks. Knowledge objects can be combined, manipulated and transmitted in different ways. Markets will be created where knowledge objects can be bought and sold (such as in project Alba described on page 279).

6 *From intellectual capital to tradable knowledge assets.* Many companies will start to identify and measure their intellectual capital – in databases, in human competencies, trademarks etc. Once identified these then become opportunities for packaging and resale, perhaps several times over. For example, publishers have sold their mailing lists for many years, but many other companies are now realizing the opportunities from trading their databases, e.g. fleet car managers and car reliability information.

7 *From knowledge centres to knowledge hubs and networks.* Although aggregating knowledge and knowledgeable people at knowledge centres gives critical mass, a more effective model may well be local nodes of expertise interconnected through human and computer networks, i.e. the virtual knowledge centre.

8 *From knowledge maps to knowledge navigators/agents.* Maps are static representations of objects, and without extensive real-time map-making capability (which could happen in the future) we need other ways to find existing and emerging knowledge. These will be human brokers (people with know-where and know-who), navigation aids on websites and increasingly intelligent software agents that dynamically seek out changing and new knowledge.

9 *From knowledge communities to knowledge markets.* Knowledge communities provide an effective vehicle for knowledge exchange. But as knowledge acquires value, and becomes 'productized' as objects

(Trend 5) these communities will develop payment mechanisms and other trappings of a marketplace. The phrase 'a penny for your thoughts' may assume real meaning as people have microchips embedded under their skin which handle knowledge transfer and micropayments under directives from the human brain!

10 *From knowledge management to knowledge innovation.* Knowledge management as a transition phase to something more fundamental. Management implies custodianship and managing what you know – innovation is creating something new and better, and that surely must be the ambition of all of us.

Source: I³ UPDATE (No. 20), June 1998 at
http://www.skyrme.com/updates/u20.htm

These specific trends are just one perspective of what is happening in the wider knowledge agenda. As noted in Chapter 1, today's knowledge agenda emerges from several evolving megatrends. It is the result of a confluence of developments in the socioeconomic environment, management thinking and technology (Figure 10.2).

As practised in organizations, knowledge management is, as has been demonstrated in Part C of this book, a blend of hard and soft factors such as ICT insfrastructures and organizational culture. Recently apparent among leading practitioners are more sense of cultural aspects, the traditions of oral story-telling and the influence of academic thinking. Current best practice in knowledge management is daily becoming more widely known, through conferences, books, articles and the sharing of knowledge by successful practitioners. However, if collectively we are to develop better futures through knowledge, what should now be the focus

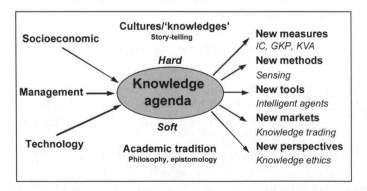

Figure 10.2   The evolving knowledge agenda

of our thinking and experimentation? What should we plan to embed into future practice? I suggest the following five themes:

- *New measures.* As is happening at the enterprise level in Skandia and at country level through the work of organizations like the OECD, the WEF and the IMD, non-financial measures that will guide us to the future need to be developed. Intellectual capital measures are a start, but we need other measures such as KVA (knowledge value-added) and GKP (gross knowledge product).
- *New methods.* Many enterprises have quickly recognized that knowledge initiatives are not simply making information accessible on an intranet, but also involve changes in human behaviour and culture. New methods and practices are needed in almost every aspect of office work – running meetings using structured dialogue, developing better ways of sensing significance in a sea of data.
- *New tools.* Chapter 3 highlighted many technological solutions that enlarge the scope of knowledge from individuals to the organization as a whole, such as document management, computer conferencing and knowledge management suites. New tools that will work more intuitively and symbiotically with humans to enhance individual knowledge and understanding include intelligent agents, visualization and mapping tools.
- *New markets.* New electronic markets will evolve as places to exchange and commercially trade domain-specific knowledge. They will provide for trading of explicit knowledge (information) as well as giving access to communities and individual experts.
- *New perspectives.* The pivotal role of knowledge in all aspects of society, not just in business, means that individuals and organizations will need to take a much wider perspective of the environment in which knowledge is used. A key strand that is likely to emerge is that of knowledge ethics, raising issues over the ownership and governance of knowledge, and how important knowledge can be made widely available for the public good.

Several of these themes have already been covered in earlier chapters. Knowledge markets and knowledge ethics merit more attention here.

Knowledge markets

The selling of explicit knowledge on-line in the form of information is not new. But developments on the Internet will increase the variety and scope significantly. With micropayment mechanisms, it will be possible for people to find and pay for relatively small amounts of information or knowledge, costing perhaps only a few cents, on a pay-as-you-go basis.

It will also be possible to sell virtual consultancy, on-line advice by the minute or per problem solved, and run collaborative knowledge events. Precursors of such markets are those of Knowledgeshop, iqport and ideaMarket.[5] These have knowledge stores where content creators have deposited information and other knowledge products, and details of on-line events. Knowledge providers receive royalty payments of up to 50 per cent as items are bought.

However, even these are rudimentary compared with what is possible. Imagine a networked consultancy like TelTech (page 55) operating entirely on the Internet with connections being made in real time and pricing taking place dynamically according to supply and demand. Developing a vision along these lines is Bright: 'the network for smarter networking'.[6] Primarily focusing on the domain of leading edge management knowledge, its key elements are:

- an accreditation process by which information assets are reviewed by experts, graded and priced with consent from the provider;
- a content 'wrapper' that provides information about the content of the knowledge asset; this is classified and indexed according to a knowledge thesaurus; the content might simply be the credentials and contact details for an expert consultant (a piece of know-who);
- a technology platform (iqport) for secure trading that allows pay-per-view and micropayments, and provides billing services that enable content providers, the platform provider, intermediaries, accreditors and others to receive a percentage of the revenues;
- dynamic pricing according to supply and demand;
- web conferencing tools for virtual collaboration, running communities and on-line events.

Such a development is indicative of the trend to package knowledge objects for resale. Another example is that of trading designs in the semiconductor industry (see panel opposite).

Knowledge ethics and governance

Ethical considerations are growing in importance in many organizations. They recognize their role in being part of an inclusive society in which the profit motive is not the be all and end all. They have to meet the aspiration of a broad group of stakeholders and trade in a manner consistent with the values of the communities within which they operate. Ethical considerations also arise in knowledge management. How far should an organization exploit an individual's prior or private knowledge

---

Alba – an example of intellectual property trading

The semiconductor industry is a good example of the trade in intellectual property. The next generation of computers will be based on systems on a chip. These combine functions that conventionally are on different chips and linked on a circuit board. Development times and costs are reduced by reusing subcomponents from different chips and mixing and matching them in new ways. The design and marketing of subcomponents, which are in effect blocks of intellectual property (IP), has become an industry in itself. A collaborative initiative between Scottish Enterprise, Cadence Design Systems, IBM and other organizations, project Alba provides an electronic network that provides a market place for these virtual components. Intellectual property blocks are traded and new designs can be validated to check that they do not infringe existing IP.

---

for its own benefit? What rights does an employee have to share in the rewards of such knowledge? A frequently cited reason against knowledge sharing is the concerns of some individuals that the organization want to pump them for all they are worth and then dispense with their services.

Such issues, though, pale into insignificance when the ownership of knowledge for the public good is concerned. How much should knowledge that can widely benefit the human race be kept as proprietary knowledge that is tightly controlled by an owner trying to maximize their commercial interests? Nowhere more stark is this debate than in the field of biotechnology and genetic engineering. Pharmaceutical companies are hunting down ancient tribal remedies based on the knowledge of the medicinal properties of plants, with a view to patenting them. Patents are also being sought for naturally occurring genes. Commenting on this emerging field of bio-prospecting, Tim McGirk writing in *Time* asks: 'Should a government, company or scientist have the right to claim ownership to the innermost workings of a living organism?'[7]

Proponents argue that finding the right genetic material is like finding a needle in a haystack and this effort should be justly rewarded, e.g. through patent protection. Others question what benefits will be shared with a tribe like the Onge tribe of the Indian Ocean whose herbal brew may hold the key to a cure for malaria.

Another example that has caused much heated debate is that of so-called terminator technology, where genetic engineering produces seeds that produce only one crop. The offspring seeds do not germinate, so farmers have to buy new seeds from the supplier each year. The terminator patent is jointly owned by Delta & Pine Land (D&PL), a subsidiary of Monsanto, and the US Department of Agriculture, since the technology development was jointly developed with support from public research funds. When D&PL sought exclusive licensing rights, there was an outcry against such commercial exploitation of what opponents called an 'immoral technology' and the need to protect 'the fundamental right of farmers to save seed and breed crops', especially poor farmers in rural economies.[8] The organization orchestrating a worldwide protest, Winnipeg-based Rural Advancement Foundation International (RAFI), commits itself to 'the sustainable improvement of bio-diversity and the socially responsible development of technologies useful to rural societies'. The recent developments in patenting genetic knowledge have raised its concerns about the impact of intellectual property rights on world food security.

There are other issues of knowledge governance that raise their heads owing to technological advances. How should knowledge markets, as discussed above, be regulated? What controls are needed to tame 'wild agents' – autonomous intelligent agents with undesirable characteristics that either through poor design or malice roam networks causing havoc with legitimate trading? IBM research has already shown that agents who trade with each other, left to their own devices, are likely to create wild fluctuations in market prices.

An existing knowledge market, financial futures, gives a foretaste of the challenges that lie ahead. Finance is a key resource in today's economy. Yet it has moved well beyond its initial role of a medium of exchange or a key factor of production (one of the trio: land, labour and capital). Money is a tradable commodity. For years there have been markets in stocks and shares, bonds, foreign exchange. Now there are markets in financial futures and a whole host of other ingeniously devised financial derivatives. These products are the result of knowledge innovation, the creative application of knowledge. These markets, as noted earlier, are only peripherally connected to other markets such as that in goods and services. In the UK, for example, the daily trade in derivatives is half of the country's annual GDP. What value does such trading bring to furthering a true knowledge society where desirable outcomes are successful businesses of all sorts and quality of life for citizens?

Traders in financial derivatives leverage large amounts of finance from small investments. Market values fluctuate significantly and fortunes are made and lost almost in microseconds. Economics Nobel prize-winners provided the fundamental ideas behind derivatives trading at Long-Term Capital Management (LTCM). But more established financial institutions had to bail it out as its financial position became untenable. In the regular stock market, intervention has been needed to halt computer trading when price swings get too violent. Will knowledge markets evolve in the same way, needing bodies to govern them, analogous to the Securities and Exchange Commission?

Knowledge scenarios

Consideration of the trends and issues described earlier leads to several possible scenarios of how the networked knowledge economy might develop:

- *Money rules OK.* The knowledge economy never materializes to any great degree. The emergence of third world countries into newly industrialized nations and people's innate desire for material goods sustains value in traditional goods and services. Scarcity in key materials, the power of financial institutions and large conglomerates, and nations at war, all restrict investment in knowledge industries and help reinforce traditional vehicles of wealth.

- *Knowledge rich vs knowledge poor.* A divided world with knowledge haves and knowledge have nots. Traditional economies coexist with the new. Within developed countries society is divided between the educated rich who have global connections, access to knowledge and latest technology and those who simply survive at subsistence level. Imbalances in regulation lead to a reinforcing cycle of continued investment in knowledge rich countries. Today, for example, Pfizer refuses to invest in India because of its weak IPR regime.

- *Techno-dependency.* The world becomes over-reliant on technology, which increasingly lets us down in unexpected ways. First, there are relatively minor disruptions in telecommunications traffic and a small percentage of companies go out of business because of the millennium bug. Later, weak points in the Internet give way causing more disruption. A foretaste of this occurred in August 1997, when human errors caused failures of significant portions of the Internet. This is compounded by intelligent agents playing havoc in previously stable enterprise computer systems. Intellectual energy is diverted simply to restoring stability in systems and reverting to the relatively stable computing environment of the late 1990s.

- *Knowledge idealists vs knowledge imperialists.* Two types of community emerge based on different value sets. One recognizes the commercial value of knowledge and believes that it should be traded as any other economic commodity. The other believes in knowledge as a public good. It pitches big corporations with financial power against individuals or collectives, as in the clashes already noted in the field of genetic patenting. The idealists create self-contained enclaves or knowledge kibbutzim networked globally into an alternative economy.

- *A collaborative sustainable knowledge economy.* All nations and individuals with different value-sets harmonize their differences to address common global problems and coexist peacefully. Concerted intelligence is directed to addressing both the economic problems of the third world and the environmental problems of the developed world. There is high investment in lifelong education and knowledge-intensive activities around the world. There is universal access to basic information and knowledge, yet mechanisms to give knowledge creators and exploiters due rewards. There is more equality of opportunity and less imbalance between rich and poor, yet meaningful incentives for individuals to achieve more than average prosperity. Everybody achieves personal fulfilment.

At the time of writing, any of these seems a potential alternative. As the future unfolds and our understanding of the knowledge economy improves, other plausible futures may become apparent. Equally there may be scenarios that combine elements found in each of the ones above. For example, some groups or even countries may exclude themselves from the third scenario and become the knowledge-rich of the second. Although my personal preference is for the last scenario, this is will only happen if there is a collective will to make it happen, combined with commitment and access to knowledge and other resources.

Knowledge networks for knowledge

As the interest in knowledge grows, there is a corresponding growth in the number of networks and communities that are collaboratively exploring the developments and addressing the implications. The Knowledge Ecology Network (KEN), mentioned in Chapter 6, has over 300 members organized into small groups that are developing guidelines, creating knowledge architectures and looking at the needs of knowledge professionals. Created by George Pór and colleagues at Co-I-L (Community Intelligence Laboratories) it uses web conferencing (Caucus) to gel a network of knowledge professionals from around the world to further the ideal of 'unleashing the capacity of knowledge professional to self-organize into a global network of mutually supportive relationships'. It plans various knowledge products and services that will help both individuals and organizations gain value through knowledge. Other networks and individuals are thinking along similar lines – of elevating knowledge networking from a narrow organisational perspective to a broader base socioeconomic force that can change the world.

Kenniscentrum CIBIT in Holland, is host for the International Knowledge Network. It is aimed more squarely at promoting good knowledge management practice within organizations. It runs events, carries out regular studies and runs a discussion forum. In fact there are a growing number of websites, such as Karl Erik Sveiby's (http://www.sveiby.com.au) that offer much useful information and opportunities for discussion (see Postscript A).

Another organization is the Washington-based Knowledge Management Consortium (KMC).[9] A society of knowledge managers, practitioners, and scientists, it brings together individuals and organizations 'to develop a shared vision, common understanding, and aligned action about knowledge and knowledge management'. It has groups working on standards and is developing a certification programme for knowledge managers and knowledge management engineers, professionals, technologists and instructors. It now has chapters in several countries.

As knowledge management grows in importance, we can expect to see many more such organizations and networks vying for the attention of professionals. Like other knowledge networks, teams will gel around key issues and agenda items. The networks and teams will interconnect through boundary spanning individuals, and their activities will overlap and co-ordinate in different ways. There is one network, however, that has a vision that goes farther than any of these. It has a programme that to my mind epitomizes the essence of the networked knowledge economy, and will drive us towards the future of our final scenario – the sustainable networked knowledge economy. The network is the ENTOVATION Network of Global Knowledge Leaders and the programme is the development of the Global Knowledge Innovation Infrastructure (GKII).

Global Knowledge Innovation Infrastructure

The ENTOVATION Network is a network of over 3000 individuals in fifty-five countries around the world who have come into contact with the work of Debra Amidon and her vision of the knowledge innovation.[10] One of its unique features is that it transcends every business function, industry and region of the world. All have a contribution to make towards the collaborative enterprise of tomorrow. Core members from around the world were surveyed for the Global Knowledge Leadership Map (http://www.entovation.com/kleadmap/). Results were premiered at the Twentieth Annual McMaster Business Conference (20 January 1999) in Hamilton, Ontario, Canada, in a presentation 'Tour de Knowledge Monde.'

Representatives from over thirty countries responded with their reflections and aspirations. Their responses reflected many different perspectives but displayed some common threads. First, the transformation to the knowledge economy is more a function of behaviour and culture change than technology. Second, these changes are difficult, but well worth the effort. Amidon summarizes:

> Clearly, knowledge is seen as the engine for value-creation. What lies in the future is/must be grounded in values, competencies and the quality of relationships. It is an economy of open access rather than knowledge being perceived and managed as a 'private good.' The reasons are because of the bountiful nature of the resource and its quality to multiply as it is shared with others.
>
> This new economy we are innovating works for the people creating a world free of poverty, disease and violence. It is an economy directed toward sustainable development placing knowledge at the point of need or opportunity. It is an economy that is transnational in scope – balancing the local/national needs with a global scope. The driving mandate is one of creating a society with a better quality of life and increased standard of living worldwide. And the initiative begins with the individual – where knowledge resides![11]

How can this collective vision be built? Amidon argues the need for a specially built global infrastructure for knowledge and innovation. This is the premise behind the GKII, an idea first described in Chapter 10 of her book, *The Ken Awakening*. She envisages bringing together both practitioners and theorists into a community of knowledge practice – a 'world trade of ideas' – that reconciles the technological, behavioural and economic issues of participants from around the world.

The GKII will provide a vehicle to leverage the different competencies in ways that support local and global efforts simultaneously. In knowledge management work we have seen how good generic knowledge principles developed in one area, such as the US Army's 'After Action Review' can be successfully transferred into other enterprises, as at BP Amoco. The main focus of the GKII is therefore to provide forums for *structured dialogue* around the knowledge innovation. It will have a research agenda based on practical experimentation, host a world congress and launch knowledge innovation awards. The GKII was formally launched at the Banff Management Centre in Alberta, Canada, in November 1998. Banff's spectacular setting provides a great stimulus for creative thinking and inspiration while the not-for-profit Banff Centre provides a unique blend of three kinds of knowledge – the Centre for Management, the Centre for Cultural and Performing Arts and the Centre for the Environment. Geographically it is a bridge between East and West.

The GKII is perhaps the ultimate exemplar of a knowledge network to build the collaborative enterprise. Globally dispersed participants will bring their knowledge to bear on key problems and issues in the form of a global learning 'collaboratory' (a contraction of collaboration laboratory). Prototypes will be developed of new knowledge. Ideas will be converted into action, either new processes or perhaps collaboratively created new products and business opportunities. The agenda will stimulate collaboration across the different boundaries – of function, industry and geography.

The future is what we make of it

Many readers of this book will be in organizations that have embraced knowledge management as a worthwhile management practice. They may even be successfully exploiting some of the strategy levers described in Chapter 2! But as this final chapter suggests, there is still much to do before the benefits of knowledge are fully realized. There is scepticism among a fair number of senior executives I meet, who feel that knowledge management is indeed a passing fad.

It is instructive to look at how some other one-time 'fads' have evolved. Few large companies today do not practice total quality management, at least in some form. Quality has become embedded in all their products and processes even though you will frequently find companies who are not practising what they preach. Similarly, most organizations have introduced some form of business process re-engineering, even if not as radical as Hammer and Champy envisaged.[12] Both concepts, unlike a passing fad, have matured into a set of desirable management practices, that in turn have stimulated a thriving industry for experts, suppliers of tools and techniques, training and other services. Because of its fundamental importance, there is every likelihood that knowledge management will do the same if properly applied.

For me, the exciting possibilities that surround the exploitation of knowledge are not just in commercial organizations. They are in enterprises of all types that serve society as a whole. And by enterprise, I mean any purposeful initiative. As we look around the world today and see all the problems and opportunities that exist, yet at the same time a wealth of human talent, it surely does not take rocket science to think of the tremendous possibilities for creating better and more fulfilling futures for everyone on the planet? No, what it takes is purposeful knowledge networking of human intellect, globally, and augmented as never before by knowledge technologies. That is fundamental to building the collaborative enterprise. I hope that the perspectives given in this book will help you in that quest.

Notes

1   Schwartz, P. (1991). *The Art of the Long View: Scenario Planning – Protecting your Company against an Uncertain World*. Doubleday.
2   Godet, M. (1982). From forecasting to 'la prospective': a new way of looking at futures. *Journal of Forecasting*, 1, pp.295.
3   Skandia AFS (1996). The future as an asset. In *Power of Innovation: Intellectual Capital Supplement*, Skandia AFS interim report, p. 8.
4   Mercer, D. (1998). *Future Revolutions*. Orion. The methods are described in Mercer, D. (1995). Scenarios made easy. *Long Range Planning*, **28**(4), 81–6.
5   htpp://www.ideamarket.com, http://www.knowledgeshop.com and http://www.iqport.com
6   http://www.bright-future.com
7   McGirk, T. (1998). Dealing in DNA. *Time*, 30 November, pp. 60.
8   Rural Advancement Foundation International (1998). Say no to terminator. http://www.rafi.org/usda.html
9   Knowledge Management Consortium (KMC) at http://km.org.
10 Amidon, D. M. (1997). *Innovation Strategy for the Knowledge Economy: The Ken Awakening*. Butterworth-Heinemann.
11 Global Knowledge Leadership Map. *I³ UPDATE*, Special Edition at http://www.entovation.com (January 1999). The map itself is at http://www.entovation.com/kleadmap/
12 Hammer, M. and Champy, J. (1994). *Reengineering the Corporation: A Manifesto for Business Revolution*. HarperBusiness.

Postscript

Free Internet update

As highlighted in Chapters 1 and 4, the Internet is affecting every business, publishing included. An increasing number of useful source references, as exemplified in this book are now Internet URLs (uniform resource locators). More importantly, the production cycle of a printed book, such as *Knowledge Networking* means that there may be more up to date and relevant material by the time it reaches you the reader.

As a special service to our readers, the author is maintaining updates and current awareness of the topics covered in this book. You can access these through the Butterworth-Heinemann knowledge management web site at:

http://www.bh.com/knowledgemanagement

This site will keep you abreast of developments, keep you informed of new publications in the field, and provide links to valuable knowledge management resources, such as those listed in the *Knowledge Management Yearbook** and the author's own website at:

http://www.skyrme.com

In the spirit of knowledge networking, the author welcomes comments, updates and dialogue via email at david@skyrme.com to form part of the evolving base of knowledge which you can access through Butterworth-Heinemann.

*Cortada, J. W. and Woods, J. A. (1999). *The Knowledgement Management Yearbook 1999–2000*. Butterworth-Heinemann.

References

Allee, V. (1997). *The Knowledge Evolution: Expanding Organizational Intelligence.* Butterworth-Heinemann.

Amidon, D. M. (1997). Customer innovation: a function of knowledge. *Journal of Customer Relationships* (5), pp. 28–35.

Amidon, D. M. (1997). *Innovation Strategy for the Knowledge Economy: The Ken Awakening.* Butterworth-Heinemann.

Angehrn, A. (1997). Designing mature Internet business strategies: the ICDT model. *European Management Journal*, **15**(5), August.

Angehrn, A. (1998). The strategic implications of the Internet. INSEAD Working Paper.

Bacon, F. (c.1598). *Religous Mediations: Of Heresies.* The Latin original is 'nam et ipsa scientia potestas est', literally 'knowledge itself is power'.

Bandler, R. and Grinder, J. (1981). *Frogs into Princes: Neuro Linguistic Programming.* Real People Press.

Belbin, M. (1993). *Team Roles at Work.* Butterworth-Heinemann.

Beer, S. (1994). *Beyond Dispute: The Invention of Team Syntegrity*, John Wiley & Sons.

Boisot, M. H. (1995). *Information Space: A Framework for Organizations.* Routledge.

Bolles, R. N. (1998). *What Color Is your Parachute: A Practical Manual for Job-Hunters and Career Changers.* Ten Speed Press.

Brooking, A. (1996). *Intellectual Captial: Core Asset for the Third Millennium Enterprise.* International Thomson Business Press.

Buchanan, D. A. and McCalman, J. (1989). *High Performance Work Systems: The Digital Experience.* Routledge.

Burk, C. F. and Horton, F. W. (1998). *InfoMap: A Complete Guide to Discovering Corporate Information Resources.* Prentice Hall.

Business Week (1997). Getting to eureka, 10 November.

Business Week (1997). Vital statistics for the real-life economy, 29 December, p. 34.

Business Week (1998). Do the math – it is a small world, 17 August, pp. 77–8.

Business Week (1998). The new economy starts to hit home, 23 March, p. 36.

Chang, P. and Ferguson, N. (1996). The data warehousing boom. *Conspectus*, February, pp. 2–3.

Chase, R. (1997). The knowledge-based organization: an international survey. *Journal of Knowledge Management*, **1**(1), September, pp. 38–49.

Chaston, I. (1995). Danish Technological Institute SME sector network model: implementing broker competencies. *Journal of European Industrial Training*, **19**(1), pp. 10–17.

CIO Magazine, 1 May 1995.

Cleveland, H. (1989). *The Knowledge Executive*. E. P. Dutton.

Coles, M. (1998). Managers tackle world-wide teams. *Sunday Times*, 8 March, p. 7.24.

Computing (1995). Fears slow down teleworking, 27 April, p.46.

Covey, S. R. (1992). Habit 3: put first things first. In Covey, S. R. *The Seven Habits of Highly Effective People*. Simon & Schuster.

Davidow, W. H. and Malone, M. S. (1992). *The Virtual Corporation*. HarperBusiness.

Deal, T. E. and Kennedy, A. A. (1982). *Corporate Cultures: The Rites and Rituals of Corporate Life*. Addison-Wesley.

DEC Computing (1996). Engineers create a global office, 10 April, p. 13.

Dempsey, M. (1996). Phone service transformed. *Financial Times*, FT-IT, 6 November.

Digital Equipment Corporation Second Quarter Report (1987).

Drexler, A. B. and Sibbert, D. L. (1993). *The Drexler/Sibbert Team Performance Model*. Graphic Guides.

Drucker, P. F. (1988). The coming of the new organization. *Harvard Business Review*, **66**(1), January–February.

Drucker, P. F. (1989). *The New Realities: In Government and Politics; In Economics and Business; In Society and World View*. Harper & Row.

Drucker, P. F. (1993). *The Post Capitalist Society*. Butterworth-Heinemann.

Durham University Business School (1997). Realising the potential of self-employment. *Small Business Foresight Bulletin No 7*.

Edvinsson, L. and Malone, M. S. (1997). *Intellectual Capital*. HarperBusiness.

European Commission (1994). *Europe's Way to the Information Society: An Action Plan*. COM(94) 347 final, July.

European Commission (1993). *Growth, Competitiveness, Employment: The Challenges and Way Forward into the 21st Century*.

European Commission (1994). *Europe and the Global Information Society: Recommendations to the European Council*, 26 May.

European Commission (1996). *ACTS Programme Guide*, DGXIII-B.

European Commission (1997). *A European Initiative on Electronic Commerce*. Communication to the European Parliament, COM(97)157.

European Commission (1997). *ACTS 97 Overview*. DG XIII-B, EC, August.

European Commission (1997). *Europe at the Forefront of the Global Information Society: Rolling Action Plan*.

Financial Times, 8 September 1993.

Flexible Working Practices Team (1993). *Case Study: The Crescent*. Digital Equipment.

Fortune (1997). Most admired companies, 3 March.

Garten, J. E. (1998). Why the global economy is here to stay. Cited in *Business Week*, 23 March, p. 9.

Garvin, D. (1993). Building a learning organization. *Harvard Business Review*, July–August, pp. 78–88.

Gibson, D. V. (1994). *R&D Collaboration on Trial: The Microelectronic and Computer Technology Corporation*. Harvard Business School Press.

Gillett, S. E. and Kapor, M. (1997). The self-governing Internet: coordination by design. In *Coordination of the Internet* (B. Kahin and J. Keller, eds) MIT Press.

Gimpel, J. (1992). *The Medieval Machine: The Industrial Revolution of the Middle Ages*. Pimlico.

Godet, M. (1982). From forecasting to 'la prospective': a new way of looking at futures. *Journal of Forecasting*, **1**, pp. 293–301.

Hall, B. P. (1994). *Values Shift*. Twin Lights.

Hamel, G. and Prahalad, C. K. (1994). *Competing for the Future*. Harvard Business School Press.

Hastings, C. (1993). *The New Organization: Growing the Culture of Organizational Networking*. McGraw-Hill.

Hawley Committee (1995). *Information as an Asset: The Board* Agenda. KPMG.

Hickman, C. R. and Silva, M. A. (1987). *The Future 500: Creating Tomorrow's Organizations Today*. Unwin Hyman.

Hildebrand, C. (1996). Experts for hire. *CIO*, 15 April, pp. 32–40.

HMSO (1986). *Performance Review in Local Government: A Handbook for Auditors and Local Authorities*.

Hofstede, G. (1991). *Cultures and Organizations*. McGraw Hill.

Honey, P. (1992). *The Manual of Learning Styles*. Peter Honey Publishing.

IMD (1998). *World Competitiveness Yearbook, 1998*. IMD, Lausanne, June.

Innovation Research Centre (1998). *Annual Innovation Survey*. Henley Management College and Coopers & Lybrand.

Institute for the Future and the Gallup Organization (1998). *Workplace Communications in the 21st Century*. Pitney Bowes.

Jarvenpaa, S. L. and Leidner, D. (1998). Communications and trust in virtual teams. *Journal of Computer Mediated Communications*, **3**(4), June 1998.

Jarvenpaa, S. L. and Shaw, T. R. (1998). Global virtual teams: integrated models of trust. In: Sieber, P. and Griese, J. (eds.). *Organizational Virtualness*. Simowa Verlag, pp. 35–52.

Johanson, R. et al. (1991). *Leading Business Teams*. Addison-Wesley.

Johnson, C. (1997). Leveraging knowledge for operational excellence. *Journal of Knowledge Management*, **1**(1), September, pp. 50–5.

Katzenbach, J. and Smith, D. (1992). *The Wisdom of Teams*. Harvard Business School Press.

Kelley, R. and Caplan, J. (1993). How Bell Labs creates star performers. *Harvard Business Review*, July–August, pp. 128–39.

Kinsman, F. (1987). *The Telecommuters*. John Wiley & Sons.

Kozmetsky, G. (1994). *Technology Transfer in a Global Context*. Working Paper No. 294-04-01, Institute of Creativity and Capital, University of Texas at Austin.

KPMG (1998). *The Knowledge Management Annual Survey*. KPMG.

Kroeber, A. L. and Kluckhohn, C. (1952). *Culture: A Critical Review of Concepts and Definitions*. Vintage Books.

Kumar, K. and Willcocks, L. (1996). Offshore outsourcing: a country too far? RDP96/1, Templeton College, Oxford.

Kuntz, W. and Rittel, H. (1972). Issues as elements of information systems. Working Paper No. 131, Institute of Urban and Regional Development, University of California at Berkeley.

Lipnack, J. and Stamps, J. (1986). *The Networking Book: People Connecting with People*. Routledge & Kegan Paul.

Lipnack, J. and Stamps, J. (1993). *The Team Net Factor: Bringing the Power of Boundary-Crossing into the Heart of Your Business*. John Wiley & Sons.

Lipnack, J. and Stamps, J. (1994). *The Age of the Network: Operating Principles for the 21st Century*. John Wiley & Sons.

Lloyd, B. (1990). Office productivity – time for a revolution. *Long Range Planning*, **23**(1), February, pp. 66–79.

Lloyd, P. and Boyle, P. (eds) (1998). *Web Weaving: Intranets, Extranets and Strategic Alliances*. Butterworth-Heinemann.

Lorange, P. and Roos, J. (1992). *Strategic Alliances: Formation, Implementation and Evolution*. Blackwell.

Manasco, B. (1997). Should your company appoint a chief knowledge officer? *Knowledge Inc.*, **2**(7), July, p. 12.

Martin, J. (1998). *Cybercorp: The New Business Revolution*, p. 130, Amacom.

Martinussen, J. and Jantzen, O. (1994). Business networking – a transferable model for a European SME support structure. *TII/Focus*, August.

Masuda, Y. (1980). *The Information Society as a Post-Industrial Society*. Institute for the Information Society, Tokyo.

Masuda, Y. (1990). *Managing in the Information Society*. Basil Blackwell.

McConnachie, G. (1997). The management of intellectual assets. *Journal of Knowledge Management*, **1**(1), September, pp. 56–62.

McGirk, T. (1998). Dealing in DNA. *Time*, 30 November, pp. 58–64.

Mercer, D. (1995). Scenarios made easy. *Long Range Planning*, **28**(4), pp. 81–6.

Mercer, D. (1998). *Future Revolutions*. Orion.

Merline, K. (1998). Schlumberger creates cutting-edge KM network. *Knowledge Inc.*, **3**(3), March, pp. 1–5.

Michuda, A. (1998). Building a practical framework for knowledge and idea sharing success. Teltech Resources, at *Facilitating Corporate Innovation via Knowledge Management* conference, ICM, New York, April.

Moran, N. (1998). Tensions rise between governments and the world of business. *Financial Times*, FT-IT, 1 April, XII.

Morita, A. (1986). *Made in Japan*. E. P. Dutton.

Murray, P. and Myers, A. (1997). *The Facts about Knowledge*. Cranfield School of Management, cited in *Information Strategy*, September 1997.

Myers, I. B. (1993). *Introduction to Type*. Consulting Psychologists Press.

Naisbitt, J. (1982). *Megatrends: Ten New Directions Transforming our Lives*. Warner Books.

Naisbitt, J. and Aburdene, P. (1990). *Megatrends 2000*.

Nonaka, I. (1991). The knowledge-creating company. *Harvard Business Review*, November–December.

Nonaka, I. and Takeuchi, H. (1995). *The Knowledge Creating Company*. Oxford University Press.

O'Hara-Devereaux, M. and Johansen, R. (1994). *Globalwork: Bridging Distance, Culture and Time*, pp. 157–170. Jossey Bass.

Oppenheim, C. (1995). Tangling with intangibles. *Information World Review*, December, p. 54.

Pedler, M., Burgoyne, J. and Boydell, T (1994). *A Manager's Guide to Self-Development*. McGraw-Hill.

Pesch, U. (1998). On-line collaboration in the production of Teleworx magazine. *Proceedings of On-line Collaboration '98, Berlin*, June, pp. 57-9. ICEF.

Peters, T. (1987). *Thriving on Chaos: Handbook for the Management Revolution*. Macmillan.

Pink, D. (1997). Free agent nation. *FastCompany*, (12), p. 131.

Polyani, M. (1966). *The Tacit Dimension*. Routledge & Kegan Paul.

Pór, G. (1998). Knowledge ecology and communities of practice: emergent twin trends of creating true wealth. *Knowledge Summit '98*, Business Intelligence, London, November.

Prokesch, S. E. (1997). 'Unleashing the power of learning': an interview with John Browne. *Harvard Business Review*, September–October, pp. 147–68.

Reuters Business Information (1996). *Dying for Information: A Report on the Effects of Information Overload in the UK and Worldwide*. Reuters.

Reuters Business Information (1998). *Glued to the Screen*.

Rheingold, H. (1994). *The Virtual Community: Finding Connection in a Computerized World*. Minerva Press.

Rhodes, J. and Thame, S. (1998). *The Colours of Your Mind*. Collins.

Rinaldi, A. H. (1996). *The Net: User Guidelines and Netiquette*.

Ring, P. S. and Van den Ven, A. H. (1992). Structuring interorganizational relationships. *Strategic Management Journal*, **13**(2), pp. 483–98.

Roos, J., Roos, G., Edvinsson, L. and Dragonetti, N. (1997). *Intellectual Capital: Navigating in the New Business Landscape*. Macmillan.

RSA (1995). *Tomorrows Company: The Role of Business in a Changing World: Inquiry Final Report*. RSA, John Adam Street, London.

Sadtler, D., Campbell, A. and Koch, R. (1997). *Breakup!: When Companies are Worth More Dead than Alive*. Capstone.

Sanger, I. (1998). Stock options: Lou takes a cue from Silicon Valley. *Business Week*, 30 March, p. 34.

Savage, C. M. (1996). *Fifth Generation Management: Co-creating through Virtual Enterprising, Dynamic Teaming, and Knowledge Networking*. Butterworth-Heinemann.

Schwartz, P. (1991). *The Art of the Long View: Scenario Planning – Protecting your Company against an Uncertain World*. Doubleday.

Scott Morton, M. S. (ed.) (1991). *The Corporation of the 1990s*. Oxford University Press.

Seely Brown, J and Solomon Gray, E. (1995). After reengineering: the people are the company. *FastCompany*, **1**(1), pp. 78–82.

Segil, L. (1998). *Intelligent Business Alliances*. Century Business Books.

Senge, P. M., Roberts, C., Ross, R. B., Smith, B. J. and Kleiner, A. (1994). *The Fifth Discipline Fieldbook: Strategies and Tools for Building a Learning Organization*. Nicholas Brealey.

Skandia AFS (1996). The future as an asset. In *Power of Innovation: Intellectual Capital Supplement*, Skandia AFS interim report.

Skyrme, D. (1998). *Measuring the Value of Knowledge*. Business Intelligence.

Skyrme, D. J. and Amidon, D. M. (1997) *Creating the Knowledge-Based Business: Key Lessons from an International Study of Best Practice*. Business Intelligence.

Smith, G. (1997). Intangible assets in corporate valuation: an investor's view. At Business Intelligence Conference, *Turning Knowledge into a Corporate Asset*, London, October.

Stewart, T. A. (1991). Brainpower. *Fortune*, 3 June.

Stewart, T. A. (1997). *Intellectual Capital*. Nicholas Brealey Publishing.

Sveiby, K. E. (1997). *The New Organizational Wealth: Managing and Measuring Intangible Asset*. Berrett Koehler.

Sveiby, K. E. and Lloyd, T. (1987). *Managing Know-How*. Bloomsbury.

Tampoe, M. (1993). Motivating knowledge workers. *Long Range Planning*, **26**(3), pp. 49–55.

Taylor, J. (1995). The alternative office. *Flexible Working Conference*, IBC, November.

The 21st century economy: keeping growth strong. Special Feature, *Business Week*, 31 August 1998.

The Teleworking Handbook. TCA.

The Times (1998). The workplace revolution. Special supplement, 20 July.

Toffler, A. (1973). *Future Shock*. Pan.

Tuscany high tech network. *R&D Management*, **26** (1996) pp. 199–211.

US Department of Commerce (1998). *The Emerging Digital Economy*, April. US Department of Commerce.

Verespej, M. A. (1996). The idea is to talk. *Industry Week*, 15 April, p. 28.

Wall Street Journal, 5 March 1997.

Willard, N. (1993). Information resources management. *Aslib Information*, **21**(5), May.

Williams, A., Dobson, P. and Walters, M. (1989). *Changing Culture*. Institute of Personnel Management.

Wissema, J. G. and Euser, L. (1991). Successful innovation through inter-company networks. *Long Range Planning*, **24**(6), pp. 33–9.

World Bank (1998). *World Development Report 1998/99: Knowledge*. Oxford University Press.

World Economic Forum (1998). *Global Competitiveness Report, 1998*. WEF, May.

Wyllie, J. (1998). The economics of intangible value. In *Collaborative Innovation and the Knowledge Economy*. The Society of Management Accountants of Canada.

Index